mutual Reflections

Jews and Blacks in American Art

◦ MILLY HEYD ◦

RUTGERS UNIVERSITY PRESS
NEW BRUNSWICK, NEW JERSEY, AND LONDON

LIBRARY OF CONGRESS CATALOGING-IN-PUBLICATION DATA

Heyd, Milly.
      Mutual reflections : Jews and Blacks in American art / by Milly Heyd.
         p.   cm.
      Includes bibliographical references and index.
      ISBN 0-8135-2617-5 (cloth : alk. paper). — ISBN 0-8135-2618-3 (pbk. : alk. paper)
      1. Jews in art.   2. Afro-Americans in art.   3. Afro-Americans--Relations with Jews.   4. Stereotype (Psychology) in art.   5. Art, American.   6. Art, Modern—20th century—United States.   I. Title.
N7415.H49   1999
704.9'4990904924--dc21   98-34696
                                                             CIP

British Cataloging-in-Publication data for this book is available from the British Library

Manufactured in the United States of America

Interior Design: Judith Martin Waterman

contents

LIST OF ILLUSTRATIONS   vii

PREFACE   xi

INTRODUCTION
Blacks and Jews in American Culture   1

CHAPTER 1
African Americans Mirroring Jews   18

CHAPTER 2
Jews Mirroring African Americans: The Vision   48

CHAPTER 3
Jews Mirroring African Americans: On Lynching   86

CHAPTER 4
Working Together: The Civil Rights Movement   117

CHAPTER 5
"Hot" versus "Cool": Involvement and Detachment   151

CHAPTER 6
Postmodernism: Addressing Racial and Ethnic Stereotyping   176

CHAPTER 7
Conclusion   208

NOTES TO PAGES   219

INDEX   241

Illustrations

FIG. 1, Timothy Cook, *Untitled*, 1996.   2

FIG. 2, John Biggers, *Crossing the Bridge*, 1942.   11

FIG. 3, John Biggers, *Middle Passage*, 1947.   12

FIG. 4, Lila Oliver Asher, *Expulsion of Hagar*, 1961.   14

FIG. 5, Henry Ossawa Tanner, *A View in Palestine*, 1898–99.   20

FIG. 6, Henry Ossawa Tanner, *The Wailing Wall*, 1897.   21

FIG. 7, Henry Ossawa Tanner, *Nicodemus Visiting Jesus*, 1899.   24

FIG. 8, Abel Pann, *Sacrifice of Isaac*, 1943.   25

FIG. 9, Henry Ossawa Tanner, *Head of a Jew in Palestine*, 1899 and ca. 1920.   26

FIG. 10, Winfred Russell, *A Study*, 1923.   27

FIG. 11, E. M. Lilien, *Joshua*, 1908.   34

FIG. 12, Aaron Douglas, *Untitled*, 1925.   35

FIG. 13, Aaron Douglas, *Invincible Music: The Spirit of Africa*, 1926.   36

FIG. 14, Abel Pann, *The Creation*, 1923.   37

FIG. 15, E. M. Lilien, *The Jewish May*, 1902.   38

FIG. 16, Aaron Douglas, *Into Bondage*, 1936.   39

FIG. 17, Aaron Douglas, *Untitled*, 1930.   40

FIG. 18, Meta Warrick Fuller, *Ethiopia Awakening*, 1914.   42

FIG. 19, Yitzhak Danziger, *Nimrod*, 1939.   43

FIG. 20, Romare Bearden, *Sermons: The Walls of Jericho*, 1964.   45

FIG. 21, Romare Bearden, *Eighth Avenue Market: New York City*, 1935.   46

FIG. 22, Ben Shahn, *The Credo*, 1954.   49

FIG. 23, Jacob Epstein, *Cursed Be the Day Wherein I Was Born*, 1913–4.   51

FIG. 24, Chaim Gross, *Mother Carrying Child*, 1926.   56

FIG. 25, Chaim Gross, *Mother Carrying Child*, 1926.   57

FIG. 26, Chaim Gross, *Jazz*, 1929. 58

FIG. 27, Chaim Gross, *Walking Negress*, 1928. 59

FIG. 28, Chaim Gross, *Pregnant Negress*, 1930. 60

FIG. 29, Chaim Gross, *Shulamit*, 1930. 61

FIG. 30, *Der Hammer*, 1928. 63

FIG. 31, Harry Gottlieb, *I Am Black But Comely*, 1925. 65

FIG. 32, Lucienne Bloch, *The Playground*, 1936. 67

FIG. 33, Philip Evergood, *The Dream Catch*, 1946. 68

FIG. 34, Raphael Soyer, *City Children*, 1952. 72

FIG. 35, Raphael Soyer, *Village East Street Scene*, 1965–66. 74

FIG. 36, Raphael Soyer, *Amos on Racial Equality*, 1965–66. 75

FIG. 37, Raphael Soyer, *Waiting Room*, 1940. 76

FIG. 38, Isaac Soyer, *Employment Agency*, 1937. 77

FIG. 39, Jacob Epstein, *Head of Paul Robeson*, 1928. 78

FIG. 40, Moses Soyer, *Portrait of Eartha Kitt*, 1964. 80

FIG. 41, Moses Soyer, *Gwen and Jacob Lawrence*, 1962. 81

FIG. 42, Benny Andrews, *Portrait of Raphael Soyer*, 1966. 82

FIG. 43, Raphael Soyer, *Portrait of Benny Andrews*, 1974. 83

FIG. 44, Daniel La Rue Johnson/Thomas Stilz, *Over Here, Over There*, 1970. 84

FIG. 45, Daniel La Rue Johnson/Thomas Stilz, *Over Here, Over There*, 1970. 85

FIG. 46, Harris, *Christmas in Georgia, A.D.*, 1916. 89

FIG. 47, Cornelius Johnson, *Prejudice*, 1927. 90

FIG. 48, Peshka, *Black on White*, 1936. 92

FIG. 49, Romare Bearden, *The Ghost Walks*, 1936. 93

FIG. 50, William Gropper, *Political Cartoon*, 1930. 94

FIG. 51, William Gropper, *Southern Landscape*, 1945. 95

FIG. 52, William Gropper, *Lynch*, 1949. 95

FIG. 53, Hugo Gellert, *Spike lynch terror! Save the Scottsboro boys!*, 1934. 96

FIG. 54, Romare Bearden, *The Real Judge at Scottsboro*, 1935. 97

FIG. 55, Peshka, *Black on White*, 1937. 98

FIG. 56, Julius Bloch, *The Lynching*, 1932. 102

FIG. 57, Julius Bloch, *Horace Pippin*, 1943. 103

FIG. 58, Louis Lozowick, *Lynching (Lynch Law)*, 1936. 104

FIG. 59, Harry Sternberg, *Southern Holiday*, 1935.   105

FIG. 60, Adolf Wolff, *The Lynch Law*, 1931.   108

FIG. 61, Aaron Goodelman, *The Necklace*, 1933.   109

FIG. 62, Seymour Lipton, *Lynched*, 1933.   110

FIG. 63, Pat Ward Williams, *Accused/Blowtorch/Padlock*, 1986.   114

FIG. 64, Jack Levine, *Birmingham '63*, 1963.   118

FIG. 65, *Freedom Fighters* (button), 1964.   119

FIG. 66, Ben Shahn, *Thou Shalt Not Stand Idly By*, 1965.   120

FIG. 67, Ben Shahn, *Martin Luther King*, 1965.   126

FIG. 68, Ben Shahn, *Frederick Douglass*, 1965.   127

FIG. 69, Ben Shahn, *James Chaney*, 1965.   128

FIG. 70, Ben Shahn, *Andrew Goodman*, 1965.   129

FIG. 71, Ben Shahn, *Michael Schwerner*, 1965.   130

FIG. 72, Cliff Joseph, *Hands of Freedom*, 1965.   134

FIG. 73, Lila Oliver Asher, *Homage to Ben Shahn*, 1966.   135

FIG. 74, Chaim Gross, *Martin Luther King*, 1968.   137

FIG. 75, Chaim Gross, *Namibia*, 1973.   138

FIG. 76, Jacob Lawrence, *Praying Ministers*, 1962.   140

FIG. 77, George Segal, *The Bus Riders*, 1964.   141

FIG. 78, Charles Alston, *Walking*, 1958.   142

FIG. 79, Cliff Joseph, *Heirs to the Kiss of Judas*, 1966.   143

FIG. 80, Cliff Joseph, *My Country Right or Wrong*, 1968.   145

FIG. 81, David Hammons, *Rabbi*, 1960s.   146

FIG. 82, Benny Andrews, *The Seder*, 1960.   148

FIG. 83, Benny Andrews, *The Student*, 1991.   149

FIG. 84, Larry Rivers, *African Continent and African*, 1969.   153

FIG. 85, Larry Rivers, *Imamu Baraka Reading (LeRoi Jones)*, 1970.   158

FIG. 86, Larry Rivers, *America's Number One Problem*, 1969.   160

FIG. 87, Larry Rivers, *Caucasian Woman Sprawled on a Bed and Eight Figures of Hanged Men on Four Rectangular Boxes*, 1970.   162

FIG. 88, Larry Rivers, *A Slave Ship*, 1970.   166

FIG. 89, Frank Bowling, *Middle Passage*, 1970.   167

FIG. 90, Larry Rivers, *I Like Olympia in Black Face*, 1970.   170

FIG. 91, Ben Shahn, *May 5, 1949.*   171

FIG. 92, Alex Katz, *Vincent and Tony,* 1969.   175

FIG. 93 and 94, Jonathan Borofsky, *Dream # 1,* 1972–73.   178

FIG. 95 and 96, Jonathan Borofsky, *Dream # 1,* 1972–73.   179

FIG. 97, Jonathan Borofsky, *I dreamed I was walking down the stairs into the subway,* 1978.   181

FIG. 98, Jonathan Borofsky, *I dreamed that blacks were marching for freedom,* 1975.   184

FIG. 99, Jonathan Borofsky, *Riot Police in Capetown,* 1987.   187

FIG. 100, Jean-Michel Basquiat, *St. Joe Louis Surrounded by Snakes,* 1982.   188

FIG. 101, Jean-Michel Basquiat, *Jack Johnson,* 1982.   189

FIG. 102, Richmond Barthé, *The Boxer,* 1942.   190

FIG. 103, Benny Andrews, *The Champion,* 1968.   191

FIG. 104, Art Spiegelman, *Maus II: And Here My Troubles Began,* 1986, 1990, 1991.   194

FIG. 105, Art Spiegelman, *Maus II: And Here My Troubles Began,* 1986, 1990, 1991.   195

FIG. 106, Barbara Kruger, *All Violence Is the Illustration of a Pathetic Stereotype,* 1991.   199

FIG. 107, Barbara Kruger, *Untitled (Speak for Yourself),* 1986.   204

FIG. 108, Ben Shahn, *Welders, or, for full employment after the war, Register/Vote,* 1944.   205

FIG. 109, Howardena Pindell, *Autobiography: Air/CS560,* 1988.   211

FIG. 110, Philip Pearlstein, *Model with Minstrel Marionettes,* 1986.   214

FIG. 111, Art Spiegelman, *Valentine's Day,* 1993.   215

FIG. 112, Gerda Meyer-Bernstein, *Phoenix,* (1994).   217

preface

As a student of art history at the Hebrew University of Jerusalem, I was fortunate to study American art with Professor Milton Brown, who spent a sabbatical leave teaching in our department. In his classes Professor Brown emphasized, whenever relevant, the social dimension and left-wing ideology of American artists, including Jewish-American artists. I was also fortunate to consult him again in America, on the topic of the present book. Another formative influence on my understanding of American art was Professor Avram Kampf, whose pioneering work on the modern Jewish experience and the visual arts also dealt with leftist Jewish-American artists who looked at social issues through the lenses of the writings of the Hebrew Prophets. Following in my mentors' footsteps, I taught courses on American art as part of my joint appointment in the departments of Art History and American Studies.

This book is an outgrowth of a joint research project that I undertook some years ago with Ezra Mendelsohn of the Hebrew University. It was Professor Mendelsohn, a specialist in modern Jewish history, who first drew my attention to the relationship between Blacks and Jews in America and introduced me to the extensive literature on this topic. He also guided me in the subject of Jewish-American history, including the important issue of the relationship between the Jews and the left.

The path to this book was paved by an article on the Soyer Brothers that Professor Mendelsohn and I published in *Jewish Art* (1992–93). Then we taught together a course on Jewish artists in America, in which we analyzed some of the issues and images discussed in this book. Professor Mendelsohn wrote the first version of an article summarizing our joint research, entitled, "Jewish Identity and the Artistic Representation of the Other," which has not been published. This work, as well as the published article on the Soyers, contained in embryonic form some of the material presented in this book. All in all, I am deeply indebted to Professor Mendelsohn for his invaluable insights, without which this book would not have been written. He drew my attention to some of the artists whose works are discussed here, and I am indebted to him for much of the historical analysis presented here. Obviously, Professor Mendelsohn is absolved from all responsibility for the book's shortcomings.

At some point we decided to continue our work on the subject separately. This book has become a specifically art historical work, applying iconographic, stylistic, and

psychological-interpretive analyses, based on interviews of some of the artists (both African Americans and Jewish Americans) and on archival research of primary sources.

I spent the spring term of 1996 at the Institute for Advanced Studies at the Hebrew
University as part of a group that dealt with "The Visual Dimension of Modern Jewish
Culture," led by Professors Ezra Mendelsohn and Richard Cohen. I am grateful to the
institute for enabling me to pursue my research, for covering the expenses of some of the
photographs reproduced in the present book, and for the enlightening comments from
the participants in the seminar discussions: Professors Ezra Mendelsohn, Richard Cohen,
Zvi Jagendorf, Walter Kahn, Barbara Kirschenblatt-Gimpel, and Vivien Mann. Professor Judith Wechsler's constructive criticism of my discussion of Ben Shahn's visual images that address the Black cause helped me to see the connections between the visual
and the civil rights activities of the artist. In addition, my research also has benefited from
the generous financial support of the Hebrew University Internal Funds.

Much of the research and writing of this book was done during a sabbatical leave at
Princeton University in 1996–97. I was privileged to enjoy the hospitality of the Department of Art and Archaeology, to profit from valuable discussions with its chair, Professor John Wilmerding, whose work on American art in general and the relationship of
Winslow Homer to the image of the Black in particular were eye-opening, and to ex-
change views with Professor Tod Potterfield and Dr. Margaret Vendryes. The latter's
article on the difference between African Americans and White Americans in the portrayal of lynching helped me to locate the position of Jewish-American artists in this
context. Professor Thomas Kaufmann Dacosta directed my attention to the importance
of the role Jewish patrons played in promoting African-American art.

In Princeton I was also able to consult Professor Arnold Rampersad of the African
American Studies Program. I am grateful to him for sharing with me his knowledge of
the Harlem Renaissance, the biography of Langston Hughes, and the poetry of Waring
Cuney. Professor Albert Raboteau was not only willing to look at some of the visual data
and to lend me books, but also enlightened me on the question of the Exodus in African-
American theology.

I owe a debt of gratitude to Professor Matthew Baigell, a scholar in American art
whose work on Jewish-American and African-American artists was a source of inspiration for my book, and whose intellectual interest, warmth, and support were instrumental to my work.

Moreover, I would not have been able to carry out my work without the professional expertise and generous help of the librarians at the Marquand Library in Princeton. Janice Powell, Denise Gavio-Weinheimer, and all the staff members have created a
very congenial environment, and they made my stay there a very enjoyable experience.
Emily Belcher of Firestone's African-American seminar library shared with me her knowledge, and I am very grateful for her assistance and good advice. During my research I was
also helped by the staffs at the Hebrew University and Jewish National Library, the

libraries of the Israel Museum, the Moorland-Spingarn Research Center, Howard University, the Archives of American Art (New York), the New York Public Library, and the Schomburg Center for Research in Black Culture, where I would like to thank especially Tammi Lawson.

Special thanks are due to Bernarda Bryson Ben Shahn for giving me permission to use restricted material in the Archives of American Art. I am also indebted to Joan Rosenbaum, the director of the Jewish Museum, New York, who encouraged and allowed me to study the reception of the museum's important exhibition, *Bridges and Boundaries: African Americans and American Jews*, in the museum's archives. Likewise, I received encouragement and archival material from the Menil Foundation. The list of museums and galleries that cooperated with my research is too long to be included in the preface and is instead acknowledged in the photographic list. I am also indebted to all the artists who were willing to discuss their works with me and without whom this book would not have been completed.

Mira Reich edited the original manuscript with great care. I enjoyed working with staff members of Rutgers University Press. I especially want to thank Leslie Mitchner for expressing deep interest in my book and helping me in the various stages of production. Thanks are also due to Paula Kantenwein and Brigitte Goldstein. Eric Schramm added the final touch in his dedicated copyediting of the book. It should be noted that quotations from my interviews with artists and other subjects are left as spoken and not supplemented with bracketed words, in order to preserve the flavor of the original statements.

I would like to conclude the preface with a word of appreciation to Professor Ziva Amishai-Maisels, a teacher, friend, and colleague, for working on and encouraging her students and colleagues to study modern Jewish identity in modern art. I learned a lot from her intellectual and moral courage in dealing with painful subjects in her work.

This book would not have been written without David, to whom I am grateful not just for his Supererogation and Toleration but also for driving me to various galleries, artists' studios, and archives throughout America, for listening critically to what I had to say, for encouraging me not to give up, and for his overall support throughout our life together. And the last warm word is to my socially and politically conscious son, Uriel, who is always present, even when far away.

Mutual Reflections

Blacks and Jews in American Culture

Two figures mirroring each other, attached by a looping chain shackled to their ankles, stand before an outline map of the United States of America. Each pulls in the opposite direction, in a kind of coordinated tug-of-war. The common chain is about to snap asunder. The two figures represent an African American and a Jewish American sharing a parallel fate. This image is a linoleum print done by Timothy Cook (fig. 1, 1996) as an illustration for an article entitled, "Who is the Jew? A Question of African-American Identity," which appeared in the first issue of *CommonQuest*, "the Magazine of Black Jewish Relations," published by Howard University and the American Jewish Committee, in spring 1996.

The drawing, for all its seeming simplicity, contains several layers of historical reference. The similar clothes and the faces differentiated almost entirely by shading convey the notion of people of the same (working) class joined in a struggle to throw off their chains and become free and equal members of their society. This anachronistic, even nostalgic, view is almost demolished by the effect of the two protagonists facing off and trying to become free of each other. The question of which is more chained to the other is not addressed, so the struggle is apparently on equal terms. The symmetrical image is a counterpart to Cornel West's analysis of the relationship between the two groups: "Yet, ironically, Jews and Blacks have been linked in a kind of symbiotic relation with each other. Whether they are allies or antagonists, they are locked into an insepa-rable embrace principally owing to their dominant status of degraded Others.[1]

The title *CommonQuest* would seem to respond to the historical level of the draw-ing—a common quest for freedom. In the course of time, the struggle of the two pro-tagonists has become a struggle between themselves as much as against their society. The "common quest" has become a search for a separate identity, a struggle in which every man is for himself. Like two prisoners forcibly fastened to each other, the two figures' only chance of freedom is through joint struggle. Yet there comes a moment when the two can fully liberate themselves only in terms of shattering the common

FIG. 1. Timothy Cook, *Untitled*, in *CommonQuest*, spring 1996 (vol. 1, no. 1), Linoleum print. Courtesy of Timothy Cook.

chain. What the cartoon suggests, therefore, is a paradoxical relationship in which the prospect of achieving the common goal of liberation and integration in American society is predicted to be breaking apart. The image throws light on the complexity of the present relationship between the two communities.

CommonQuest is a contemporary endeavor to readdress and reassess the charged account of these two "others" in American society. The publication is surely well timed, answering a demand as well as a need for reviewing the respective histories of Blacks and Jews in America. A sense of urgency is expressed both by the title graphic (note the intentional omission of spacing in *CommonQuest*) and by the coeditor in formulating the magazine's raison d'être: "Much in black and Jewish life fascinates. The need to dispel myths about each other is urgent. Mutual stakes in a just and civil society bind us together. . . . We offer no bromides of brotherhood, no romance of Selma days."[2]

Relations between Jewish Americans and African Americans have always been of a special character. Although for different reasons—ethnic and religious on the one hand and racial on the other—Jews and Blacks have long been considered as outsiders or "others" (to use contemporary terminology), not belonging to the mainstream of American society.[3] They also share a history in which their appearance was assigned a derogatory role. In both cases physical attributes were negatively evaluated and treated as alien. Linda Nochlin writes: "Stigmata of stereotypical Jewishness" consist of "frog-like mouths, the large uncomely noses, the squinty eyes, and the weak, hunched-over physiognomies."[4] But also, "similar deviations have been read into the thick lips and dark skins of the Black." These attitudes are derived from the classic Greek "universalist notion of the 'normal' (or 'beautiful')."[5]

Sander Gilman has shown that Western physiognomy and character studies, from Johann Caspar Lavater in eighteenth-century Europe through Robert Knox in mid-nineteenth century America, associated Jewish and African features with certain character traits.[6] Hence, the analysis of Jews' and Blacks' mutual reflections should take into account the fact that both were perceived as different and were subjected to negative stereotyping focusing on the perception of their outward appearance.

These are external racist and anti-Semitic points of view. However, there is also a sense in which the notion of otherness is internal, as can be seen in W.E.B. Du Bois's reflections about otherness as implying a state of dual existence. Perhaps Du Bois's classical definition of the Black experience as a "double-consciousness," a "two-ness," that "sense of always looking at one's self through the eyes of others," can be borrowed and applied to the American Jewish experience.[7] With Du Bois's sense of duality in mind, I would argue that there is something unique in the way many African Americans and Jewish Americans look at each other. This mutual interest conveys a heightened awareness of the other, which is also self-awareness. The common attitude lends the Jewish–Black connection a special fascination.

The sculptor William Zorach was born in 1889 in Euberick, Lithuania, and emigrated with his Jewish family to the United States in 1893. In his autobiography, he reminisced: "I did a head of Dr. W.E.B. Du Bois which was presented to the Schomburg Collection on his ninety-second birthday. I felt there should be some real record in the way of a portrait of this fine gentleman and scholar who had devoted his life to the Negro people and their problems, who had edited and published *The Crisis* ever since our early days in the Village, and who was living in our neighborhood on Brooklyn Heights."[8]

Ezra Mendelsohn has pointed out the analogies between the two groups. Both underwent profound demographic, economic, social, and cultural changes due to mass immigration to North American cities (one group from the American South, the other from Eastern Europe). New York became a common metropolis and Harlem, once partly Jewish, developed into the center of a Black political and cultural renaissance.[9] Having started their lives in the big city as working people, Blacks and Jews were often attracted to socialist and communist ideas. Quite a few Jewish-American and African-American artists participated in the activities of the John Reed Club of artists and writers. The appeal of radical left-wing ideals was associated with the general universalistic weltanschauung of secular American Jews and their effort to become integrated in the host society.[10]

Another feature of these analogies relates to the parallel debates within the two communities about alternative ideals of integration and national self-determination. The ideology of assimilation in the Jewish case was challenged by Zionism, and in the Black case by cultural nationalism such as that of Marcus Garvey.[11]

Notwithstanding these rapprochements, the course of the relations between the two communities is full of vicissitudes. There were periods of close alliance and a sense of common aspirations and destiny; but there were also rough edges and misunderstandings on both sides. Ambivalence is perceptible in various publications that address the two groups' respective attitudes. The title of Jonathan Kaufman's *Broken Alliance*, a book discussing "The Turbulent Times between Blacks and Jews in America," and the title of the 1992 exhibition at the Jewish Museum, New York (the first to address the visual dimension of this experience)—*Bridges and Boundaries: African Americans and American Jews*—both carry conflicting overtones.[12] Each of these titles is based on a duality, a switch from hope to disappointment, from attachment to rift. The jacket design for *Broken Alliance*, by Jack Ribik, alludes in the cracked lettering of the title to the archetypal image of the broken Tablets of the Law, signifying the breaking of the covenant between God and his people.

This ambivalence runs as a leitmotif through many of the essays in the Jewish Museum exhibition catalogue. Thus on the one hand Jack Salzman describes the Jewish–Black relationship as a "strong alliance," a "bridge," and even a "grand alliance," and on the other hand challenges the very existence of such grand notions, suggesting the possibility that they are but a "myth."[13] Clayborne Carson contrasts "mutually supportive relations" with "mutually hostile relations." He distinguishes between Jews and Blacks as sharing "common experiences" of oppression and the two minorities sharing "common experiences as a culture" within the political left.[14] Writing about Jews and Blacks working together in the civil rights movement, Taylor Branch offers the title "Blacks and Jews: The Uncivil War." His article questions the implied evolution from "mutual empathy" to "racial hatred."[15]

A typical example of this kind of ambivalence can be found in Du Bois. He had close contacts with Jews such as Joel Spingarn, a leader of the National Association for the Advancement of Colored People (NAACP), and to whom he dedicated his autobiography. However, as the recently published critical edition (1997) of *The Souls of Black Folk* shows, the original manuscript of the chapter titled "Of the Black Belt" refers to the Jew as the "heir of the slave-baron" and contains sentences such as: "Here and there are tales of projects for money-getting, born in the swift days of Reconstruction, 'improvement' companies, wine companies, mills and factories; nearly all failed, and the Jew fell heir." The editors' commentary on this text spells out the to-and-fro movement in the various editions regarding Du Bois's use of the word "Jew" in contexts of land exploitation in the South. His original 1903 formulation "reflected a larger turn-of-the-century anti-Semitic discourse which he had learnt and absorbed as part of his nineteenth-century education." In later editions, partly under the impact of the Holocaust and also with the intention of avoiding offense, Du Bois was willing to omit some phrases that could be interpreted as anti-Semitic, but he left others in, confident that "my evident reputation as being indebted to Jewish culture would absolve me from blame of unfairness."[16]

And how are we to evaluate the contrasting interpretations of phenomena that were central to the relationship between the two communities? Persecution, for example, was taken on the one hand as a source of common understanding and mutual empathy; but on the other it was understood as pulling people apart by committing the persecuted party to "intensify a protective ethnocentrism that makes for antagonism toward all other groups, including other minority groups."[17] Similarly, suffering is taken by the writer James Baldwin as imposing a greater duty on Jews toward Blacks since "the Jew should 'know better.'"[18] Yet suffering has an equal potential for turning the victim toward defensive and aggressive behavior. Or consider another example: when Jews accept this assumed responsibility and express their identification with Blacks in various activities on the basis of their own experience of suffering and persecution, they are at times perceived as looking down at their fellow community, as caring for their own interests, or trying for domination and control. What is read by one as showing sincere altruistic concern is read by the other as patronizing and condescending.[19]

Baldwin analyzes "the Negro's ambivalent relation to the Jew." He identifies with the Hebrew Scriptures story of the path from slavery to freedom in the flight from Egypt (some popular hymns and stories come from that source), yet the Jew is also the Christ-killer who failed to accept the savior. Baldwin describes a widespread Black attitude of hatred toward the Jew, arising from encounters with Jewish small tradesmen, rent collectors, real estate agents, and pawnbrokers—all associated with the American business tradition of exploitation.[20]

Later variants of this fundamental ambivalence can be found in the emergence of Black Power and the Nation of Islam, their opposition to Zionism and to the State of Israel. This ambivalence was by no means confined to the Black side. Mutual accusations of Blacks as anti-Semitic and of Jews as racists have become part of the uneasy relationship. These recriminations were heard in the Crown Heights riots in 1993, which took place in an area where ultra-Orthodox Jews live in proximity to Blacks. Another context of friction was the national debate on affirmative action in which Jews were both among the strong advocates of the policy and those who often fell victim to it (as in the famous case of *Bakke*), a situation that was bound to create mixed feelings within the two communities.

To further illustrate the complexity of the relationship between Jews and Blacks in America, we should remember that the mutual interests of the two groups emerged from different historical sources. Jews became involved in the Black cause through their interest in social issues and their association with left-wing culture, often calling on the social teaching of the prophets. As Avram Kampf first noted, "Many Jewish artists expressed now not only their immediate personal experience as immigrants but tapped the roots of their social values anchored in the prophetic tradition."[21] The origins of Black interest in the Jewish people were of a religious nature, based on the fundamental role of the biblical ideas of "Exodus," "the Chosen People," "the Promised Land." These ideas were adopted by Black culture from the Hebrew Scriptures and their references transferred from the ancient Israelites to modern-day Blacks. In the words of Du Bois: "Emancipation was the key to a promised land of sweeter beauty than ever stretched before the eyes of wearied Israelites."[22]

Albert Raboteau has investigated the role of the Exodus story in slave religion, where it was perceived as "an archetypal event." The biblical story played a part in the articulation of the slaves' sense of "historical identity as a people." By identifying with it "they created meaning and purpose out of the chaotic and senseless experience of slavery." It also enabled them "to project a future radically different from their present."[23]

The book of Exodus, as Michael Walzer has shown, has played a tremendous role in liberation movements throughout history.[24] It was particularly relevant to Black history: like the ancient Israelites, Blacks were living in their homeland before their enslavement; like the ancient Israelites, they maintained a strong sense of their identity throughout their exile; like the Jews in their exilic history, they associated suffering with a privileged standing in the eyes of God; and of course, like the Jews, they always sang and prayed for liberation and the return to the Promised Land (symbolic or actual).

The actual encounter of Blacks with real-life Jews in America could not leave them indifferent. In everyday life they did not necessarily encounter socially conscious, well-wishing Jews. The gap or dissonance between the character of the local Jewish landlord and the heroic biblical figure, as well as the gap between the Old and New Testament, is an important factor in the split between the "Israelites" and the Jews. As we saw above, both Du Bois and James Baldwin express these contradictions. Langston Hughes, who, as will be discussed in chapter 1, wrote "America," a poem in which Black and Jewish boys are mirror-images, named his second book *Fine Clothes to the Jew*:

> When hard luck overtakes you
> Nothin' for you to do
> Gather up yo' fine clothes
> An' sell 'em to de Jew.[25]

Typical of such historically significant encounters, the fact that the motivating forces behind the attraction of each group to the other were different only added to the uneasiness of the relationship and to the inevitable tension. While the traditional attraction of Jews to Black issues was universalistic in tendency, based on a comprehensive social outlook, that of Blacks to Jews was originally particularistic, having to do with deep metaphors and images unique to Black culture and to the religiously based understanding of Black history.

Bearing in mind the complexity of the two people's association, let us turn to the art world. An important aspect of the relationship between Jews and Blacks in the arts is philanthropy. Patronage has played a major role in art throughout history, and even though philanthropy is often associated with a sense of supremacy, the art world could not have survived and flourished without it. By supporting Black artists, Jewish-American philanthropists became part of the long history of patronage in the arts. And although the full account of their enterprise still remains to be written, even a short survey shows that during the crucial stage in the launching of Black art in modern urban society, these philanthropists had a vital influence. Fellowships given by these donors enabled artists to study abroad, mainly in Paris, or to travel to places related to African-American ancestry.[26]

The main Jewish-American sponsors of Black art were Otto Kahn, the Spingarn family (Joel and Amy Spingarn, and Joel's brother, Arthur), Julius Rosenwald, and in some cases the Guggenheim Foundation. The Spingarn medal was instituted in 1914 by Joel Spingarn (chairman of the NAACP, 1914–19, 1931–35, and president of the NAACP, 1930–39), who gave it annually "for the highest achievement by an American Negro." The award was continued after his death by his brother Arthur. Jacob Lawrence was a recipient of the prize in the visual arts for his work as an artist, teacher, and humanist. In 1921 Amy Spingarn established a separate prize for the visual arts. This was given under the aegis of *The Crisis* (the monthly magazine of the NAACP founded by Du Bois and subtitled, "A Record of the Darker Race") to "persons of Negro descent in order to encourage their aptitude for art expression." The painter Laura Wheeler Waring benefited from the award for "Negro achievements in the Fine Arts." After graduating from the Pennsylvania Academy of Fine Arts, the grant enabled her to study at the Académie de la Grande Chaumière in Paris in 1924–25.[27]

Otto H. Kahn awarded an annual prize to a Black artist as part of the Harmon Foundation's early activities. The Foundation's exhibition catalogue of 1931 hails Kahn's "current knowledge of, and keen concern in the Negro as he progresses towards greater achievement and wider recognition in the field of the visual arts."[28] It was to him that Hale Woodruff appealed for help in 1928 when they were both in Paris and the painter was in dire straits. In 1933 Sargent Johnson was awarded the Otto Kahn prize for his ceramic bust *Sammy*.[29] In 1930 Arthur B. Spingarn, in collaboration with Mrs. John D. Rockefeller, the collector and bibliographer Arthur A. Schomburg, and the critic Alain Locke, also contributed toward art prizes given by the Harmon Foundation.[30]

Many leading black artists were encouraged to pursue their careers by Julius Rosenwald (1862–1932), the president of Sears Roebuck, who established the Julius Rosenwald Funds (1917–1948). Rosenwald was sympathetic to the ideas of Booker T. Washington and was involved in building vocational schools for Blacks.[31] He was also interested in medical and health institutions and in providing fellowships for Blacks in various academic fields. In his writings about philanthropy, he discussed the historical place of patrons in Western art, mentioning among others the Medicis: "The Medicis have been exonerated for much of their cruelty because of their sympathetic support of artistic expression." However, as for the American scene, Rosenwald did not advocate philanthropy for the arts:

> As America absorbs her frontiers, and as wealth mellows in the possession of the third and fourth generations, doubtless there will be a revival of interest in the creative expression. Meanwhile philanthropy probably does well to concentrate upon those things which are in accordance with America's present peculiar genius: intensive accumulation of knowledge (as well as wealth) and the active application of scientific findings to organize social welfare.[32]

Thus spoke a first-generation-coming-to-wealth Jewish philanthropist. These declarations notwithstanding, Julius Rosenwald by no means refrained from supporting Black artists. His legacy was continued after his death. In 1929 Augusta Savage was awarded successive fellowships for studying in Paris; the award was increased from $1500 to $1800 per year "in special recognition of her merit and her problems in supporting herself." This was a means of overcoming racial discrimination, since she had previously been rejected by the Fontainebleau summer art school. She kept her contacts with the Rosenwald Fund in 1940, when she set up an exhibition in Perrin Hall, Chicago. Introduced by the head of the Rosenwald Fund to a socially prominent audience, she described what she had had to endure in order to become an artist.[33]

Richmond Barthé was awarded a Julius Rosenwald fellowship on his return to Chicago in 1930 "for his continued development." Following his success in New York, his Rosenwald grant was renewed.[34] Aaron Douglas received the Rosenwald fellowship for studies in the South and in Haiti in 1937.[35] It was given to him for creative art in portraits and character sketches. In 1940 Eldzier Cortor received a fellowship to go to the Sea Islands off the Carolina and Georgia coasts, where he could immerse himself in the traditions of people who had retained many African attitudes to their environment.[36] One of the most prominent African-American artists, Jacob Lawrence, won three successive Julius Rosenwald Fund fellowships when he was only twenty-one years old, enabling him to continue painting when the Works Progress Administration, under whose auspices he had been working at the time, discontinued its activities.[37]

In 1941 Charles White was awarded a Julius Rosenwald Fellowship for a year's work in the deep South. This fellowship enabled White, a native of Chicago, to reconnect with the region from where his parents and grandparents had come. After this, he was to be included in a show in December 1941 at the Downtown Gallery in New York, owned by Edith Halpert, who was engaged in discovering and exhibiting the "wealth of talent there was among Black artists." However, the attack on Pearl Harbor caused the cancellation of the show. The paintings were shown in the following year at the New York ACA Gallery owned by Herman Baron, who was also engaged in promoting Black artists.[38]

In 1946 the sculptor and painter Elizabeth Catlett won a Rosenwald fellowship to complete a series of paintings, lithographs, and sculptures, on the role of Negro women in America. The fellowship's renewal in 1947 enabled her to study in Mexico where she became close to the Muralists.[39]

Archibald Motley, who was "committed to portraying the variety of types of indi-viduals, colors and shades of those who inhabit the African American communities" (to quote Samella Lewis), won the Guggenheim Fellowship in 1929.[40] Richmond Barthé received the Guggenheim fellowship twice, in 1940 and 1941.[41] Ellis Wilson, after sub-mitting drawings of defense workers in an aircraft engine factory, was awarded a Guggen-heim fellowship, which was later renewed.[42]

However, financial support was not the only point of interaction in the art world, as the case of the painter and sculptor John Biggers and the psychologist and educator Viktor Löwenfeld indicates. Biggers, born in 1924, and the Jewish-Viennese Löwenfeld enjoyed a relationship based on reciprocity, a give and take from which the two gained much in their respective development. Since an excellent catalogue with illuminating articles accompanied a 1995 Biggers retrospective, I will not go into a detailed analysis of his work, but will only use his example to highlight a different model of alliance.[43]

The story of this relationship goes back to the rise of Nazism and the dismissal of Jewish scholars in Germany and Austria from their jobs as the result of racist policies. In *From Swastika to Jim Crow*, Gabrielle Simon Edgcomb studies fifty-one individuals and nineteen institutions where refugee scholars came to hold faculty positions in histori-cally Black colleges. Her book tells the story of crosscultural meeting points between two different groups of people, both victims of racist oppression and persecution. In universities and colleges such as of Atlanta, Fisk, Howard, Lincoln, Spelman, Knoxville, Hampton, and others, these refugees learned "to reassemble the pieces of their lives and careers."[44] They could identify and see the similarity between their circumstances and segregation in the South. The illustration on the book jacket, which juxtaposes a "white-only" cab and a "Nur für Arier" (Aryans Only) bench, is a visual analogy to the title. In many cases these changes in work environment were perceived by the European schol-ars who found a new home in Black institutions as an experience that "changed and enriched our lives in significant ways, both intellectually and emotionally."[45]

The collaboration of Viktor Löwenfeld and John Biggers is the only example in Edgcomb's book dealing with the art world. Löwenfeld, a refugee from Vienna, was en-gaged in transforming the department of industrial art at Hampton Institute into an art department. He believed that talented people could become artists in their own right and did not have to limit their aspirations to carrying out the designs of others. Biggers, later an important artist, an art educator, and a professor of art, came to Hampton College in 1941 from Gastonia, North Carolina, with the intention of becoming a plumber.[46] Löwenfeld's evening art classes changed his destiny. Giving up plumbing "meant a tre-mendous risk," recalls Biggers, "because making a living was extremely important. So, when I enrolled in Viktor's evening drawing class a new world began."[47]

The close interaction between the two was both artistic and personal. Artistically, Löwenfeld, who later wrote *Creative and Mental Growth*, a textbook on art education, encouraged his students to be true to themselves.[48] In other words, the creative was closely related to the mental, and the mental meant finding one's sources of creativity not in the external world, but rather in the internal. Black students were encouraged to engage in self-expression that would bring them nearer to their own roots. "I began to see art . . . as a responsibility to reflect the spirit and style of the Negro people," Biggers reported.[49] Most importantly, Löwenfeld brought Black students into close contact with African art, which, as Biggers himself admitted, did not appeal to him in the beginning, and he could not understand "why Löwenfeld wanted us to look at the ugly stuff!"[50] Löwenfeld taught Biggers "the profound meaning of it, the great meaning of African art, its humanistic tradition and how old all this must have been. . . . I realized that I had a heritage, and inheritance that I was entirely unaware of before."[51] For the teacher it was crucial to build a link between Black students and their African heritage. Furthermore, "in drawing, students no longer felt the need to make faces look Caucasian." In the days when African-American artists preferred to travel to Europe (mainly Paris) to study the masters, old and new, Löwenfeld believed that they should also go to Africa. With his encouragement, Biggers later did.[52]

On the personal level, the relationship between Biggers and Löwenfeld was that of shared intimacy between two persecuted people. Biggers remembers the day Löwenfeld read him a letter from the State Department, telling him that his family had perished:

> Now this was—this was one of the—again one of the most horrendous experiences I've ever had because a human being was telling me that his family—and he named them—were victims; they had been burned. . . . And I had heard of neighbors whose—members of the families had been lynched. But I realized that race and color might not have any meaning at all when it comes to terrifying experiences in this world. . . . I always felt a relationship with Viktor because he had shared this with me. I felt the relationship had truly crossed all country and racial barriers, so that those barriers were crossed now.[53]

Perhaps the best visual example illustrating the experience of crossing the barriers is Biggers's painting *Crossing the Bridge* (fig. 2, 1942), in which the artist shows the wandering of a Black family, carrying their meager possessions—on the head, on the back, in a cart—as they move over a bridge from one world to another. The imagery recalls the theme of the "Wandering Jew."[54] Another illustration of shared destiny can be seen in Biggers's elongated drawing on corrugated board, *Middle Passage* (fig. 3, 1947). Rather than depicting a whole slave ship, the artist concentrates on a fragment of the hull, thus enhancing the sense of congestion in the multilevel bunks in which people were caged. This image, in which the disproportionately huge hands suggest a great need, is reminiscent of the famous photographs of inmates of Nazi concentration camps. Once more, probably due to his familiarity with the Holocaust experience through Löwenfeld's accounts, Biggers draws a visual analogy between the Black and the Jewish lot in his depiction of the misfortunes of Black people.

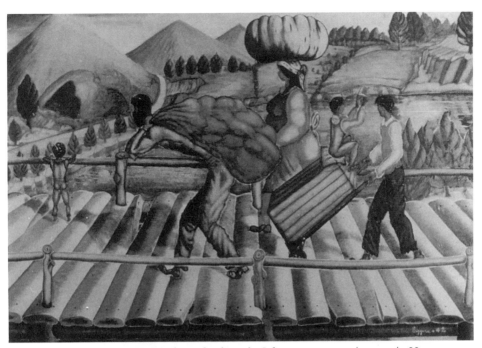

FIG. 2. John Biggers, *Crossing the Bridge* (1942), Oil on canvas, 30 $^1/_2$ x 45 $^1/_2$. Hampton University Museum, Virginia. Courtesy of John Biggers.

Biggers became an artist of Black life. His paintings and sculptures attest to the hardships of his people, as can be seen in paintings such as *Crucifixion* (1942), *Night of the Poor* (1948), and the *First Shotgun, Third Ward #1* (1966). He sometimes made punning allusions to European works of art to which he had been introduced in Löwenfeld's art classes. In *Gleaners* (1943), the artist alludes ironically to Millet's naturalistic painting: rather than harmoniously and rhythmically gathering the wheat, here the protagonists walking on a railroad track collect the scattered pieces of coal that fall off passing trains. However, Biggers also celebrates the beauty and rhythm of the Black people and Black life. In various paintings and murals, such as *The Web of Life* (1975–76), a mural for the science building of Texas Southern University, the artist delved into the mysteries of the life cycle, inspired by his sojourn in Africa.

Another common denominator between Biggers and Löwenfeld was their intellectual curiosity. When Löwenfeld moved to a new position as professor of art education at Pennsylvania State University, Biggers followed him there and acquired a master's degree. At the beginning of the 1950s, when Biggers did research for a YWCA mural, *The Contribution of Negro Women to American Life and Education* (Houston), Löwenfeld suggested that the research become a doctoral dissertation. In 1954 Biggers became a full professor at Texas Southern University. Löwenfeld himself remained engaged with African-American art, in both his teaching and his writing.[55] Biggers has acknowledged

FIG. 3. John Biggers, *Middle Passage* (1947),
crayon on corrugated board, 9 $^1/_8$ x 12 $^1/_4$.
Collection of the artist, courtesy of John
Biggers.

Löwenfeld's impact on his own teaching and on his students: "I have several ex-students who are teachers now, who paint, too, and we compare our work and discuss the meaning of painting. Löwenfeld and his tremendous insight always comes into the conversation."[56]

Other important African-American artists who encountered Löwenfeld during their stay at Hampton were Elizabeth Catlett and Charles White. While White executed a mural commission, Catlett taught at Hampton when Löwenfeld was the department chair. He became a personal friend and mentor. According to Samella Lewis, Löwenfeld "had an intense concern for human dignity. This insistence on dignity, a constructive solution to Elizabeth's concerns about injustice, has colored Catlett's work ever since."[57]

Another example of close collaboration between a Black academic art institution and a Jewish professor can be seen in the career of Lila Oliver Asher, an artist and fine arts teacher, who was born in Philadelphia in 1921. For forty-four years (1947–1991), Asher taught in the art department at Howard University, the oldest academic art department in Washington D.C. Throughout her stay she was the only White member of the department. Her appointment was initiated by Franz Rapp, a refugee from Nazi Germany and former director of the Munich Theatre Museum. In the early days she had close contacts with the department's founders, James V. Herring and the art historian James Porter, whose pioneering book *Modern Negro Art* became a classic. Asher's own minority perspective encouraged her sensitivity to the Black minority. In her graphic art and her sculptures womanhood in general and the theme of mother and child in particular play a central role. She often uses black and white linocuts to depict symbiosis and commitment between African-American mothers and their children. The image of Hagar in her linocut *Expulsion of Hagar* (fig. 4, 1961), a prototype of the rejected maidservant cast out into the desert, conveys the African-American artistic equation of Hagar's Egyptian ancestry with Africa, making her a symbol of African-American slavery.[58] In Asher's image the expulsion is conveyed through the dominating outstretched patriarchal hand of Abraham in the foreground, while Hagar and Ishmael fade away in the background. Asher's iconographic choice is reminiscent of the work of Edmonia Lewis, the first major sculptor of African-American and Native-American origins, whose work *Hagar* (1875) signifies the expulsion from Africa to slavery.[59]

The 1991 retrospective at the Howard University Art Gallery, "Lila Oliver Asher: The Years at Howard, 1948–1991," was an unusual event. Although there is no written policy on the matter, the focus of Howard exhibitions has been on African-American artists. Among Asher's students were leading artists and art historians such as Romare Bearden and David Driskell, who also wrote the introduction to the catalogue, associating Lila Asher with the department's "glorious past." As for her teaching,

> The writer remembers poignantly the clarity with which Asher taught, extolling the virtues of keenly observing the beauty of the human figure. The memorable lectures she delivered to a small class of students in the early

FIG. 4. Lila Oliver Asher, *Expulsion of Hagar* (1961), linocut. Collection of the artist, courtesy of Lila Oliver Asher.

1950s have served as model lesson plans for those of us who have made teaching a lifelong commitment. I am grateful to have been Asher's student four decades ago, her colleague at Howard University in the 1960s and most importantly have over forty years counted her among treasured friends.[60]

It is not surprising that Lila Asher's work became part of the Barnett-Aden collection in the Museum of African American Art in Tampa, Florida. Two of her sculptures, both entitled *Female Figure* (1983), are in this collection.[61]

The abundant literature on the relationship between African Americans and Jewish Americans does not sufficiently acknowledge the existence of a visual dimension. In fact, only one text is specifically devoted to this subject, *Bridges and Boundaries*, the catalogue of a courageous and thought-provoking exhibition at the Jewish Museum in New York in 1992. Organizers were comprised of two museum staff members and Gretchen Sullivan Sorin, an African-American social historian. A combined venture with the NAACP, the exhibition aimed to examine the relationship between African Americans and Jewish Americans in the twentieth century, revealing a complex and dramatic story of cooperation and conflict.[62] Although the catalogue contains significant articles on the background of the relationship between Jews and African Americans, the essay on the art itself is fragmentary and does not do justice to either the scope of the works exhibited or the individual artists and major works shown. Exhibits by leading artists, such as Philip Guston, Larry Rivers, and Art Spiegelman, are not even mentioned in the catalogue. It has been noted that "art . . . plays a curious role in the exhibition, often as supplementary illustration."[63] Ron Harrington, writing for *Black Ivory*, also wished that the exhibition and the book "should have had more in common."[64]

The present book attempts to deal with the various visual languages, the thematic concerns, and the developments and changes in the way artists of both backgrounds have viewed each other during the last hundred years. It follows and elaborates the approach of the Jewish Museum exhibition by studying artists pursuing positive visions as well as those reflecting harsh realities (both expressed by ideologically committed artists of the left), but widens the chronological scope. Accordingly, I looked for the beginning of this visual dialogue in the early portrayals of Jews by the Black artist Henry Ossawa Tanner at the turn of the nineteenth century. I also hope to fill a lacuna in the *Bridges and Boundaries* exhibition regarding the Harlem Renaissance of the 1920s, drawing an analogy between the New Negro and the New Jew. The last part of the book deals with artists working in the final third of the twentieth century: those personally involved in their lives and through the expression of their private dreams, and those working in a post-modernist vein, emphasizing the role of language and text in the visual arts. The use of language has proved particularly effective in articulating social and racial issues.

The book investigates artists of both groups in their mutual rapport, each group examining "the other" which becomes a journey of self-discovery as well. This examination, which rests on mirroring, also at times leads to disillusionment and criticism. As a general overview, the artists discussed belong to two categories, reflecting two modes of thought: first, the typically ideological, the "engaged artists," either the African Americans involved in formulating their own artistic language, or the Jewish Americans socially and ideologically committed to the Black cause in the 1930s and during the civil rights movement; and second, the "engaged/disengaged" artists of the end of the twentieth century, who use the relation between the visual and the verbal image as a means of evoking ambiguities. Artists of this second category have been posing questions rather than giving definite answers, problematizing issues rather than raising banners. However, even in this skeptical mode, the fact that artists of the two communities are rubbing shoulders with each other demonstrates that they cannot completely break apart.

The book, therefore, has two emphases, starting with those who have the answers and ending with those who raise questions. It combines a thematic with a chronological approach. Due to the multifaceted nature of the visual material, the analysis cannot follow a purely chronological line, thematic considerations at times overriding the historical narrative.

The topic is also relevant to the growing awareness of the place of ethnicity and race in contemporary society and culture. Contemporary discourse, shying away from the "ivory tower" mentality of modernism, introduces the cultural impact of minorities into the study of culture and art. The visual material naturally lends itself to contemporary methodology, which includes both "high" and "low" art as equally legitimate topics in the study of social and cultural trends. The study examines painting, sculpture, cartoons (in both the Jewish-Yiddish and African-American press), comics, and installations. The often personal involvement of artists in the social themes underlying their works made it necessary to search archival material as well as to conduct interviews, when possible.

In contrast to the abundant literature dealing with the social and political relationships between the two communities, parallel studies of the visual dimension are strikingly absent.[65] A possible explanation for this absence may lie in the predominance of abstraction in the modernist language of art, which does not lend itself to the articulation of social issues. Although major Jewish-American artists contributed to the formation of abstract art, and some of them were surely personally concerned with racial justice, these issues did not play a role in their artistic creation. At the same time, figurative artists wishing to express an ethnic or minority identity were by and large marginalized, both in the case of artists concerned with their own identity and in that of artists interested in the identity of the other. Hence abstraction, advocated by Modernism as well as by critics such as Harold Rosenberg and Clement Greenberg, who happened to be Jewish, influenced the art world in general and the research undertaken by scholars in particular. The admonitions of these critics were addressed equally to Jewish and Black artists as well as to other particularistic trends.

There is a fundamental difference in the way ethnic identity can be ascribed to

artists of the two groups discussed in this book. Whereas it would be a fair generaliza-
tion to say that most Black artists identified themselves as engaged in the art of Black
people, most Jewish-American artists would not consider themselves as engaged in Jewish art. Nevertheless, the underlying assumption of this book is that the way racial issues
are portrayed by artists of Jewish origin reflects the typically universalist interests of
much of secular post-Enlightenment Jewish culture.

The formative environment of Jewish-American artists was typically urban and
northern. These artists, who emerged in the 1920s and 1930s, were either first-genera-
tion American born or, more likely, immigrants. They did not experience nature and the
place of human beings in it in the same way as did American artists who had been deeply
rooted in the country for many generations. An example of the latter is Winslow Homer.
As John Wilmerding has shown, Homer, in *The Gulf Stream* (1899), in contrast to negative portrayals of Blacks, identifies in this seascape with the image of the lonely Black
man drifting in a boat. Wilmerding drew attention to the only existing photograph of
Winslow Homer in which the artist (himself a loner) is seen next to the Gulf Stream,
suggesting this circumstance as an indication of Homer's identification with the painted
figure.[66]

Life in the big city, in tenement housing, led to close association and shared daily
experience of Jews and members of other minorities, including Blacks. The artists of
these groups came from this milieu, being typically associated with the social realism of
the "Ashcan school."[67] Their left-wing inclinations and their sensitivity to social issues
were shared by many African-American artists. The remark by the Black painter Aaron
Douglas that "the Negro artist, unlike the white artist, has never known the big house.
He is essentially a product of the masses," is applicable to the Jewish-American artists of
the first half of the twentieth century.[68]

However, these distinctions between urban and nonurban perceptions of African-
American life rapidly became blurred after the middle of the twentieth century, when
most of the art scene, non-Jewish as well Jewish, moved to the big cities. Andy Warhol,
Duane Hanson, and James Rosenquist are typical examples in that period of non-Jewish
artists who raised Black issues and fought racism in art in a powerful and socially conscious way.

Thus, although there is a long tradition of mutual examination of Blacks and Whites
in American art, some of it based on conflict and animosity, some on sympathy and
common struggle, there is a particular, even unique character to the reciprocal gaze of
Jews and African Americans. This is associated with their common status as minorities
in an often intolerant society, sharing some fundamental goals of recognition and integration but also competing in forming group identities in the larger society. It is this
unique historical position, which is so poignantly portrayed by the tragic tug-of-war of
the two figures chained to each other in *CommonQuest* that justifies a systematic study of
the mutual reflection of Blacks and Jews in American art.

CHAPTER I

African Americans mirroring Jews

Our Negro American painter of outstanding success is Henry O. Tanner. . . . Though a professed painter of types, he has devoted his art talent mainly to the portrayal of Jewish Biblical types and subjects, and has never maturely touched the portrayal of the Negro subject.[1]

Thus said Alain Locke, speaking with the voice of the Harlem Renaissance, in an article that has become a classic on African art and its role in the formation of African-American "racial art." Locke's concern with Tanner's preferences is associated with the former's search for an authentic "African idiom." Ironically, the likelihood of finding this authentic idiom for African-American art in African art is mediated by the enumeration of the many cases in which African art influenced modernist painting in general. Locke implies that as Picasso, Matisse, Derain, Modigliani, Epstein, Lipchitz, and others found direct and profound inspiration in African art, so could an African American like Tanner.[2]

Indeed, Henry Tanner was an outstanding artist who gained recognition abroad as well as in America. Furtheromore, independent of his artistic success, Tanner was the first Black artist to portray Jews. I would like to argue that his choice of Jewish characters expresses his own sense of "otherness." Tanner finds in the Jewish "other" an echo of his own racial difference. In this sense, Locke's reading of Tanner's art seems to minimize the deeper motivation behind the images. Tanner's focus on Jewish biblical types went beyond a mere attraction to orientalism.

Henry Ossawa Tanner was born in Pittsburgh in 1859, the son of a minister who eventually became the Bishop of the African Methodist Episcopal Church. The father was a scholar, a prolific author, and an editor of journals that went beyond the church. Obviously, Tanner was exposed to the biblical narrative through his father's sermons and scholarly writings. A student of Thomas Eakins at the Pennsylvania Academy of the Fine Arts and then in 1881 of Benjamin Constant at the Académie Julien in Paris, Tanner can be described as a man torn between three worlds: America, Paris, and African-

American culture. This agrees with the observation of poet Paul Laurence Dunbar (1872–1906) that the Black writer not only lives in two worlds but also writes for two worlds. In Tanner's case there were even three.[3]

This fragmented identity is reflected in Tanner's expatriate life of forty-six years in Paris. He did not follow Eakins's advice to remain in America as a way of becoming a great American painter and even told "coloured artists who sought his help. . . that they could have it as artists, not Negroes."[4] Paris, the cosmopolitan center of the art world at the time, was for Tanner a universalistic refuge from his multifaceted identity. For him art, in its pure form, meant abstracting oneself from particularity, whether local or racial.

Tanner himself was exposed to racial and ethnic stereotyping and unpleasantness as a student at the Pennsylvania Academy. In a chapter in his memoirs with the racist heading "The Coming of the Nigger," Joseph Pennell, artist and later member of the National Academy, wrote how the easel of the "negro" (who does not even merit a name) was taken to the street one night, "and though not painfully crucified, he was firmly tied to it and left there." Pennell goes on to draw an analogy between Black and Jewish artists: "Curiously, there never has been a great Negro artist or a great Jew artist in the history of the world." He seems to enjoy his racist and anti-Semitic remarks which today sound farcical: "The only 'black' man—and he called himself a Moor—was Del Mazo. Rembrandt and Turner *were accused* of being Jewish, but they *never admitted* it during their lives."[5] Artists of both groups are charged with hiding their true identity. Being Jewish is seen in terms of misdeed and the most absurd of all—Pennell was only too eager to include Rembrandt and Turner among the "convicted."

Tanner visited the Holy Land twice, for six weeks in 1897 and again in 1898 for six months. These journeys provided the artist with "an insight into the country and the character of the people."[6] He was able to sense the sadness of the land through its landscape and its population and was attracted to the religious ardor of the Jewish worshipers. Thus the Judean mountains are described in a somber tone: "Those great barren hills that can blossom like a rose, with irrigation, were to me a natural setting, a fitting setting, to a great tragedy. The country, sad and desolate, is big and majestic."[7]

The melancholy romantic mood is reflected in a landscape, *A View in Palestine* (fig. 5, 1898–99) depicting a vast panorama of the Judean Hills from a high vantage point, leaving a very narrow strip for a skyline. Rather than depicting the harsh light, Tanner turned to the heaviness of the strong shadows, juxtaposing fading olive green vegetation with the stark heaviness of the Judean mountains' stoniness. Yet notwithstanding the specific location, the landscape conveys a certain primordial quality. Horizontally undefined with no vertical objects to suggest a framing boundary, it seems to expand to both sides, creating the illusion of unlimited space. The spiritual response vis-à-vis infinity, the "Sublime," associated with American panoramic landscapes (and with German Romanticism), is projected by Tanner onto the majestic view of the hills in Judea. The typically contemplative and religious attitude of American landscape painting

FIG. 5. Henry Ossawa Tanner, *A View in Palestine* (1898–99), oil on canvas, 23 x 37 $^3/_4$. Frances Lehman Loeb Art Center, Vassar College. Gift of Mrs. Walter Driscoll (Margaret L. Weyerhaeuser, class of 1923), Mrs. F. Rodman Titcomb (Elizabeth L. Weyerhaeuser, class of 1915), and Robert J. Siversten (Sarah Weyerhaeuser, class of 1930). 1946.3.3.

is applied quite naturally to the depiction of the Holy Land, although the lush green of America and Europe had to be replaced by the dryness of the land and its lackluster vegetation.

Tanner's characterization of the landscape, in word and painting, drawing an analogy between the land and its people in a national sense, is an extension of the attitude to American geography in which "nature and nation have been mutually dependent in defining one another."[8]

Although nature serves as a metonym for the people, Tanner also took a closer look at these people's history in *The Wailing Wall* (fig. 6, 1897). His interest in the Western Wall shows his understanding of what the place stood for in the eyes of the worshipers. With Black history in mind, the double function that prayer served in the time of slavery, and the coded language of Black spirituals, Tanner was aware of the dual function of prayers at the "Wailing Place." He depicted the site as symbolizing the destruction and the hoped-for revival of the old Temple, an image that became a visual icon for a specific national struggle, constantly repeated by artists in the nineteenth and twentieth centuries. Tanner painted the wall and worshipers with great empathy and an emphasis on the group as well as on the individual: "Nor do I forget the deep pathos of 'Jews' Wailing Place'—those tremendous foundation stones of that glorious temple that stood upon Mount Moriah, worn smooth by the loving touch of tearful and devout worshippers from all over the world, under the scornful gaze of the to-day Turkish conqueror."[9]

FIG. 6. Henry Ossawa Tanner, *The Wailing Wall* (1897),
oil on canvas, 25 $^{1}/_{2}$ x 19 $^{1}/_{4}$. Museum of Art, Rhode Island School of Design.
Gift of Mr. and Mrs. Leonard Granoff.

Like the tragedy of the desolate landscape, Tanner perceived the tragedy of the people in their subjugation to a foreign occupier. He evidently identified with the oppressed Jews, who nevertheless maintained their faith. This seems to echo the strong belief of Tanner's father, Benjamin Tucker Tanner, who in *The Negro's Origin and Is the Negro Cursed* declared: "The genealogical table of the Negro, written in his own flesh, remains. Ages of scourging have not sufficed to erase it. Written by the finger of God, it is more enduring than the stones of Sinai."[10]

Benjamin Tanner compared the genealogical persistence of Black identity with that of the Jewish people as symbolized by the "stones of Sinai," an abstract reference to Moses' Tablets of the Law. For Henry Tanner the grand stones of the Wailing Wall were the concretized symbol of Jewish perseverance, physically enduring under all hostile political oppression. The spiritual metaphor of a heavenly Sinai in the churchly father's text was transformed into a more political image of earthly Jerusalem in the painter son.

Albert Boime refers to Benjamin Tucker Tanner's direct identification of the Jew and the Negro in relation to bondage and rehabilitation. Both peoples had a mind to work, building the city of Jerusalem on the one hand and the African Methodist Episcopal Church on the other.[11] Boime reads Tanner's description of the Wailing Wall as a "displaced sense of persecution and religious compensation." He also associates Mosby's analysis of *Daniel in the Lion's Den* (1895) with Tanner's conception of the Wailing Wall.[12] According to Mosby the highly controversial Dreyfus Affair raging during his sojourn in Paris might have strengthened Tanner's sense of identification with the Jews on issues of race and persecution. This writer even asks: "Could Tanner have seen himself in the figure of the lonely, persecuted Daniel?"[13] To this we may add that Daniel played a role in Black spirituals based on biblical stories:

> Daniel was a Hebrew Child
> He went to pray to God for a while
> The King at once for Daniel did send
> And he put him right down in the lion's den.[14]

If that is indeed the case, we have gone beyond Alain Locke's conception of Tanner's art as racially detached.

While Tanner feels with Daniel, in *Nicodemus Visiting Jesus* (fig. 7, 1899) he also empathizes with the models representing the protagonists. For this painting, done in Jerusalem, Tanner chose local Yemenite Jews to sit for him. "I still remember with pleasure the fine head of the old Yemenite Jew who posed for Nicodemus."[15] In fact, it seems that both models were Yemenites. Boime brings to his reading of the painting an interpretation by Scarborough, an African-American critic, according to whom Tanner's biblical figures were successful because he showed "the Jew as he must have lived and looked nearly twenty centuries ago." Scarborough related the artist's sensitivity to the way Jews are supposed to have looked in the distant past to his own racial self-awareness. This, as well as Tanner's own remark on the Yemenite Jew, is rightly perceived by Boime to be "a displaced and codified ethnic assertion that has implications for the African Methodist Episcopalian Church as well."[16]

To take these insights a step further, Tanner may have chosen the Yemenites not only because of their "Semitic features," but primarily because of the color of their skin. Let us bear in mind that Tanner's biblical protagonists were usually White (e.g., *Daniel in the Lion's Den*, 1895; *The Resurrection of Lazarus*, 1896; *The Return of the Holy Women, Two Disciples at the Tomb*, 1904–05). The African-American art historian James Porter makes a point of his surprise at the "whiteness" of Henry Tanner himself when he first met him.[17] Since Tanner was of mulatto descent, he might have seen Yemenites as people with whom he could sympathize; he could have been attracted to them as representing the dark-skinned people of the White race. From his perspective, they could have been equated with the "Jewish Negro."[18]

Among the Christians of the American Colony in Jerusalem whom Tanner could have met, the Yemenite Jews found particular favor and interest. In the words of a modern historian, "the encounter of these Christians with the Yemenite Jews was electrifying." The colony was struck by the Yemenites' "dark skin with dark hair and dark eyes." It should be noted that when the first Yemenite Jews came to Palestine, mostly in 1881–82, the authenticity of their Jewishness was questioned by some members of the old Jewish community in Jerusalem.[19] Besides, they were traditionally artisans, known for their intricate jewelry. Tanner may have been aware of the low social status of this group and their experience of being rejected by their co-religionists.

Tanner's *Nicodemus Visiting Jesus* (John 3:1–3) is a night scene. This choice of subject stems from Black history. Henry Louis Gates's remark that "the slaves metaphorically 'owned' the night, while the master owned the day" can be applied to Tanner's painting.[20] The practice of night rituals, according to Mosby, is the result of forbidding slaves to engage in religious practices during the day. Full-fledged Sunday night services are still performed by many African-American and evangelical denominations.[21] Romare Bearden and Harry Henderson emphasize Nicodemus's New Testament status as a "ruler of the Jews," meeting secretly with Jesus. Furthermore, since Nicodemus converted, the story "is analogous to tales of slaveholders who, in secret conversations with abolitionists, became converted to their cause."[22] Tanner in his mystical night scene depicting Nicodemus visiting Jesus thus creates through the darkness of the Yemenite model a bridge between the races, between the biblical past and the present, and between subjugated peoples.

Tanner seems to have anticipated the employment of the Yemenite Jews as models at the Bezalel Art School, which was established in Jerusalem in 1906 as part of the search for the cultural rebirth of the Jewish people in their homeland. For the Bezalel artists, such as Abel Pann, who was born in Latvia in 1883 and emigrated to Palestine in

FIG. 7. Henry Ossawa Tanner, *Nicodemus Visiting Jesus* (1899), oil on canvas, 33 $^{11}/_{16}$ x 39 $^{1}/_{3}$. Courtesy of the Museum of American Art of the Pennsylvania Academy of the Fine Arts, Philadelphia, Joseph E. Temple Fund.

1913, as for Tanner, the Yemenites served as images on which to project their biblical fantasies. An example is Pann's pastel of Sarah, bejeweled in traditional Yemenite costume, and intended as an illustration to Genesis 12:14: "When Abram was come into Egypt the Egyptians beheld the woman that she was very fair." The *Sacrifice of Isaac* (fig. 8, 1943) became a leitmotif in Pann's art from the 1920s through the 1940s. In the 1943 version, drawn in response to World War II, Pann deviates from the biblical story and traditional portrayals of the theme. There is no ram as substitute, and the possibility that Isaac will indeed be sacrificed is suggested. The head tilted upward of the trapped son resembles that of a Yemenite youth.

As for Tanner, his biblical themes should not be separated from his portrayal of Jews as such, as in *Head of a Jew in Palestine* (fig. 9, 1899 and ca. 1920). According to the information on a paper label at the lower left of the stretcher, the painting, originally made in Palestine, was redone at a later date in Europe. Mosby, one of the authors of the Tanner exhibition catalogue for the Philadelphia Museum of Art, holds that this paint

FIG. 8. Abel Pann, *Sacrifice of Isaac* (1943), pastel. Collection Itiel Pann,
courtesy of Itiel Pann, Jerusalem, Israel.

ing is based on the same model, namely a Yemenite Jew, as the *Nicodemus Visiting Jesus*.
However, the later portrait shows a face not at all typical of a Yemenite. Mosby traces the
difference to the style of the beard and tries to explain it by the reworking of the picture.[23]
However, the striking contrast between this head and the typical Yemenite lies more
generally in color and features. The personage has light-colored Western, European Jewish (Ashkenazi) looks. There are two possible ways of accounting for the difference
between the head of Nicodemus and that of the portrait. Either Tanner has physically
"bleached" the dark-looking figure of the 1899 painting, altering some of the facial traits,
or the painting was based on a different model altogether, a non-Yemenite. In either case
the final painting in conjunction with the early one indicates Tanner's dual attraction to
and wavering between two racial types as projected on Jewish models in Jerusalem. It is
known that thanks to his reputation as a painter of Jewish types, the artist was commissioned to paint the portrait of Rabbi Stephen Wise, an important religious leader in
America, but the painting has been lost.[24]

Tanner's identity quest as reflected in his choice of biblical themes, manifested at
the turn of the nineteenth century and the beginning of the twentieth, revived at a later
stage, toward the end of his life. His ambivalence emerges again in the painting called

FIG. 9. Henry Ossawa Tanner, *Head of a Jew in Palestine* (1899 and ca. 1920), oil on canvas, 24 x 21 $^1/_8$. National Museum of American Art, Smithsonian Institution, gift of Mr. and Mrs. Norman B. Robbins.

FIG. 10. Winfred Russell, *A Study*, oil on canvas (lost) in *Opportunity* (1923).
Courtesy of the National Urban League.

Judas. Although the work was destroyed by the artist, there is a photograph of Tanner standing beside it, published in the *Baltimore Afro-American* (1937). According to this news item: "The famed 78-year-old artist is shown beside his painting of the penitent Judas. The picture above in his Paris studio on the Boulevard Saint Jacques, was destroyed by the artist after completion, because he was dissatisfied with it."[25]

Tanner deviates from the traditional iconography of the theme of Judas as the betrayer of Christ for thirty pieces of silver, depicting the disciple in the pose usually associated with the return of the Prodigal Son. Could this concept refer to his personal involvement with the theme, his sense that by living in Paris he had betrayed his people, his repentance, and his continued hesitation leading to his dissatisfaction with the portrayed image and its destruction? The *Judas* thus suggests that Tanner did not achieve a sense of equilibrium toward the end of his life but remained torn between the various realms of his existence.

Tanner's portrayals of Jews raise a question which is relevant to the entire scope of the present book, namely that of the relationship between type and stereotype. As a matter of fact these two terms describe the same phenomenon: the characterization of an individual as belonging to a group. The normative attitude to a type leads to the concept of the stereotype. Historically speaking, contemporary discourse dealing with the "other" focuses on stereotype in the negative sense, whereas artists concerned with the emergence of racial and ethnic identity at the turn of the nineteenth century were engaged in the quest for a positive representation of a type. Linda Nochlin problematizes the issues concerning "Jewishness" as a "visual trope" and asks how a distinction can be made between "an image of Jews which is anti-semitic and one which is 'positive.'"[26] In other words, should a "Jewish nose" always be interpreted in the negative sense? Tanner looked for Hebraic types; his *Raising of Lazarus* (1896) comprises a group of figures with "Hebraic faces of all ages."[27] These recur in other scenes such as *Two Disciples at the Tomb* (1906). The common denominator of all these protagonists is the traditionally crooked "Jewish nose." Nochlin's notion of the contextuality and intentionality of the artist's portrayal as a means for understanding what is behind the choice for a representation of a Jew can be applied to Tanner, who looked for types to represent the biblical themes. Hence, a Lazarus representing "the struggle and hopes of Black Americans,"[28] with a very distinctive "Jewish" nose, does not carry a condemnatory connotation, but is rather a depiction of a type in a descriptive way. A contemporary reading of Tanner's Hebrew types as negative stereotypes would therefore be anachronistically wrong.

When we return to the reworked *Head of a Jew in Palestine*, we are confronted by the bust of a patriarchal figure, in a contemplative mood. The high brow, long beard, aquiline nose, and heavy gown create a sense of authority and command. A pertinent comparison can be made with the study of the head of a Jew done by another Black artist, Winfred Russell, published in an issue of *Opportunity: A Journal of Negro Life* (1923) as an illustration for an article on Black artists, titled *A Study* (fig. 10). The writer reviews the state of Black art in America and hails the few recognized Black artists, "who gained prominence after years of the most trying circumstances" and who should serve as role models for the younger generation of artists. The article mentions particularly the position of Henry Tanner as a preeminent and "leading painter of the race."[29]

A comparison between Tanner's *Head of a Jew in Palestine* and Russell's study reveals that both were attracted by the solemnity and intellectual power of the figures, depicted with emphasis. However, whereas Tanner's image is majestic, Russell's head is more realistic, and less idealized. The article does not mention Jews, but the very choice of a typically Jewish portrait illustrating an article on Black artists indicates the continuous interest of Black art in Jewish themes.

The attitude of Black writers to Jews can be further considered in the context of the Harlem Renaissance. In spite of present-day criticism, *The New Negro*, edited by Alain Locke, is still the definitive text, the Bible of the Harlem Renaissance, "that dramatic upsurge of creativity in literature, music, and art within black America that reached its zenith in the second half of the 1920s."[30] Arnold Rampersad comments on the paradoxical role of Locke, who never lived in Harlem, nor in the South, where most Blacks were still living at the turn of the century. Although Locke was much influenced during his studies in Germany by Herder's ideas of "the folk," Rampersad remarks that his "sense of the folk was mainly theoretical."[31] In that respect he reminds one of Theodor Herzl, the founder of modern Zionism, who also came from an upper middle-class background and who did not live among the masses he wished to lead. Both leaders had never actually lived in the regions from which "their people" were expecting to be liberated.

While Locke tries to place Harlem in the context of world events, referring to India, China, Egypt, Ireland, Russia, Bohemia, Mexico, and Palestine, *The New Negro* also has numerous allusions to the Jewish people. There are no fewer than thirty six references to "Jew," "Jews," "Judaism," "Zionism," "Hebrew," and "Israel." Jews serve as a comparative model against which to examine Black identity. In the "Foreword" Locke takes "Palestine full of renascent Judaism" as the model for the "New Negro."[32] In his essay "The New Negro," Harlem is compared to "the home of the Negro's 'Zionism.'" Furthermore, he writes, "as with the Jew, persecution is making the Negro international."[33]

In the year that *The New Negro* was published, Langston Hughes's poignant poem "America" appeared in *Opportunity*.[34] According to Rampersad, this poem is related to a voyage that Hughes, accompanied by Locke, made to Venice in 1924. During their stay Hughes insisted on visiting the Jewish Ghetto.[35] The term "ghetto" appears in the poem, in both the Jewish European and in the African-American context. "America," written in monologue form, draws an analogy between the "little dark baby" and "the little Jew baby" in their relationship to America. America is defined in terms of "dream," "vision," "the star seeking I." Looking at the past, the poem creates a neat parallel:

> Out of yesterday
> The chains of slavery;
> Out of yesterday,
> The Ghettos of Europe;
> Out of yesterday,
> The poverty and pain of the old, old world,
> The building and struggle of this new one, . . .

There is a sense in which the two boys' appearance is seen in terms of the reconciliation of rather surprising opposites:

> You and I,
> You of the blue eyes
> And the blond hair,
> I of the dark eyes
> And the crinkly hair.
> You and I
> Offering hands
> Being brothers,
> Being one,
> Being America. . . .

Another contributor to *The New Negro* draws an analogy between the West Indians and the Jews, both being "ambitious, eager for education, willing to engage in business, argumentative, aggressive and possessed of great proselytizing zeal for any cause they espouse."[36] The book also includes an article on the raison d'être of the independent Howard University, called "the National Negro University." The author offers as an analogy the Jewish universities of America and Palestine (as well as Catholic and Protestant institutions) that, like the Negro university, are designed to investigate the particularistic nature of each culture; he writes that while in the Jewish case the universities derive their inspiration from the "elders of Israel," the future leadership of the Black institution should emerge from within the Negro race since its elders were not Black but missionaries.[37]

Writing on city life, Charles Johnson contends that in contrast to those demanding "a United Negro Trades Union" structured like the "United Hebrew Trades," the Blacks are generally skeptical and individualistic.[38] James Weldon Johnson proclaims the superiority of Harlem in the American context. Unlike the alien languages of immigrants, such as Yiddish or Italian, the language of Black Harlem is English. "Harlem talks

American, reads American, thinks American."[39] With all the power of the repeated analogy between the plight of the African Americans and other ethnic minorities, this quotation highlights the distinctive local position of the Blacks who are not newcomers but rather an integral part of the linguistic culture. To the Harlem Renaissance this was a source of pride and hope, as is most notably reflected by the literary contribution of the Black Renaissance in poetry, fiction, and drama.

In his article on "The Negro Spirituals," Alain Locke sees similarities between African-American folk songs and the Psalms—the expression of Jewish spiritual experience—which according to Du Bois are the only parallel to Black folk songs.[40] This analogy is fictionalized in the dramatic story "Fern" (excerpted from *Cane*) by Jean Toomer. The story deals with the mystical power of music transcending the two cultures. The writer draws an analogy between Fern's nose, which is described as "aquiline, Semitic," and the songs of the Jewish cantor. Her image evokes strong feelings of sorrow, like the effect of the cantor's voice. The story ends with a mystical experience. Fern sings convulsively, "mingled with calls to Christ Jesus. And then she sang, brokenly. A Jewish cantor singing with a broken voice."[41] She loses her own identity as she becomes merged with the Jewish cantor—the physical and spiritual lead to complete identification.

Toomer's story has been criticized by other scholars. Rampersad queries whether Toomer was not out of place "in a brave new world of Negro-ness," since he himself resented being referred to as a "Negro" (despite his Black ancestry).[42] And Henry Louis Gates, while analyzing Toomer's complex personality and his reception by various critics, also sees Toomer in terms of "racial castration."[43] It is worthwhile noting that the reaction to Toomer's writings can be compared to the criticism of Henry Tanner's painting and for similar reasons. Moreover, it is striking that both artists, Toomer and Tanner, who were able to form a bridge between the two peoples, were partly rejected by their fellow Blacks as not genuinely expressing "Negro-ness." And we are reminded of the observation by Locke quoted at the beginning of this chapter, referring to Tanner's neglect of Black subject matter.

Though in his critique of Tanner, Locke specifically highlights content matter, he is in fact mainly concerned with style. African art is "classic" in its lesson of discipline and is perceived as the most stylized form of art. The newly acquired respectability of the African idiom should serve as a basis for a racial idiom. "Racial art" ought to be inspired by the limitless wealth of the decorative aspects and symbolic nature of the folk tradition in African art.[44]

Locke's phrase, "Palestine full of renascent Judaism," takes us to another realm of comparison, that of national and racial revival in the arts, that of the New Negro and the New Jew. Although the Hebrew Renaissance in the arts preceded World War I, the two artistic revivals have some features in common. In both cases, obvious differences notwithstanding, the cultural and artistic revivals were an integral part of the struggle for self-definition. The artists of the Harlem Renaissance and of the Zionist movement in Palestine were both engaged in an intensive search for particular forms of expression that would define their respective identities.

Bezalel, the first art school in Palestine, was founded in Jerusalem in 1906 by Boris Schatz (born in 1866 in Latvia) and other immigrant artists from Eastern Europe. Since the early Zionist congresses, these artists were engaged in a visual attempt to conceptualize the image of the New Jew. The school was designed to concentrate on both arts and crafts in a way that would reflect the local and "authentic" characteristics of the New Jew.

As is well known, there was a movement within the Harlem Renaissance to go back to the sources, to ancestry, to African art, to Ethiopia. The Zionist revival in the arts also believed in returning to the origins—the Bible, as well as artistic images having a flavor of the East, which in practice produced a mélange of styles (Sumerian, Ancient Egyptian, African, Yemenite, even Far Eastern). These stylistic interests were continued during the 1920s and the 1930s with the development of other artistic centers in Palestine and with the emergence of the Canaanite movement. For both the "New Jew" and the "New Negro" the revival in the arts stemmed from a reaction to a Eurocentric conception of the world, which of course was impelled by anti-European trends within the arts of Europe itself. These comparisons are relevant beyond the exact dates of the revivals, namely not just 1906 (Bezalel) and 1925–29 (Harlem Renaissance), but to trends leading to or following the two revivals.

The reaction was best manifested in the desire to return to what each of these cultures believed to be their ideal past. For both, revival also meant a reversal of physical stereotypes and a proud representation of those bodily features that were traditionally used as a means of denigration. In the illustrations to the Bible by the Bezalel artist E. M. Lilien (born in 1874 in Drohobycz, Galicia), the aquiline noses of his heroes is stressed as part of the wish to assert their Semitic identity as a source of pride. Lilien's *Joshua* (fig. 11, 1908) which depicts Theodor Herzl in an oriental garb and Assyrian beard, carrying a sword, is a case in point. And similarly, Aaron Douglas's cover illustration for *Opportunity*, done in the same year as the publication of *The New Negro* (fig. 12, December 1925), shows a dignified profile of an African-American youth, the protruding lips accentuated by the white background. His image in the forefront is complemented by the ideal city in the distance.

The element of self-awareness and pride is emphasized by Mary Schmidt Campbell in her introduction to the Studio Museum in Harlem's publication in homage to the Harlem Renaissance, "They were among the first Americans to celebrate Black history and culture and they were the first artists to define a visual vocabulary for Black Americans."[45]

Moreover, for the visionaries of the Hebrew and Harlem Renaissance, there was a gap between vision and reality. Boris Schatz's utopic book, *Jerusalem Rebuilt*, completely ignores the local situation, the poverty, the hunger, even the starvation, experienced especially during World War I.[46] As recent criticism of the Harlem Renaissance has remarked, "It was difficult to conceive of the horribleness of the American scene for black people during the era in which Locke produced his classical collection."[47] For these utopists art's being at odds with reality provided an escape mechanism from a harsh reality.

Another common denominator between the art of early Zionism and the Harlem Renaissance is the ideological commitment. For both groups, art had a message, and modernism's "art for art's sake" was a luxury they could not afford. Art as the salvation of mankind has been an underlying assumption behind many facets of Modernism. However, for both the New Jew and the New Negro, salvation was perceived in terms of its people. Each faced the conflict of particularism-segregationalism vs. universalism. An artistic form that could readily express the particularist aspect of a culture was book illustration, which played a role in both revivals.

An instructive example, one of many possible comparisons, is that between Aaron Douglas's *Invincible Music: The Spirit of Africa* (fig. 13, 1925, from the page opposite the article "The Negro Digs Up His Past" in *The New Negro*, published also a year later in *The Crisis*), and Abel Pann's *The Creation* (fig. 14, 1923), in his illustrations to the book of Genesis. Douglas, born in Kansas in 1899, was the leading African-American illustrator of *The New Negro*, and a student of the Bavarian portrait illustrator of *The New Negro*, Winold Reiss.[48]

Douglas's emulation of African art was not viewed favorably by James Porter, who argued that his work lacked dynamism and "in its general effect bears but scant relationship to the powerful forms and religious message of African Negro Art."[49] Kirschke's comprehensive recent monograph on Douglas's art rejects these criticisms, claiming that no Black artist was as authentic as Douglas in his depiction of Black life and adaptation of African art. She holds that his immersion in African art was also related to his wish to reach the common people and his belief that the connecting thread uniting Blacks of all nationalities was Africa.[50] It has been pointed out that there is a recurrent theme among writers in the New Negro movement, namely birth and rebirth.[51] The Douglas illustration expresses spiritual birth. In *The Spirit of Africa*, the dark silhouette rises from the earth, whose contours merge with those of the drum in a flat, Egyptian-like, two-dimensional manner. The figure's head is tilted upward, at a sharp, exaggerated angle, toward the schematically depicted leaves that suggest heavenly rays.

In Abel Pann's vision, Adam crouches in a fetal position while his elongated neck and "primitivistic" head are directed toward the ray of light representing God's creative power. In the two examples the moment of creation or birth can be seen as alluding to the artists' act of creation as well as to the birth of a people.[52]

Side by side with scenes of creation and birth, one naturally finds in the two revival movements scenes of longing, which call for twin-focal compositions. The protagonists are placed on one side while the object of yearning is located at the opposite end. Consider, for instance, E.M. Lilien's illustration for the *Songs of the Ghetto*, "The Jewish May"

FIG. 11. E. M. Lilien, *Joshua* (1908), illustration in *Die Bücher der Bibel*, The Hebrew University, National Library, Jerusalem, Israel.

FIG. 12. Aaron Douglas, *Untitled*, cover of *Opportunity* (December 1925). Courtesy of the National Urban League.

FIG. 13. Aaron Douglas, *Invincible Music: The Spirit of Africa*, illustration, *The Crisis* (February 1926), with permission.

FIG. 14. Abel Pann, *The Creation*
(1923), color lithograph.
Collection Itiel Pann, courtesy of
Itiel Pann, Jerusalem, Israel.

FIG. 15. E. M. Lilien, *The Jewish May*, illustration in *Songs of the Ghetto* (1902),
The Hebrew University National Library, Jerusalem, Israel.

(fig. 15, 1902). A bearded Jew, chained by thorns, raises his arms toward the rays of the
sun representing Zion and freedom. In *Into Bondage* (fig. 16, 1936) Douglas's slave
raises his chained arms toward the light, which again represents the hope of liberation
from slavery. In a later depiction published in *Opportunity* (fig. 17, February 1930), the
theme is no longer a narrative but is conveyed by a rhythmical gesture. The artistic
language is more abstract as the protagonist's raised hands reach out toward a circle
representing craving for wholeness.

Alain Locke was critical of Meta Warrick Fuller's work as wavering between abstract expression, which he considered to be imitative, and racial expression, which he
valued only as experimental.[53] However, her *Ethiopia Awakening* (fig. 18, 1914), which
predated the Harlem Renaissance, became a symbol of birth and rebirth. The motif of
awakening both as an actual birth and in a metaphorical sense of creative rebirth was
portrayed by Rodin, with whom Fuller studied in Paris. In his *Adam* (1888), a male nude
exemplifies this role; for Fuller it is a clothed woman. The woman becomes a personification of the land of dreams—Ethiopia. Ethiopia was the focus of African-American longing. It was associated with the (Black) Queen of Sheba as well as with the political
independence of a Christian community. It is noteworthy that the symbol of national
awareness is, as described by Mary Schmidt Campbell, "a woman awakening from the
deep sleep of the past."[54] She is modeled on an Egyptian source, but the head is the
artist's. The awakening figure is emerging from the frozen stance of an Egyptian sculpture.

Unlike Alain Locke, David Driskell hails *Ethiopia Awakening* as "a truly Pan-Africanist

FIG. 16. Aaron Douglas, *Into Bondage* (1936), oil on canvas, 60 x 60.
Collection of The Corcoran Gallery of Art. Museum Purchase and Partial Gift of
Thurlow Evans Tibbs, Jr., The Evans-Tibbs Collection.

FIG. 17. Aaron Douglas, *Untitled*, illustration in *Opportunity* (February 1930).
Courtesy of the National Urban League.

work of art," evidence of the hereditary union between Black Africa and Black America. He also associates this image of rebirth with the biblical prophecy in Psalms 68:31, "Princes shall come out of Egypt; Ethiopia shall soon stretch out her hands unto God."[55] In this image, iconographically alluding to the resurrection of Lazarus, Fuller merged past and present, the personal with the social and racial, a cross-centuries Queen of Sheba. Albert Raboteau has shown that in the post-slavery period Black Americans often read their future in Psalm 68:31, a text complementary to that of Exodus: "In addition to linking the present with the mythic past, they joined it to a mythic future." The linkage gave meaning to Black suffering.[56]

Nimrod (fig. 19, 1939), by Yitzhak Danziger, was made in Palestine from a local Nubian red-hued sandstone. The personage occurs in 1 Chronicles 1:10 "And Cush [Hebrew for Ethiopia] begat Nimrod: he began to be mighty upon the earth." Nimrod is a hunter whose name in Hebrew connotes rebellion. The sculpture is a nude youth whose features have an Egyptian model, the statue of Pharaoh-Hephren (4th Dynasty). A hunting bird is perched on the shoulder. In spite of his rebellious connotations and nudity, he does not comply with the physicality of a "macho" character, but, as recent critics hold, he is rather vulnerable in his disposition.[57] Danziger belonged to the Canaanite movement, which held that the rebirth of the Jewish people in their ancestral country could be achieved only by a return to the original identity of the people who settled the land of Israel in ancient times. This meant a complete break with the two thousand years of Jewish diaspora culture and an identification with the local regional population. The choice of the sandstone, which was brought from Petra, partly because of its earth colors and local connotations, but also in order to rebel against classical materials such as marble or bronze, accords with the search for roots in the distant past. By fragmenting the body, which is devoid of legs, the image alludes to fragments of ancient archaeological relics, stating its relation to the past.[58]

Worlds apart, *Ethiopia* and *Nimrod* express rebellious aspirations and similar deep yearnings for a pure source of identity, unmarred by the long history of persecution and oppressed culture. Note the contrast between the upper and lower part of the body in the two sculptures: in one case the legs are wrapped, in the other completely missing. Both make an effort to free themselves from their captivating immobility. They are both majestic in their freshness, in their ancient looks.[59]

As we have seen in the introduction, the Hebrew Scriptures played an important role in the formation of Black spiritual culture. The connotations evoked by *Ethiopia Awakening*, as well as the biblical illustrations done by Aaron Douglas, are a visual manifestation of this tradition. Black artists' reaction to Tanner's turn-of-the century biblical depictions and their own personal development was twofold: the biblical personages became Black, in an attempt to bring them closer to the Black audience; and there was a change in style as artists turned to the modernist idiom. These two factors can be demonstrated in the works of Aaron Douglas, William H. Johnson, and Romare Bearden.[60]

18. Meta Warrick Fuller, *Ethiopia*
Awakening (1914), bronze, 67 x 16 x 20.
Schomburg Center for Research in
can Sculpture, Art and Artifacts
ision, The New York Public Library,
or, Lenox and Tilden Foundations.

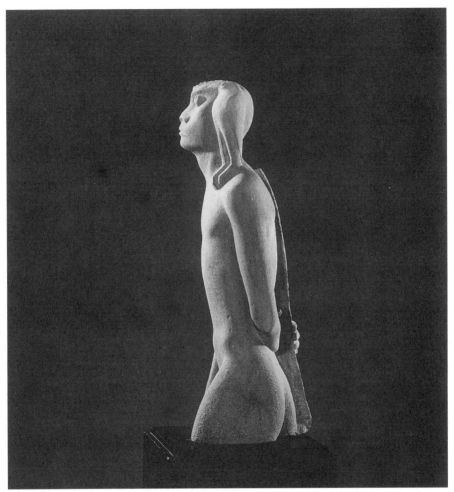

FIG. 19. Yitzhak Danziger, *Nimrod* (1939), Nubian sandstone, 37 $^{1}/_{2}$ x 13 x 13. Collection Israel Museum, Jerusalem. Courtesy of Israel Museum and Sonia Danziger.

A special emphasis related to Exodus can be found in Aaron Douglas's painting *Let My People Go* (1928), in which a Black angel blows a trumpet, while the other partici-pants, in rhythmical movements, heads tilted upward, convey the sense of ecstasy as they sing the eponymous spiritual.[61] William H. Johnson shared the practice of illustrat-ing Black spirituals, integrating religious and social messages in his painting. According to David Driskell: "In *Swing Low, Sweet Chariot* [c. 1944], Johnson shows the lyrical finesse of his work and his narrative skill. A chorus of Black angels, who resemble the women seen frequently in Johnson's paintings of everyday scenes, are lined up in midair waiting, with white horse and chariot, to carry home an aging Black male, modestly clothed in short pants, who is about to receive the rewards for his good life."[62]

A sophisticated collage work is Romare Bearden's *Sermons: The Walls of Jericho* (fig. 20, 1964) coinciding with the civil rights movement. Here the tumbling walls are inter-preted as consisting of Black faces, African masks, and Western architecture. The col-lage seems to be the most appropriate way to suggest the tension between fragmentation (the collapsing walls) and the possibility of a new construction in which a new power, represented by the African Masks, emerges. The walls also carry an apocalyptic tone, a necessary step toward redemption.

Whereas the artists so far presented emphasized the racial component of Black art, a radically opposite perspective on the issue of racial and ethnic art was forcefully offered by Meyer Schapiro in the middle of the 1930s.[63] Schapiro, a Jewish art historian who at that time was a Marxist, conducted a frontal attack on the widespread belief that art is essentially rooted in national and racial identity. He flatly denied the biological unique-ness of any art style—be it French, German, Jewish, or Negro. Furthermore, he re-garded the tendency of many Black artists to cultivate an African style as doubly dangerous: on the one hand, such an attempt can yield only derivative, pseudo-African art; on the other, it plays into the hands of the reactionary forces within the dominant White Ameri-can culture in its attempt to segregate Blacks in their own marginalized domain.

It is noteworthy that Schapiro referred in analogical terms to the same issue in Jewish art. He again denied any essential Jewish character that might be discovered in the works of Jewish artists of various European countries and styles. He claimed that there is no such thing as Jewish style, since Jews adopted the styles of the people among whom they were living. The absurdity of attributing style to Jews as such is illustrated by the possibility of imputing to them almost every style in modern art. Anti-Semitic critics who alleged that Jews had an evil role in the creation of modern art attributed to Jewish intellectualism the creation of abstract art. To Jewish emotionalism, they attributed ex-pressionistic art, and to Jewish practicality, realist art. Although he did not explicitly refer to the group of revivalist Zionist artists of the Bezalel school, it seems quite clear that Schapiro would have directed similar criticism against this kind of attempt to create a nationally based art style.

We should bear in mind that Schapiro was writing in the midst of the struggle

FIG. 20. Romare Bearden, *Sermons: The Walls of Jericho* (1964), photomontage, 11 3/4 x 9 3/4. © Romare Bearden Foundation/Licensed by VAGA, New York.

Eighth Avenue Market, New York City

(Sketches from an Art Student's Notebook by Romare Bearden)

FIG. 21. Romare Bearden, *Eighth Avenue Market: New York City* (1935), drawing in *Opportunity* (January 1935). Courtesy National Urban League.

against fascism, and hence the idea of national or "Volk" art was anathema to him. He believes in class as the deep explanation of art styles and forms, and that shared history and social conditions matter more in the definition of art than the race or nationality of its creators.

A striking and most illuminating comparison with Schapiro's views can be found in a forceful survey by Alain Locke of the history and contemporary state of Black art, published just two years after Schapiro's article.[64] In this retrospective essay, Locke adopts a broader view of Black art than the one he expressed in *The New Negro* over ten years earlier. This change is the result of the development of Black culture itself since the height of the Harlem Renaissance into the late 1930s. "Negro expression," wrote Locke, has "veered away from racialism and sharply repudiated historical romanticism, and while still continuing some of the folk interests of cultural racialism, it is definitely realistic, socialistic, and proletarian." Locke explained this shift of focus as related to a historical process in which an oppressed group first molds its particular self-identity as part of its racial liberation, and then goes on to struggle for social liberation. He also sees the Depression as a formative factor, creating heightened social sensitivity that effected the switch of cultural interest to "proletarian" concerns. The disillusionment of the elite pointed to the necessity of addressing the social issues in order to make a difference. Almost exactly like Schapiro, Locke writes that the story and history of Black art cannot be told separately from the general historical account of the styles in which Black art developed. But being on the whole less judgmental and normative than Schapiro, Locke insists that in Negro art the racial concern always remains and cannot be ignored. Negro art reflects its period but is "always caught up in the texture of a racially determined phase, as might also be expected."

In the spirit of Schapiro's approach, reflected also in the late article by Locke, we may conclude the present chapter with an illustration by Romare Bearden in *Opportunity* (fig. 21, January 1935). Bearden, born in North Carolina in 1911, became a major African-American artist known later for his collage work, his art teaching, and his scholarly writing on African-American art. The illustration consists of four sketches from his notebook as an art student, depicting *Eighth Avenue Market* in New York City (1935). These sketches, done during the Depression in a style less habitual to Bearden, show the proletarian anxieties of two ethnic groups sharing the same fate. The sheet deals with the common life of Jews and Blacks on a class basis. It depicts the meeting ground between members of the lower class of both groups in the Eighth Avenue market of New York, in their common struggle for survival, facing the hardship of daily existence.[65]

The works presented in this chapter have shown what Jews signified for African-American artists at the turn of the nineteenth century and the beginning of the twentieth: identification, religious quests, problems of identity—racial and stylistic, as well as those relating to class issues. They all acted as a mirror in which one minority group tried to identify itself through another.

CHAPTER 2

Jews mirroring African Americans
The vision

> I have the right to believe freely. To be a slave to no man's authority. If this
> be heresy, so be it. It is still the truth. To go against conscience is neither
> right nor safe. I cannot . . . will not . . . recant. Here I stand . . . no man can
> command my conscience.

These words are inscribed on the painter's palette in Ben Shahn's *The Credo* (fig. 22, 1954). The combination of title and image lends the painting the status of a personal and artistic identity card. The head of the artist (in profile), emphasizing his inward looking eye, and the above text are inseparable, and together form the shape of a palette, enclosed by the artist's hands holding his tools. The declarative nature of this self-presentation is further reinforced by the use of the religious term "credo."

However, although Shahn's statement in its credo-title has specific religious overtones (it quotes from Martin Luther's speech at the Diet of Worms in 1521), there is a shift from the religious to the social sensibility in his own understanding of the ideas of freedom, authority, conscience, and above all the opposition to slavery and subjugation. Shahn is a modern, secular artist who is fighting for artistic freedom, social liberation, and racial justice. One of his constant commitments as an American Jew was to the struggle for the freedom and equality of all people.

The mirror metaphor used in the previous chapter will be shown in this chapter to be double-faced. If earlier I examined how Jews were reflected in African-American art, in this chapter and the next I will investigate how Black topics were perceived by Jewish-American artists. Twentieth-century Jewish-American artists frequently depicted Black subjects and themes in a way that expressed their search for their own identity. As the case of Henry Ossawa Tanner shows, Jewish themes entered African-American art before African-American themes found a place in the works of Jewish-American artists. This was due to the fact that Black artists entered the art world before Jewish Americans

FIG. 22. Ben Shahn, *The Credo* (1954), gouache, 31 x 22 $^1/_2$.
© Estate of Ben Shahn/Licensed by VAGA, New York. Collection
Bernarda Ben Shahn, photograph, courtesy of Bernarda Ben Shahn.

began to participate actively in it. However, once Jewish-American artists engaged in the
Black cause, they did so in a persistent and often passionate manner.

The Jewish concern with Black topics will be discussed under two aspects: the
positive vision in this chapter and the grim reality in the next. Owing to the complexity
of the tale to be told, the analysis will not always follow a purely chronological line.
Furthermore, the reciprocal nature of the act of mirroring requires us to take into account the African-American point of view whenever this is relevant to the narrative.

Matthew Baigell has proposed that the attraction of many Jewish-American artists
to socially and politically oriented art evolved from memories of oppression in Eastern

Europe, from the Hebrew Scriptures tradition of charity and social concern, and also from "the opportunity to play a participatory role in American art." This description is applicable to most of the artists presented in my discussion of Jews mirroring African Americans. Furthermore, Baigell also comments on these artists' shared experiences with African Americans; they who were all simultaneously trying to enter "the mainstream of American art."[1]

Baigell's three-fold explanation of the socially involved art of many Jewish Americans may serve us well in articulating the "visionary" aspect of their representation of Black issues. The historical experience of persecution and the liberating one of the transition to the New World, with its open-ended promise, could easily suggest a potential for similar promise to another oppressed people, the Blacks in America. But beyond this formal similarity, as immigrants these artists were equally in search of their specific identity in America, and they often articulated their social and artistic responses in a language related to their Jewish upbringing. This could take the form of an appeal to the canonical Jewish sources of social justice (the biblical prophets) or the use of Hebrew texts in a work of art. And last but not least, drawing upon Baigell's third explanation, becoming American was a paramount goal for immigrants in general and for artists in particular. It meant participation in the struggle for justice in America, for the equality of all Americans, and in the case of artists, the adoption of new artistic languages. It is only natural that immigrants attempting to assimilate in the host society tend to ally themselves with those ideologies that support the cause of full equality of all subgroups in the greater society and their universal claim to assume an American identity. Left-wing ideologies were instrumental in the striving for this egalitarian goal, and it was no coincidence that Jewish and African Americans often found themselves on a common front in the 1930s.[2]

Theorists discussing the relationship between politics and art have argued that a work of art is often not merely the outcome of a political situation or "the result of a political intent" but "may itself constitute a political act or statement."[3] This is evident, with few exceptions in the case of most of the artists to be presented in the next three chapters.

The relationship between Jews and Blacks is often conveyed through the image of the child as "Father of the Man." Childhood serves here as a natural focus for the projection of deep hopes but also of disillusionment. High expectations may lead to disappointment. Although this chapter will focus on the positive vision, the historical starting point is rather somber. The earliest example of a Jewish-American artist's involvement with the Black cause is Jacob Epstein's early sculpture *Cursed Be the Day Wherein I Was Born* (fig. 23, 1913–14, exhibited in 1915), a stark lament, dramatic in style and existential protest. Alain Locke's list of modern artists influenced by African art included Jacob Epstein. However, Epstein's early sculpture is unique in the context of this list in that it uses African art in a sense that goes beyond the formal aspects, and strikes at the heart of

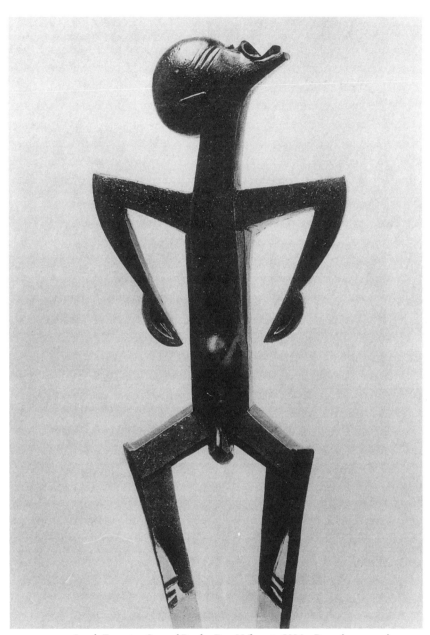

FIG. 23. Jacob Epstein, *Cursed Be the Day Wherein I Was Born* (1913–14), plaster and wood painted red, H: 45.5. Present whereabouts unknown. Permission Jackie Epstein.

the plight of Black people at the beginning of the century. Western artists who were inspired by African art separated form from content, supplying their own content to the African form. Since they were engaged in the formal language of African art, they never attempted to relate the style to the living circumstances of Black culture. Epstein, although not simply restating the traditional meaning of African art in the African context, equally differs here from the tradition emerging in Europe, in which African art was a source of influence on Modernism owing to its expressive style and structural qualities.

Epstein began collecting African art in 1907. In the 1930s his possessions included hundreds of statues, masks, and ivories. Arnold Haskell evaluated his collection as "one of the finest in the world."[4] When interviewed, Epstein was critical of the way African art was perceived by the West and was opposed to the term Primitive Art: "African art is not primitive either technically or emotionally; on the contrary, it is often extremely subtle and sophisticated, and many of the masks express emotions of great complexity."[5] He sees its artistic merits (simplification, directness, union of naturalism and design, striking architectural qualities) but is also aware of its religious functions in tribal ceremonies such as initiations, evoking "awe and fear," as in figure 23.[6]

The immediate influence on Epstein's *Cursed Be the Day Wherein I Was Born*, as suggested by Hugh Honour in his study of the image of the Black in Western art, was a Kota reliquary figure. And yet, although Epstein's source of inspiration was similar to that of other modernist artists, namely African sculptures in the Paris Trocadero and the British Museum, his adaptation of this art was different.[7] This particular work coincided with a 1913–14 exhibition of African art by Alfred Stieglitz (born in 1864 to a German Jewish family) in his avant-garde gallery called 291. The photographer and gallery owner was interested in the modernist qualities of the sculptures. A year later, in his Braque-Picasso exhibition, the now-classic Gabon statues were shown with the focus on the formal aspects of the objects displayed. Though Epstein and Stieglitz were involved with African art in the same years, Stieglitz in exhibiting and Epstein in *Cursed Be the Day Wherein I Was Born*, their interpretations differed.

The biblical title *Cursed Be the Day Wherein I Was Born* (quoting Jeremiah 20:14, like its close parallel from Job 3:2) is a most intense expression of existential distress as well as a metaphysical cry against injustice. Epstein used a classical African style to depict a newborn child with Black features. In this dramatic image the neck and head are stretched upward toward heaven in a position of prayer. The mouth is open in a primordial scream. This position may be understood as expressing both despair and protest, a death wish and a sense of unjust treatment. The meaning of the sculpture is also enhanced by the fusion of the African style with the Christian dimension, alluded to by the form of a cross which is created by the crying figure. Various layers of African-American history are superimposed on each other.

Jacob Epstein was born in America in 1880 to East European immigrant parents. His origins were in the Lower East Side of New York, but he later emigrated to England, where he was eventually knighted in token of appreciation of his artistic contribution. In a perceptive analysis of *Cursed Be the Day Wherein I Was Born*, Hugh Honour wrote: "No artist of the time was more acutely aware of the terrible consequences of racial prejudice. His parents had fled from Poland after anti-Jewish pogroms. He grew up in America at a time when hostility to blacks was violent. And in the Jewish community in the Lower East Side, New York, he lived on a par with members of other despised ethnic minorities."[8]

By associating this sculpture with a specific biblical text, Epstein brings together the fate of the two peoples, intertwining the cry of the Black with that of the Jewish people. The cry is archetypal: it continues a long history of the theme in art including the Hellenistic *Laocoon* and Edvard Munch's *The Scream* (1894). In this respect the cry of the Black figure can also be perceived as universal. In England, Epstein's fascination with African art and his constant sculpting of Black people were not always perceived with approval. The critic Eric Gill complained that "the primitive in Negro sculpture [terminology which Epstein rejected] answers the primitive in Epstein."[9]

No politically conscious artist could make a sculpture bearing such a title as *Cursed Be the Day Wherein I Was Born* in our times. To contemporary sensibility it would risk being interpreted as showing either a paternalistic attitude or worse, as if the artist were saying that the life of a Black man is not worth living. The work should therefore be understood in the context of the period when it was done, as an artistic gesture of sympathy with the misery of Black people. And yet the allusion to this biblical verse was not foreign to Black writers. We may recall the title of Benjamin Tucker Tanner's book, *The Negro's Origin and Is the Negro Cursed*. Today, "curse" would not be applied to ethnic identity, neither by people belonging to an ethnic group nor by those observing them.

The influence of African art in portraying suffering was not confined to the African experience. Chaim Gross used African art to mourn the fate of his sister and through her the tragedy of the Jewish people. Chaim Gross was born in Galicia in 1904, the son of a lumber merchant. He emigrated to the Lower East Side of New York in 1921, where he attended the Educational Alliance Art School. Here he met the painter Moses Soyer, and through him his twin brother Raphael, as well as Philip Evergood, Philip Reisman, Peter Blume, Saul Berman—all committed to the Black cause as an integral part of their world view and artistic expression.[10]

Gross's wooden sculpture *My Sister Sarah in Memoriam* (1947) reflects his attraction to African art. The work is dedicated to the memory of the artist's only sister, who perished in the Holocaust. It is an adaptation in a Western artistic language of a totemic Sudanese sculpture in the Dogon style, a figure with which the artist was well acquainted.[11] Although the title of the work refers only to the artist's sister, the sculpture itself depicts a mother carrying a child, thus including Sarah's fourteen-year-old daughter who died with her. The style of this Mother and Child theme combines a typically African totemic style with a traditional Western articulation of the bodily features (under the impact of

Donatello's *Madonna and Child*).[12] Gross illuminates the tragedy of the death of whole lines of family through the use of a typically African fertility theme. His analysis of African sculpture can be applied to the relationship between the present sculpture and its African source:

> Negro sculpture does two things, among many others, which I find particularly admirable. For one, it shows that fine work can be done by judiciously combining abstract and representational elements and still keep to the basic trunk form. The other is the practice of confining the limbs of a subject in the cylindrical form so that they do not project outward from the vertical axis of the wood.[13]

In Gross's work there is a painful gap between the strong symbiosis of mother and child in trunk form, the child being carved as almost part of the woman's body, and the title. The disparity between the title and the image implies a reversal of the traditional role of the mother as a life giver, a sheltering being. For the artist this contrast is doubly significant, since Sarah is one of the biblical matriarchs, and the artist's own name, Chaim, means "life" in Hebrew. The use of African artistic language to articulate the sense of personal loss and that of collective trauma is common to Gross and Lipchitz. The facial features of Lipchitz's *Mother and Child* (1941–42) are African. Lipchitz wrote, "There is despair involved in this sculpture but also, I feel, a kind of hope and optimism and even a form of aggression."[14] The choice of the African idiom of the two artists in such a charged context suggests that Jews and Blacks share a similar history.

Both Epstein's and Gross's sculptures remind us that the suffering of the two peoples always loomed in the background, even when the positive vision was the ostensible subject. Gross suggested the Black experience not only through his Holocaust memorial. This concern takes us back to the early days of his career in New York at the end of the 1920s. In the left profile and frontal views of *Mother Carrying Child* (figs. 24, 25, 1926) we see an early example of the trunklike fusion in which the child can hardly be distinguished from the carrying mother. They form a condensed block of raw matter, suggesting the primordial inseparability of the relationship. The image of the two-in-one strides forward forcefully, the dynamism enhanced by the rapid woodcarving technique. The overall effect of the sculpture is of a dedicated mother, who with strength and determination is walking forward almost as in a ritual.

Another way of making a positive statement was through experiencing the most creative aspect of Black culture—its music. Gross was attracted to the rhythm of jazz in wooden sculptures that he carved at the end of the 1920s. His *Jazz* (fig. 26, 1929), in its fine rhythmic lines, shows that he was well attuned to the voice of Black music flourishing during the Harlem Renaissance and was inspired by its originality and authenticity. He captured the rhythm and unity of the dancers' fine movements. Many publications and depictions related to jazz appeared throughout the 1920s: "Jazz at home," printed in *The New Negro*, is illustrated by Aaron Douglas's couple overtaken by the power of jazz in the midst of a repeated scheme of musical notes. The article itself questions the nature of "this taking new thing," pointing out its singularity: "Jazz is a marvel of paradox: too fundamentally human, at least as modern humanity goes, to be typically racial, too international to be characteristically national, too much abroad in the world to have a special home. And yet jazz in spite of it all is one part American and three parts American Negro, and was originally the nobody's child of the levee and the city slum."[15]

At about the same time, Langston Hughes published his book *The Weary Blues* (1926), and Louis Armstrong and Duke Ellington were gaining recognition. Miguel Covarrubias's *Dancing Couple* (1928) conveys the joy and bodily freedom of the dancers. In comparison with this image, Gross's rendering is more formal, stressing the couple's perfect unity and coordination: "*Jazz* symbolizes the spirit of a past decade. It has swing, warmth, earthiness and youthful zest," to quote Josef Lombardo.[16]

In the early days of the Educational Alliance, Gross's wooden sculptures celebrated the Black woman, expressing through such images a sense of oneness between mother and child, a longing for freedom, beauty, and fertility. This can be seen in his westernized works that observe the intimate sense of scale characteristic of African sculpture. The *Walking Negress* (fig. 27, 1928) is an upright, striding nude, echoing, though in a different style, Aaron Douglas's typical head postures (see chapter 1). Though on a small scale, the stance is proud, the woman's head confronting heaven directly. In discussing the similarities between Gross's sculpture and African art, Lombardo pointed out that African art is monumental despite its small size, and that this "heroic impression" is felt in Gross's work.[17] This insight is applicable to the *Walking Negress*. According to Renee Gross, the artist's wife, the protagonist's pose manifests that "she is in search for a better life."[18] Both the artist and his friends empathized with this sculpture, so that when Raphael Soyer painted Chaim Gross's portrait, he placed it next to this figure.[19]

The *Pregnant Negress* (fig. 28) was completed in 1930, in the same year as *Shulamit* (fig. 29). The work is obviously a reference to a biblical source, in this case the beautiful Black woman in the Song of Songs. There is a context to these works which associates the celebration of Black beauty with the Harlem Renaissance. Consider the October 1928 issue of *Der Hammer*, the Yiddish communist literary journal (fig. 30). This issue presented a Jewish recognition of the Renaissance. Poems by Langston Hughes were translated into Yiddish, next to a poem by Waring Cuney: "How Beautiful She Is." Arnold Rampersad, discussing the slow reception of Langston Hughes by the left until the publication of *The New Negro*, mentions the March 1925 issue of the *Communist Workers Monthly* as Hughes's first publication in a radical left journal.[20] The poems in Yiddish in *Der Hammer* can be added to the story of Hughes's reception. "Poem" celebrates the beauty of Black people:

FIG. 24. Chaim Gross, *Mother Carrying Child* (1926),
left profile view, lignum vitae, 14 $^1/_2$ x 6 x 4 $^3/_4$.
Courtesy of the Chaim Gross Studio Museum Collection, New York.

FIG. 25. Chaim Gross, *Mother Carrying Child* (1926),
front view, lignum vitae 14 $^1/_2$ x 6 x 4 $^3/_4$.
Courtesy of the Chaim Gross Studio Museum Collection, New York.

FIG. 26. Chaim Gross, *Jazz* (1929), mahogany, 41 5/8 x 17 x 2 1/4. Collection
Jake Milgram Wien. Courtesy of the Chaim Gross Studio Museum Collection, New York.

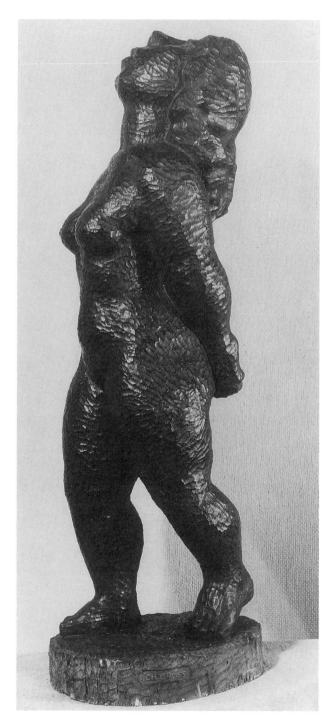

FIG. 27. Chaim Gross,
Walking Negress (1928),
lignum vitae, 35 x 9 $\frac{1}{2}$ x
12 $\frac{1}{4}$. Courtesy of the
Chaim Gross Studio
Museum Collection,
New York.

FIG. 28. Chaim Gross, *Pregnant Negress* (1930),
ebony, 25 $^1/_2$ x 8 x 6 $^1/_2$. Courtesy of the
Chaim Gross Studio Museum Collection, New York.

FIG. 29. Chaim Gross, *Shulamit* (1930), lignum
vitae, 30 inches high. Collection: Birobidjan
Museum, Russia. Courtesy of the Chaim Gross
Studio Museum Collection, New York.

The night is beautiful,
So the faces of my people.

The stars are beautiful,
So the eyes of my people.

Beautiful, also, is the sun.
Beautiful, also, are the souls of my people.[21]

The Yiddish translator used the simple title "Poem," which appeared in *The Crisis* in August 1923 (it was later replaced by "My People"). The poem expresses a correspondence between the micro- and macrocosmos, Black people and nature, body and soul. In structure it preserves the form of a dialogue between preacher and community, a call-and-response chant song, with a repeated line typical of gospel music. Since the editors of *Der Hammer* wished to emphasize beauty, they felt free to change the original heading of another poem published in translation. Waring Cuney's title "No Images" was altered to "How Beautiful She Is." The poem, which won first prize in an *Opportunity* poetry contest in 1926, characterizes the Black woman's lack of awareness of her beauty, and tries to compensate her for it through the delicate evocation of what she does not see. The poem is based on a set of comparisons in which the woman's dance between the palm trees and the reflecting river, alluding to Africa, are contrasted with modern city life where dish water cannot serve as a mirror:

She does not know
Her beauty,
She thinks her brown body
Has no glory.

If she could dance
Naked,
Under palm trees
And see her image in the river
She would know.

But there are no palm trees
On the street,
And dish water gives back no Images.[22]

There is an element of surprise at the end of the poem; "dish water" is a rude awakening from the exotic landscape capturing her beauty, and reminds her of her place in society.

It is noteworthy that two years after its publication Waring Cuney's poem was translated into Yiddish and published in the Yiddish press, with a special emphasis on beauty, expressed by the substituted title. This emphasis corresponds to Alain Locke's

FIG. 30. *Der Hammer* (October 1928),
Waring Cuney poetry, illustrations Winold Reiss.

demand that "art must discover and reveal the beauty which prejudice and caricature have overlaid."[23] The special alliance between Jews and Blacks is highlighted not only by the fact that poems of admiration of Black beauty were translated and published in a Yiddish journal, but that they were illustrated by an artist working for *The New Negro*, the Bavarian Winold Reiss, portraying the beauty of the Black woman.

The cover of *The Crisis* (fig. 31, February 1925), by Harry Gottlieb (the director of the Communist John Reed Club during the 1930s), is also dedicated to the Shulamit. Here we find direct Black and Jewish collaboration. The floral ornamentation, echoing Jewish ceremonial art such as the decorations on Torah scroll cases, frames Shulamit's words in the Song of Songs: "I am black / But comely / O, ye daughters / of Jerusalem" (1:5). The biblical text and the title of the magazine share the same space and are hand-drawn, in capital letters throughout.

This illustration resembles those of the Bezalel Art School, where the Song of Songs received a very lavish treatment in the work of Ze'ev Raban (1922). The most significant element in grasping Shulamit's role for the artists of Bezalel is their reading of the original Hebrew sentence as "I am black *and* comely" rather than "I am black *but* comely." Rather than apologetic about her blackness, the biblical heroine is, according to the new Zionist artists, proud of it. In other words, this verse is read in a nonracial way. This switch of meaning and notion of color is related to the concept of the New Jew or Jewess who would not remain indoors, but was exposed to nature, worked on the land, and was integrated with it, and thus superseded the diaspora tradition of estrangement from the natural environment. For the Zionist pioneers in Palestine, the pallid countenances of diaspora Jews symbolized their physical weakness and unhealthy way of living.

Chaim Gross's *Shulamit* should therefore be understood in this wider context. This is quite relevant to the destiny of the sculpture, since the artist gave it to the Jewish settlers of Birobidzhan, to show his support of their struggle to achieve autonomy through agriculture in the Soviet Union at the end of the 1920s.[24] It is thus significant that Gross's endorsement of this ideological settlement was done via the *Shulamit*. The sculpture acquires a symbolic meaning, connecting the Jewish people in Russia striving for autonomy with the aspiration for freedom and equality of the Black people epitomized by the beauty of the Shulamit.

Gross glorifies the beginning of life through the torso of his *Pregnant Negress*. He deviates from the traditional female torso as it was conceived in art in the post-classical era, epitomized by ancient statues of Venus. Gross replaces this notion of beauty with the beauty of the torso of a Black woman pregnant with new life. Throughout his life Gross, like Epstein, was a collector of African art, remaining consistent in his appreciation of it as classical. He also traveled to Africa, and the thoughts he expressed about African art in 1985 recapitulate the meaning of the pregnant Black torso: "For me these sculptures are as beautiful as Greek statues."[25] Further, by choosing this truncated form

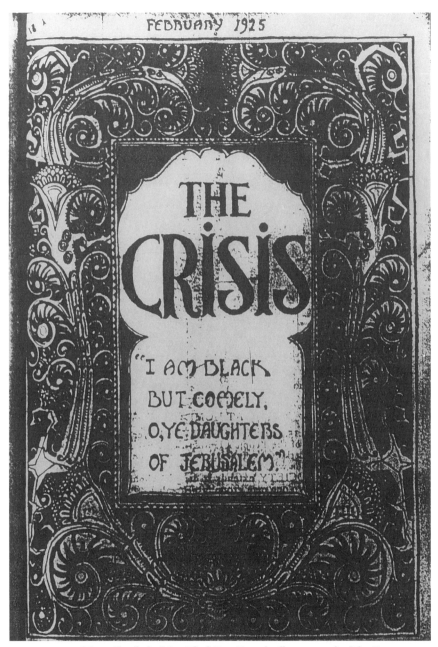

FIG. 31. Harry Gottlieb, *I Am Black But Comely*, illustration for *The Crisis* (February 1925), with permission.

of expression, rather than sculpting a specific full-length representation of a pregnant woman, Gross avoids making a descriptive image. Instead, the *Pregnant Negress* is elevated to symbolic status, glorifying the Black race and artistic creation.

Dreams and hopes for the future were persistently symbolized through images of childhood. Lucienne Bloch (daughter of the composer Ernest Bloch) portrayed her vision in a recreation room of the Black women prisoners' ward in the Women's House of Detention in New York. Her choice of a prison for her work, which was done as part of a WPA project in 1936, highlights the oppressive conditions to which Blacks were subjected. Lucienne Bloch was born to a Jewish family in Switzerland in 1909 and arrived in America at the age of eight. She worked with Diego Rivera in the early 1930s, grinding his colors for the frescoes he was doing in New York, and later took part in the American Mural Movement of the 1930s.

In her fresco *Childhood* (fig. 32, 1936, now lost), which was intended to be incorporated into a *Cycle of a Woman's Life* (never completed), the artist depicted children of mixed races together on a playground.[26] The playground perspective creates a space that distances the children from the industrial city as if to protect and shelter them. It is a dream world with trees and flowers, including a flower-seller watering his stock. A variety of games are illustrated: building a brick structure, playing a ball game, swinging, and sliding. Some children are active participants, some are viewers contemplating the scene, others are leaving the playground. The accompanying adults, both female and male, are also multiracial. An apple has been split between the children, two parts for the White boy and girl, forming one group, and another part for the Black boy. Since the children are not eating the apple but are perceived as staring at it in wonder, the apple, in itself an archetypal image, gains a charged symbolic meaning. It is also the detail Lucienne Bloch selected for comment. She was gratified by the prison inmates' reaction, and she described their excitement and the impact her fresco had on them: "In fact, in the inmates' make-believe moments, the children of the mural were adopted and named. The scene representing negro and white children sharing an apple was keenly appreciated."[27]

According to Paul von Blum, Bloch anticipated the community engagement that characterizes present-day social murals. She consulted with the inmates throughout the project and took their comments and proposals into consideration.[28] The popularity of Bloch's images among the women stands in contrast to the fate of those done by Ben Shahn for the men in Riker's Island Penitentiary. Shahn's drawings show that his design consisted of two parts: one a gruesome portrayal of cruelty in prisons in the past, the other an idealized concept of healthy conditions in modern prisons. According to the press release, Shahn's mural was rejected for psychological reasons, "because prisoners didn't like it," whereas Bloch's mural was accepted "because women prisoners thought it attractive."[29] Shahn's imagery was conceived according to an abstract traditional moral division of good versus evil; Bloch concentrated on the positive vision.

The fact that such an "innocent" topic as a multiracial playground was conceived

FIG. 32. Lucienne Bloch, *The Playground* (1936), fresco W.P.A. project (lost).

in terms of a utopic vision manifests the degree of segregation in American society of the 1930s and 1940s. It demonstrates that segregation was not found only in the South but also in New York City. Bloch's project was not received without criticism, however. It was condemned by people who claimed that taxpayers' money had been spent in order to create a pleasant setting for criminals.[30]

Lucienne Bloch's ideal playground leads us to another painting centering on a Jewish artist's reflections on Black children, this time in dream form. Philip Evergood (originally named Blashki, born in 1901 to a Jewish father from Galicia and a Christian mother) took an archetypal food image other than the apple as a sign of triumph. In his *Dream Catch* (fig. 33, 1946) an enormous fish is caught by a Black boy. The artist moves from his earlier representational art style to the language of magic realism, depicting the incongruities of dream imagery. This picture is related to Evergood's constant concern throughout his life, in his art as well as in his writings, with the fate of Black people. Expressing himself in a positive visionary mood, he wrote: "The hands of people who want peace, security, racial equality and culture reach out and *Meet* throughout our country and across the oceans and lands of the world in strength and courage to build an inevitable chain which will be called Civilization."[31] Philip Evergood believed in art as the salvation of mankind. He drew an analogy between human and aesthetic equality: "Where Human equality as well as aesthetic equality exists. Where black and white and yellow, men and women have equal opportunities for recognition and for the development of their individual talents and beauties. A world where Art is as common as head to the people and where head is as common to the artist as Art."[32]

A short detour into the artist's involvement with the Black cause may place the *Dream Catch* in a broader context. Take, for instance, his comparison of the supermarket

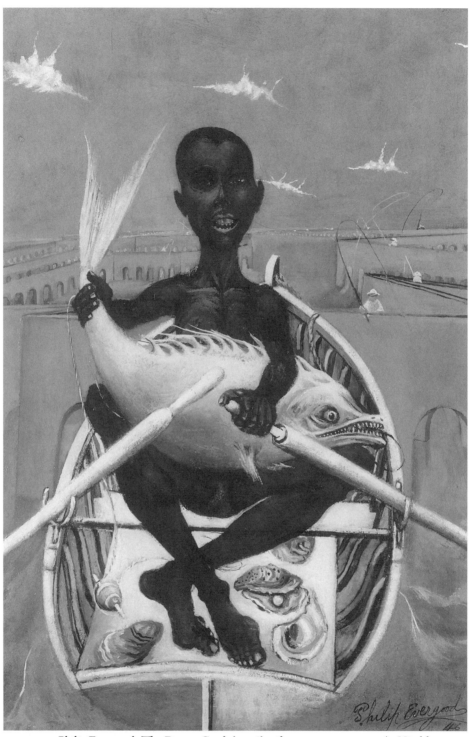

FIG. 33. Philip Evergood, *The Dream Catch* (1946), oil on canvas, 30 x 20 7/8. Hirshhorn Museum and Sculpture Garden, Smithsonian Institution. Gift of Joseph H. Hirshhorn, 1956.

culture of America with the culture of Africa. Here he reversed the then-common stereo-typical evaluation of the African countries vis-à-vis America. The people of Tanganyika, Liberia, and the Congo may be considered "primitive," in not having asbestos roofing and air conditioning, but "they are civilized as we are not" in what really matters. They represent civilization in their long history of amazing sculpture and decorative art, "handed down as a tradition from father to son, from generation to generation." This emphasis on continuity is in obvious contrast to his assessment of America's cultural assets, as well as the condition of its workers. Evergood asks: "Why don't we put our energies first into solving the monumental problems of good jobs for all—Black and White—and for making our great country free for people of any color?"[33]

In joining organizations such as the Forum for Democracy (1944), Evergood took part in sessions whose agenda included topics such as "How to Take the Problem out of the Negro Problem." Active in the activities of the Artists' Committee for the Protection of Negro Rights, he was involved in raising money to combat the deplorable housing conditions in Harlem and in the struggle to fight for equal rights for Black people. Other Jewish-American artists who belonged to this enterprise were Jack Levine, Abraham Rattner, Moses Soyer, Raphael Soyer, and William Gropper. Jewish collectors and gal-lery owners such as Herman Baron, Edith Halpert, and Joseph Hirshhorn were also sponsors of the committee. It was a joint venture whose African-American sponsors were Langston Hughes, Jacob Lawrence, and Lily Harmon. Other American artists spon-soring the committee were Milton Avery, Nicolai Cikovsky, Rufino Tamayo, and Robert Gwathemy.[34] In the 1960s Evergood collaborated with Jacob Lawrence and others in the Student Nonviolent Coordinating Committee (SNCC) by donating works of art that were sold to raise funds.[35]

Philip Evergood communicated his social concerns from the very first stages of his artistic career, when he joined the socially committed ACA Gallery in 1935. He did this following the presentation of the show *The Struggle for Negro Rights* by Herman Baron, the gallery owner. Later, writing for the Marxist publication *The Art Front*, Evergood defined his ideological position regarding American art: "We believe that artists who can see clearly the complicated structure of America and pick out its basic social pattern, who are sympathetic to its people and its culture and traditions, who are interested in psychology of the classes and groups, have the basis of saying something about America."[36]

As a matter of fact, Evergood does not depict a great number of Americans very sympathetically. His art is perceived by critics as divided into two categories: Good and Evil. Evil is signified by a business suit and a swastika, Good by the crippled and the underprivileged.[37] Black people belonged to the category of good, and he was concerned that they should be portrayed in a dignified way. The artist Elizabeth Catlett, who had spent part of her life in Mexico City, expressed her admiration for Evergood's representa-tions of "the Negro People": "As an American Negro, I was very happy to see a great advancement in your painting of your treatment of the Negro People. There is a beautiful, expressive head of a Negro sitting on a curb that impressed me very much. I think the film should be shown to working people and their impressions utilized in your future painting."[38] In a review of Charles White paintings titled, "Charles White: Beauty and Strength," Evergood hails the Marxist *Masses and Mainstream* for choosing White, "a Negro people's artist who not only can draw human beings with the dignity they deserve but who gives us a penetrating and symbolic rendering of the beauty of the Negro people."[39]

In Evergood's iconic *Dream Catch*, the hero is a Black boy. Kendall Taylor, in a study of Evergood's art, argues that his special emphasis on images of Black children stemmed from his belief that they represented "the innocent victims of racist politics in a capitalist economy."[40]

The image, which was based on an actual dream of the artist, conveys a dual perspective on its protagonist. A Black boy in a rowing boat holds a disproportionately large white fish with exaggerated carnivorous teeth. The shape of the boat is echoed in the shells on its floor. The boy himself is external to the confining boundaries of the architectonic structure seen in the background. The "miracle" of the fish is reflected in the elated, victorious expression on his face. It is a bountiful compensatory dream in which the size of the fish counterbalances the boy's need and symbolic hunger. Since the picture was based on an actual dream, it is in the nature of a transferred identification with the boy on whom the artist bestows the hope of self-fulfillment.

However, this giant catch raises questions about the nature of the fish, since the achievement suggested by the theme contradicts its stylistically frozen nature and its fixated position. There is also a catch in the dream—the fish has lost its freedom and may be foretelling the boy's fate. Is the artist also alluding to the "white whale," the representative of evil satanic powers in Herman Melville's *Moby Dick?* Evergood himself reflected on his hero's prospects: "The little black boy, doomed to a life of frustration by a discriminatory society, has made his humble conquest in a dream—that of catching a big, fat fish."[41] The duality in the boy's predicament is thus expressed both visually and verbally, but it also reflects Evergood's own self-perception.

In the year following *The Dream Catch*, Philip Evergood participated in the exhibition *Artists' Tribute in Memory of F. D. Roosevelt*, held at the ACA Gallery in 1945, a joint enterprise of Herman Baron and the artists. Art works were shown next to quotations from Roosevelt's speeches. Evergood's image, featuring a multiracial street in the background and a determined, self-confident African American in the foreground, illustrated Roosevelt's promise: "We are determined to make every American citizen the subject of his country's interest and concern, and we will never regard any faithful law-abiding group within our borders as superfluous."[42]

In his writing, Evergood attacks racial prejudices camouflaged in religious argument:

This attack against the P.C.A. of Christmas Greeting Cards by the spokesman for the Knights of Columbus is a demonstration of a particular brand of bigotry and spiritual blindness. The two cards singled out to be besmirched represent the highest *kind* of morally [*sic*] and humanitarian idealism. The mother and child by Hirsh gives dignity to the story of all mothers of all children. The negro child crowned with thorns by Wynne is a pure and fervent plea for the equality of Man. Sacrilege is the thought that a negro child can not wear a halo of purity and at the *same* time suffer the crown of thorns. I was surprised of the account of the intolerance of this attack. I am surprised that my picture showing two woodmen one a negro and one a white man both carrying a Christmas tree through the snow was not also accused of stirring up racial controversy because it was so clearly aimed at bringing about racial unity and human understanding.[43]

This text fits with the frame of mind of other "dreamers" who had visions of a different social reality and conceptualized their aspirations through the iconic nature of mother-child representations. Raphael Soyer, the twin brother of Moses Soyer, was born in 1899 in Borisoglebsk, Russia, and emigrated with his family to America in 1912. His vision relating to Black children is unequivocal.[44] On the one hand, the artist shares Lucienne Bloch's idea of the shared existence of children of all races, as can be seen in *City Children* (fig. 34, 1952). But his children, whose serious expressions reflect the realities of the gloomy modern city do not distinguish between the races. For Soyer the depiction of children being together is significant, regardless of the circumstances. This painting was shown in the 1964 exhibition *The Portrayal of the Negro in American Art*.[45] The artist expressed the belief that if such an exhibition were to be circulated throughout the country, it would improve race relations.[46]

On the other hand, perhaps also because of the pessimism of the modern street, Soyer had a more ambitious goal than mere coexistence. His left-wing background and universalistic vision led to a belief in racial fusion. A recurrent image in his work throughout the 1960s was that of a White woman nursing a Black child. The pair feature as an integral part of the painting *Village East Street Scene* (fig. 35, 1965–66) next to the poet Allen Ginsberg and the writer LeRoi Jones, as well as the painter himself. The artist here plays a triple role: he is part of the excitable street atmosphere, he is there in the guise of the artist as spectator, and he is also a commentator, conveying his universalist vision. The White woman nursing the Black baby stands next to a White child. This fusion and coexistence is conceived as a most natural part of everyday city life. Soyer explains the importance of the image of the White woman and the Black child, which he also used in his graphic work: "This is a young woman called Gypsy who had a child with a black man. I thought of this scene as mother and madonna. To me she signifies the madonna of our times. Instead of a halo she has the sign for an atomic fallout shelter."[47]

Thus, a modern Madonna is conceived as one who will bring together the Black and White races through her offspring. On the metaphoric level she also alludes to united efforts to erase racial differences.

FIG. 34. Raphael Soyer, *City Children* (1952), oil on canvas.
Collection L. Arnold Weissberger, courtesy of Mary Soyer.

Particularly interesting is another black and white variation on the theme of the Madonna carrying a Black child, which bears a biblical quotation in both Hebrew and English: "Are you not as children of the Ethiopians unto me, O children of Israel?" (Amos 9:7) (fig. 36, 1965–66). It is significant that Soyer insists on using the Hebrew version next to the English translation to state his "credo," in spite of, or rather due to his left-wing nondenominational affiliations. The authority of the biblical text, clothed in the particularistic Hebrew language, enhances the universalist vision provided by the figurative image. Many Jews on the left, despite their much heralded universalism, took pride in what they believed to be the universalist Jewish heritage, a heritage whose message they considered their own and regarded as a guide to action. The Hebrew prophets served as the proclaimers of the universal message. In *Amos on Racial Equality*, the artist deviated from the original reading of the text. Amos's text is usually understood as a derogatory analogy between the children of Israel and the Ethiopians. But Soyer reverses the meaning of the verse in order to say that in the eyes of God, Blacks are no less significant than his own people. However, what is important for our present purpose is that a modern Jewish-American artist links his own belief in racial equality to what he believes to be an ancient Hebraic tradition of social justice, even though his understanding is quite opposite the standard reading. As we have seen earlier in this chapter, this is not the only reversal of biblical meaning. Raphael Soyer uses the same inversion as the artists of Bezalel's reading of "I am black *and* comely" (replacing "I am black *but* comely" from *Song of Songs*). By these inversions of meaning, the modern left-wing ideologies add another layer to the long tradition of biblical exegesis.

Raphael Soyer's vision of the 1960s is also related to his life-long commitment to the Black cause, shared by his twin brother Moses and his other brother Isaac. Their struggle was multifaceted. During their early days in the Educational Alliance, they battled with other Jewish-American artists to include Black artists in exhibitions. In 1926 the three Soyer brothers, together with Jack Levine and Chaim Gross, wrote to Abbo Ostrowsky urging him to "hold . . . an exhibition of the promising young Negro painter, Edward Strickland."[48] In Depression-era paintings such as Raphael Soyer's *Waiting Room* (fig. 37, 1940) and Isaac Soyer's *Employment Agency* (fig. 38, 1937), these artists depict contemplative people of different races sharing a similar fate. The mood is epitomized by the harsh capitalist inscription: "All fees are payable. Cash in advance."

Moses Soyer was the art critic of the *New Masses*, and it was in this role that he hailed Black artists. Richmond Barthé was especially singled out for praise for his sculpture *The Negro Looks Forward* (1940), which was part of the Roosevelt tribute exhibition.[49] Another review is illustrated by Jacob Epstein's *Head of Paul Robeson* (fig. 39, 1928), which took as its subject the left-leaning Black singer and actor. Epstein himself was critical of America's failure "in the portrayal of the many remarkable types that compose American people . . . the negro in particular." In his own work, Epstein claims:

FIG. 35. Raphael Soyer, *Village East Street Scene* (1965–66), oil on canvas.
Private collection, courtesy of Mary Soyer.

"I myself have probably undertaken more negro portraits than any sculptors in America"—the portrait of Paul Robeson in the role of Eugene O'Neill's Emperor Jones is a case in point.[50] Here the artist executed the work rapidly so as to capture Robeson's particular mood, the spiritual expression of longing. The proud head tilted upward, as Moses Soyer sees it, "reveals strong, impressive character."[51] Paul Robeson also commented on his rapport with Epstein, writing that "he was fine, just a fine human being. I'll never forget those eyes, and the way his face would break into a smile." In spite of the short period of time," He caught—more I think than I ever put into the part of Emperor Jones—he caught the whole meaning and his feeling for my people." And Robeson also appreciated the universal quality the portrait projected: "He was way beyond the sitter, beyond just the personal thing—so characteristic of him, and of his work."[52]

Moses Soyer's own painting of a young Black woman was warmly received by

FIG. 36. Raphael Soyer, *Amos on Racial Equality* (1965–66), drawing.
Collection Rebecca Beagle Soyer, courtesy of Mary Soyer.

FIG. 37. Raphael Soyer, *Waiting Room* (1940), oil on canvas. Collection of the
Corcoran Gallery of Art, Museum purchase, William A. Clark Fund. Courtesy of Mary Soyer.

FIG. 38. Isaac Soyer, *Employment Agency* (1937), oil on canvas, $34\,{}^{1}/_{4}$ x 45.
Collection of Whitney Museum of American Art. Purchase 37.44. Courtesy of Avi Soyer.

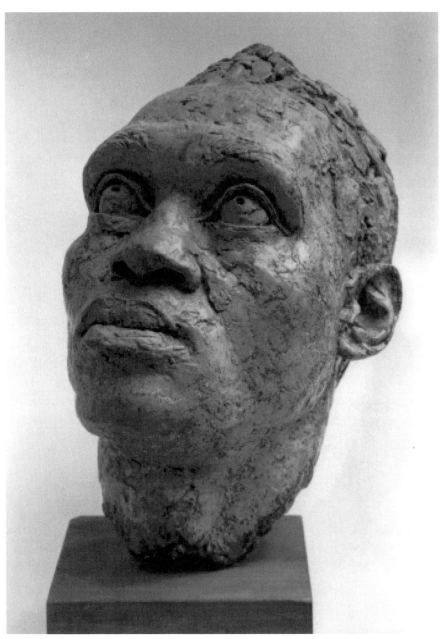

FIG. 39. Jacob Epstein, *Head of Paul Robeson* (1928), plaster, H. 33.
Collection Israel Museum, Jerusalem, Israel. Permission of Jackie Epstein.

another art critic of the journal *Art Front*: "a significance not to be overlooked . . . the Negress represented by Moses Soyer has dignity and self-assurance—she is treated as an equal."[53] An examination of the double portrait of the singer and actress *Eartha Kitt* (fig. 40, 1964) would seem to bear out this critic's remarks.[54]

In many instances the Soyer brothers' friendships with Black artists were expressed in portraits documenting these relationships. Thus, Moses' friendship with one of the leading African-American artists, Jacob Lawrence, is captured in the double portrait *Gwen and Jacob Lawrence* (fig. 41, 1962) of the painter and his artist-wife. Moses painted the close relationship of the couple through the naturalistic depiction of the proximity of the two busts, and also through the triangular composition created by their pose.

Mutual reflections can be exemplified through the gaze that two artist friends conveyed through the portraits each did of the other. Raphael Soyer, who was represented by the Forum Gallery in New York, saw to it that once the African-American painter Benny Andrews (born in Morgan County, Georgia, in 1930) decided to settle in New York in the 1960s he would be represented by the same gallery. They followed the modernist tradition of artists painting artists: in 1966 Benny Andrews painted a *Portrait of Raphael Soyer* (fig. 42), to be succeeded eight years later by Raphael Soyer's *Portrait of Benny Andrews* (fig. 43, 1974). Andrews sets Raphael in a de Chiricoesque street that provides a background to four figures that often appear in Soyer's work: a contemplative young girl seated on a chair, a nude young woman on a colorful rug, a young bearded man standing next to a brick wall, and an old man seen from the back as he leaves the scene, a mirror image of Raphael and perhaps of his brother, Moses. Raphael Soyer himself, in formal dress with a contemplative expression next to a podium, is both part of his constructed "studio" and detached from it. Andrews captures the essence of the mood of Soyer's paintings that often juxtapose generations, setting the young next to the old, the clad next to the nude—their common denominator being the introverted, detached, and melancholy disposition. Andrews fused Soyer's iconography with his own stylistic language, echoing *pittura metafisica* shadows. The shadows the figures project also suggest the double life they share: Raphael's (source images) and Andrews's (recapitulation).

In contrast to Andrews's re-creation of his painter friend's studio, Raphael Soyer's portrait of Andrews is more traditional, centering on the bust which faces the viewer. Andrews's warm and responsive, handsome, elongated features, framed by his beard as he raises a glass of wine, express a sense of immediacy, of a celebration, perhaps toasting their mutual friendship.

The Soyer brothers' association with African-American artists included constant struggles to enable Black artists to exhibit their work, the publication of reviews of Black artists and Black themes in art, and their own visual portrayal of images of Blacks that are full of empathy and insightful characterization. Raphael Soyer's later vision of White women nursing Black children as the salvation of mankind can be understood against this background as a culmination of a life-long involvement.

FIG. 40. Moses Soyer, *Portrait of Eartha Kitt* (1964), oil on canvas, 30 x 36.
Private collection, courtesy of David Soyer.

But it was the African-American artist Daniel La Rue Johnson (born in 1931 in Los Angeles, winner of a Guggenheim fellowship) who further expanded the vision of racial fusion in the 1970 exhibition *Some American History*. In his mixed media done in collaboration with Thomas Stilz, *Over Here, Over There* (figs. 44, 45), Johnson deals directly with the nursing of children in the interracial context. It is noteworthy that this vision, which goes a step further than Soyer, was part of an exhibition initiated by Larry Rivers, as a common artistic venture by Rivers and some African-American artists. (A more comprehensive discussion of this joint exhibition will be presented in chapter 5.) Johnson does not rest content with depicting a mother of one race holding a child of another, nor is he satisfied with depicting a mother of one race exclusively. He creates a dual image, with a racial mélange of nursing mothers. They are parallel images of equal status, which metaphorically also represent the joint exhibition. Through provocatively paired images the artist was busy shattering stereotypes, even if there is a slight tongue-in-cheek effect. He also articulated his thoughts about it: "It shows how black women in history have nursed white children, and how now you have only to look around to see white girls nursing black children. It says if you want some milk and you're a baby, you

FIG. 41. Moses Soyer, *Gwen and Jacob Lawrence* (1962), oil on canvas, 30 x 36.
Private collection, courtesy of David Soyer.

can go over there and get some, and you can go over here and get some, which is just
another way of saying that the lines dividing people are just a lot of bull."[55]

Johnson here challenges the cruel history of Black women and children. Through
his demand for equal nursing rights, he tries to make amends for that history. His text
accords with Jan Nederveen Pieterse's studies of the image of the "Buxom Mammy,"
stereotyping the Black woman as a good-tempered nurturing type, captured in modern
advertisements in the image of Aunt Jemima: "Slavery deprived blacks themselves from
parenthood, and in nostalgic representations of them their parental qualities are at the
service of white children, who were nurtured by black nannies. . . . Meanwhile their
easygoing servitude was turned into a commercial attribute."[56] Daniel Johnson is obviously challenging this notion with an alternative model: "As a result of history, we will
be able to say to one another, 'Don't beat me up; don't put me down because I'm black—or
because I'm white.'"[57]

Although the starting point of this chapter was the identification with the plight of
the newly born Black child, most artists of the 1930s through the 1960s whose works

FIG. 42. Benny Andrews, *Portrait of Raphael Soyer* (1966)
oil and collage on canvas, 28 ³/₄ x 29 ³/₄. Courtesy of Mary Soyer.

FIG. 43. Raphael Soyer, *Portrait of Benny Andrews* (1974), oil on canvas, 12 x 9.
Collection of the artist, courtesy of Benny Andrews.

FIG. 44. Daniel La Rue Johnson/Thomas Stilz, *Over Here, Over There* (1970), mixed media: H: 60, W: 84. Menil Collection, Houston, with permission.

are discussed here have manifested an attitude of admiration or even reverence toward the image of the Black. We saw the pride and beauty of the Black woman, the aspirations for a better future expressed through the torso of the pregnant Black woman, and also through Paul Robeson's dignified portrait. The chapter also examined dreams, the typical vehicles of vision. A Black boy with a white fish, his dream catch, contains also the frustration of the fantasy. Dreams of multiracial playgrounds led to a vision of complete fusion in the form of a mixture of races in the most intimate of relations, that of mother and child.

FIG. 45. Daniel La Rue
Johnson/Thomas Stilz,
Over Here, Over There
(1970), mixed media:
H: 60, W: 84. Menil
Collection, Houston,
with permission.

CHAPTER 3

Jews mirroring African Americans on Lynching

Scottsboro's just a little place:
No shame is writ across its face—
Its court, too weak to stand against a mob,
Its people's heart, too small to hold a sob.[1]

The other side of the wish-fulfillment world of dreams is that of reality turned nightmare. The most brutal manifestation of racial persecution and discrimination in America was lynching. From the period of Reconstruction to the mid-twentieth century, thousands of Blacks fell victim to this most cruel practice. In his macabre book *100 Years of Lynchings*, Ralph Ginzburg collected newspaper reports on lynchings without analysis of the documentary data since the facts speak for themselves.[2] And yet, in the short introduction he could not refrain from asking, "What lies at the root of race hatred?" The answer, which follows Frantz Fanon's line of argument, centers around the psychoanalytic term "projection": "Jews . . . are deceitful and money-mad; Negroes . . . are slothful and sex-mad" are his examples illustrating race-biased projections. Ginzburg connects these generalities to a specific case from the *New York Herald Tribune* dispatch of February 9, 1936. It tells of "the mob hanging a Negro, allegedly for attempted rape. The leader of the mob, it later turns out, is convicted for the very same offense he ascribed to the Negro."[3]

The artists presented in this chapter regarded their depiction of lynching as part of their struggle against racial projections and their tragic consequences. Next to George Bellows's harsh lithograph *The Law Is Too Slow* (1923), Thomas Benton's oil painting *A Lynching* (1935) and Reginald Marsh's drawing *This Is Her First Lynching*, many Jewish-American artists expressed their dismay over these horrific events. Margaret Rose Vendryes distinguishes between Black and White artists' visual conceptualization of lynching, a difference she attributes to the fact "that every black artist was a potential victim." African-American artists were not drawn to depicting the lynching spectacle; they would not be "lashing out at the oppressor." Instead they preferred to circumvent the actual "deed" itself and lament the victim through art that "possessed the tone of an appeal to the morality of the viewer, often through religious references." *The Mother* (1934), a Pietà-like representation by the African-American artist Richmond Barthé, is a case in point.[4] Yet Vendryes's argument subverts the original intention of some White artists' depictions of lynching when she states that certain lynching images by White artists bear "the same open-faced audacity that their Southern brothers used to commit the crime."[5]

This chapter focuses on the relationship between Jewish Americans and African Americans and their common concern about lynching as represented in art. Bearing in mind Vendryes's distinctions between African-American and White American artists, the question is to what extent do Jewish artists fit into these categories?

The questions Vendryes raises are as old as the history of lynching. In fact a symposium was taking place in the pages of *The Crisis* throughout 1926 on the subject, "The Negro in Art: How Shall He Be Portrayed." A questionnaire was sent to various writers, Blacks and Whites, involved in the Black cause. Among the questions: "When the artist, black or white, portrays Negro characters is he under any obligations or limitations as to the sort of character he will portray?" and similarly, "Can any author be criticized for painting the worst or the best characters of a group?" The questionnaire referred to visual stereotypes and asked whether the artist should consider the impact of painted representations on the image of Blacks in real life. There was no conclusive answer. The responses varied from those who believed in preserving the positive outlook of the community to others who believed in artistic freedom.

Another type of debate appeared in *The Crisis* (February 1937), entitled, "Do Lynching Pictures Create Race Hatred?" The editors discussed readers' letters relating to a picture of the lynching of Lint Show at Royston. According to these letters, giving publicity to such images had a tendency to increase race hatred. The policy of *The Crisis* was diametrically opposed to this suggestion, declaring that "very often the sheer horror of lynching serves to rouse ordinarily lethargic people to action."

Similar discussions were widespread in the aftermath of the Holocaust within the Jewish community. Are portrayals of victims of Nazi atrocities, particularly the visual ones, legitimate forms of artistic expression? Are they not potentially degrading even when the motive behind their creation is to commemorate and document? Do they not potentially stimulate anti-Semitism and neo-Nazism? The high degree of risk of abusing and distorting the original intention places a well-meaning artist in a particularly sensitive moral position, vulnerable to misinterpretation and unjust criticism.[6]

Lynching was a central theme in the important exhibition discussed earlier, *Bridges and Boundaries: African Americans and American Jews*. One of the aims of the show was to draw an analogy between the long history of Jewish suffering, including pogroms in

Europe, and the history of Blacks since the days of slavery. The assumption was that these histories led to an alliance, an "incident-rich relationship of two communities whose chief point of communality has always been that they were underdogs and outsiders."[7]

One of the most powerful visual images at the exhibition was a photograph labeled *A Man Was Lynched Yesterday*, a documentation of a banner that was hung out of the window of the NAACP offices in New York, reporting the bare fact that a lynching had taken place. The strength of the image lies in the mere stating of the fact in a cool, seemingly detached way, without an illustration of the actual lynching itself. The horror is enhanced by the disparity between the event and the almost matter-of-factness of the news item captured in one sentence. The catalogue pointed out that most mainstream American newspapers did not report lynchings on their front pages. However, the Black and Yiddish presses continuously gave news and featured visual material of these events.[8] In Black magazines such as *The Crisis*, *Opportunity*, and *The Afro-American*, articles and photographs as well as cartoons constantly depicted lynching images. The NAACP banner, stating "a man was lynched yesterday," played the role of a recurrent reminder on the pages of *The Crisis*. A stylized graphic sign language with the title "Social Studies in Pictures" on the pages of *Opportunity* (April 1933) also used a "cool" manner to deal with lynching. Statistical lynching data is presented through the repeated diagram of a lynched body, shocking both by its content and by the mechanical reproduction of the lynched Black man.

Visual images in African-American magazines have used various strategies to denounce lynching. These included turning the victim into a martyr of faith, and the demonic depiction of the murderers as the hooded ghouls of the Ku Klux Klan. In a 1916 print titled *Christmas in Georgia, A.D.* (fig. 46) signed by Harris, and published at Christmas in *The Crisis*, the whole White community is throwing stones and firing at the already hanged, dignified-looking man, while a majestic Christ figure clasps him to his breast saying: "Inasmuch as ye did it unto the least of these, My brethren, ye did it unto me." Associating the lynched man with Christ gives meaning to his death. The composition recalls Goya's protest painting *3 May, 1808* (1814). Here a French firing squad is seen from behind—the shooters are anonymous, dispassionate, aiming at the Christ-like Madrileno victim. The lynched figure is thus set in the broad context of the martyrdom of the oppressed in art. In the lynching scene, however, the "passions" of the actors are predominant.

An opposite type of image is Cornelius Johnson's *Prejudice* (fig. 47), also printed in *The Crisis* (March 1927). Here, the aggressor is symbolized by a demon with protruding fangs, horns, and the typical devilish clawlike hands. He is holding a rope and a gun, the attributes of lynching. And there were many cartoons depicting the Klansmen, using ironic titles, playing on and reinforcing the gap between caption and image.

The images in the Yiddish and Black press shared this type of sardonic humor, for instance in their treatment of the Ku Klux Klan. The Klan with its white sheets, pointed

FIG. 46. Harris, *Christmas in Georgia, A.D.* (December 1916),
illustration in *The Crisis*, with permission.

hoods, and midnight activities lent itself to caricature. The repeated pattern of masquer-
aders lacking individual human attributes even complies with Bergson's definition of the
comic. The cartoonists' aim was to undermine the Klan by pointing out its mechanical,
laughable aspects. These publications not only condemned the Klan's present activities
but had also protested against the visual impact of *The Birth of a Nation* (1915), the
controversial, explicitly racist film by D. W. Griffith, which has passed into cinema history and is often discussed for its aesthetic qualities rather than its racism. The film,
which glorified the Ku Klux Klan and was originally called *The Clansman*, was based on
the Rev. Thomas Dixon's anti-Black novel by that name.

This can be exemplified through the similarity between images by Peshka, pub-
lished in the Yiddish daily *Der Tog*, and those done by Romare Bearden in *The Afro-
American*. Peshka's regular column, sometimes called "Black on White," used double
meanings in relation to Black destiny. In the May 26, 1936 issue (fig. 48) the large
Klansman is hugging a smaller, hooded Black double whose robe is inscribed "Black
Legion." They are in the foreground, while a lynched man is seen hanging at a distance.
Both figures are surrounded by their instruments of death—rope, whip, gun, and tar.
According to Ezra Mendelsohn, Peshka's awareness of the Black Legion, though obvi-
ously related to the American scene, could also be a reference to the infamous "Black
Hundred" who attacked Jews in tsarist Russia. The Ku Klux Klan and a similar organiza-
tion, "Black Legion," were both anti-Black and anti-Semitic.[9] Romare Bearden's Ku Klux

FIG. 47. Cornelius Johnson, *Prejudice* (March 1927),
illustration in *The Crisis*, with permission.

Klan man, in *The Ghost Walks* (fig. 49, June 6, 1936), is of colossal dimensions, recalling Goya's *Colossus* (c. 1810). He sports a swastika on his sleeve, and masses of people with the "Black Legion" flag are walking below, alluding to an endless march.

Next to Peshka, William Gropper, a student of Robert Henri and George Bellows, continuously deplored lynchings in his painting and graphics in a mode which, "instead of the wholesome naturalistic pride of country typical of such works, [displays] a rather biting and incisive criticisms of events."[10] Gropper, born in New York City in 1897, shared Romare Bearden's attitude to the Klan. Thus, in his *Political Cartoon* (fig. 50, 1930) the Klansman becomes a giant, leading on the rabble. Other cartoons of the Klan show the influence of Goya. The print *Southern Landscape* (fig. 51, 1945) echoes the satire of the *Disasters of War*. In a later variation, *Lynch* (fig. 52, 1949), four hanged silhouettes of Black men are shown in the background, while the foreground is domi-nated by the figure of a smug, hooded Klansman who even under his disguise conveys a sense of satisfaction. Gropper included this image as part of his Warsaw exhibition in 1949. He expounded his artistic beliefs thus: "I'm from the old school, defending the under-dog. Maybe because I've been an under-dog or still am. I put myself in their posi-tion. . . . I react, just as Negroes react, because I have felt the same things as a Jew, or my family has."[11]

We can also see the affinity between the Black and Yiddish press in the various *Der Tog* cartoons and in Romare Bearden's images demanding justice in the case of the Scottsboro boys. The series of trials, from 1932 to 1935—"certainly the most sensa-tional trials in the history of the Negro at the American bar of justice"—were related to a case where nine Black youths, two of them thirteen and fourteen years old, were charged in Alabama with raping two White women on a train they were all riding. Eight were sentenced to death; however, they were retried. The defense, led by Samuel Leibowitz, saved their lives and awakened the nation and the South to Alabama's injustice. In the subsequent proceedings of the Scottsboro cases, charges were dropped against five of the boys; the other four were retried and convicted in 1937. Overall, the defendants spent no less than six and as many as nineteen years in jail. Most historians agree that they were innocent, that "the Scottsboro boys had committed no crime other than being born black."[12]

A flood of pamphlets and posters was produced during the years of the trials. The Jewish graphic artist Hugo Gellert did a poster (fig. 53, 1934) for the International Labor Defense with the caption, "Spike lynch terror! Save the Scottsboro boys!" In this power-ful image the brutality of the skeletal hand threatening the nine innocent victims (the nine Scottsboro boys) is countered by the two muscular hands forcefully breaking that threat. The skeletal arm conveys death and greed (the ring with a dollar sign inscrip-tion), while the other two hands are associated with life and determination. The use of red for the tips of the fingers pointing at the boys denotes the blood thirst of racial persecution, while the same red color of the other two hands and their instruments

FIG. 48. Peshka, *Black on White*, illustration in *Der Tog* (May 26, 1936).

suggests the socialist inspiration of this protest poster. These two hands are portrayed in a way that cannot be ascribed to a single person. The resolute smashing of the deadly attack on the boys is thus depicted as a joint act, possibly of White and Black hands. Hugo Gellert, a tailor's son, was born in 1892 in Hungary, and the sweatshop experience was formative in the development of his political consciousness.

In the November 23, 1935 issue of *The Afro-American* (fig. 54) Romare Bearden's cartoon of the Scottsboro trials portrayed a monumental image of a hooded Klansman, wearing the Klan insignia and holding a rope behind a table in a so-called "Court." There is bitter irony in the relationship between this image and the caption: "The Real Judge at Scottsboro." Peshka's parallel concern with the case can be seen in the July 1937 version of *Black on White* in *Der Tog* (fig. 55), depicting a group of four Black boys under the protection of a White motherly figure. As they were the last to be tried and eventually

"The Ghost Walks"

FIG. 49. Romare Bearden, *The Ghost Walks* (June 6, 1936), illustration in *The Afro-American.* © Romare Bearden Foundation/licensed by VAGA, New York.

convicted, they became younger and younger in the artist's eye and consequently in more need of motherly protection. They are holding a statement demanding, "Free the Scottsboro Boys," while the words "public opinion" are written on the woman's gown. The artist appeals to American public opinion as the only way to counter the injustice of the formal legal system. The female figure symbolizes the decent White people of conscience.

Persecution of Blacks on a racial basis was not the only concern Jews and Blacks had in common. The plight of Jews in Europe in the 1930s drew attention in the Black press, as did racial discrimination in America in the Yiddish. The Black press drew analogies between the fate of Blacks and Jews under the Nazis. A cartoon in *The Crisis* (June 1934, exhibited at the Jewish Museum exhibition in 1992), showed a hooded klansman with his "natural" paraphernalia, under the caption, "Nazi persecution of Jews and

FIG. 50. William Gropper, *Political Cartoon* (1930), cartoon, whereabouts unknown.

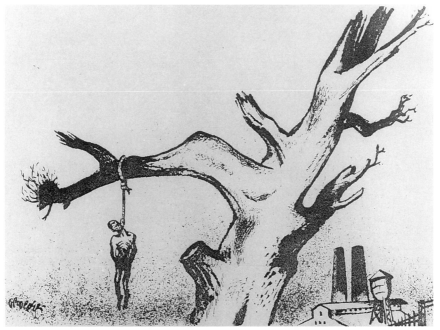

FIG. 51. William Gropper, *Southern Landscape* (1945), cartoon, whereabouts unknown.

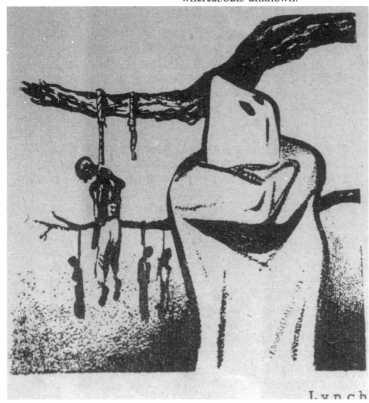

FIG. 52. William Gropper, *Lynch* (1949), cartoon, whereabouts unknown.

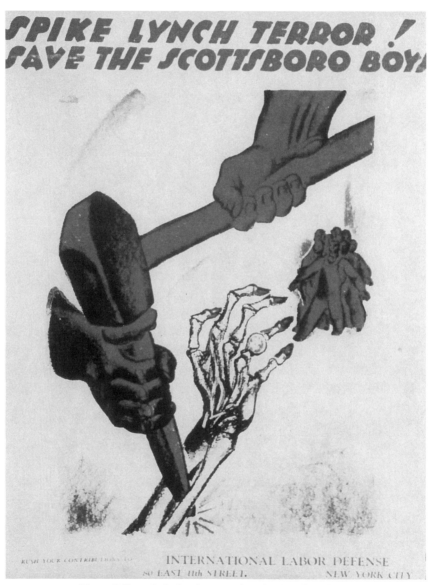

FIG. 53. Hugo Gellert, *Spike lynch terror! Save the Scottsboro boys!* (1934), poster, private collection.

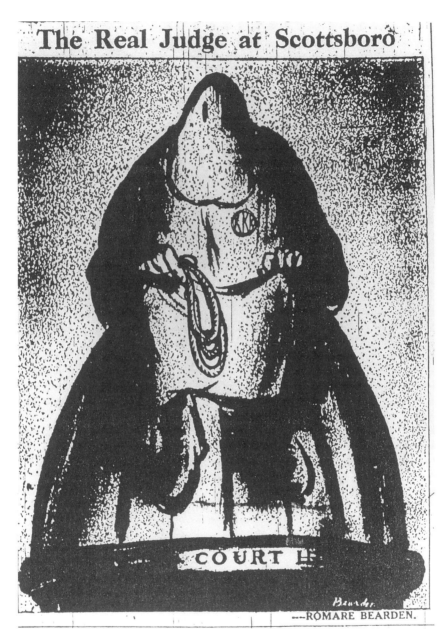

FIG. 54. Romare Bearden, *The Real Judge at Scottsboro*, cartoon in
The Afro-American, (November 23, 1935).
© Romare Bearden Foundation/Licensed by VAGA, New York.

FIG. 55. Peshka, *Black on White*, cartoon in
Der Tog (July 1937).

Negroes." A poem by the Yiddish writer Berysh Vaynshteyn, "Lynching" (1936), reiterates this analogy by conceiving lynching in Christian terminology:

> White wild hands snare you with a stray rope,
> And a July tree crucifies your Negro neck.

This association is first refuted and then reinforced in the third stanza:

> Your singing prayer wept so mournfully to God,
> But he won't appear to you, his legs burst, his nailed hands,
> He cannot even open an eye with a tear for you
> Or accept your last word as a confession—He's crucified Himself.

The moment of drawing on the two peoples' parallel histories in relation to left-wing ideologies emerges at the end of the poem, with analogies between the South and Europe. Vaynshteyn refers to Wedding, a working-class district in Berlin, known as the bastion of Communism and to Leopoldstadt, Vienna's working class district associated with left-wing parties that included a large part of Vienna's Jewish population. This was the time of the Austro-fascist regime, and all left-wing parties and movements were prohibited and oppressed. If these are words of consolation, it is indeed a very bitter one:

> Negro, the fate of destruction fell not only on you.
> Many, many die like you. Such a death is now in fashion.
> Like this they now die everywhere—
> In Wedding, in Leopoldstadt and in Carolina.[13]

In an article dealing with lynching and the struggle against it in the 1930s, Marlene Park argues that anti-lynching art grew in reaction to the Scottsboro case and then as part of anti-lynching legislative efforts. After World War II, images of lynching signifying White racism continued to appear primarily in the works of African-American artists. The article investigates two parallel exhibitions held in 1935, one by the NAACP, titled *An Art Commentary on Lynching*, and the other by the Communist John Reed Club. The exhibitions were manifestations against lynching and in support of appropriate anti-lynching legislation.[14] Park's analysis of the politics of the period, as well as her wide array of illustrations, seems to play down the role of Jewish artists in this struggle. Of the many artists dealt with in the article, only the Jewish impact of Hyman Warsager and Louis Lozowick is pointed out. However, the author completely ignores the Jewish background of many artists to whom she herself refers: Seymour Lipton, William Gropper, Julius Bloch, Adolf Wolff, Philip Evergood, Harry Sternberg, the early Philip Guston, Hugo Gellert, and Aaron Goodelman. Furthermore, William Gropper's graphic depictions of lynching at the end of the 1940s; Philip Guston's Klan themes, to which he returned in his neo-expressionistic figural imagery after his abstract period; as well as Larry Rivers's three dimensional installation dealing with lynching (1970)—

demonstrate that for these artists, interest in the topic extended beyond the period suggested by Park.

Julius Bloch's *The Lynching* (fig. 56, 1932), shown in *An Art Commentary on Lynching*, was chosen as the quintessential type representing Jewish artists' depiction of the subject in the *Bridges and Boundaries* show. Julius Bloch was born in 1888 in Kehl to German-Jewish parents and came to America in 1893, establishing his career in Philadelphia. His lynch scene should be viewed in the wider context of his overall work. It is not the only context in which the artist portrayed African Americans. In fact, in its gruesome nature it was an exception to his usual depictions. More typical were dignified, respectable portraits, such as the thoughtful face of *Deacon William Mann* (1939), holding a book as he addresses the spectator; the image of *Tom* (1938), presented to Howard University; as well as the "classic" profile of the artist *Horace Pippin* (fig. 57, 1943), a friend of Bloch's. Bloch, who became an instructor in the Philadelphia Academy, lived within the Black community of the city. In his journals he writes that he often had to justify his painting of Black people and to address the constant doubts of others about his motives for doing so. Bloch's answer is significant: "Primarily because he [the Black] makes my life a richer, happier one, inspired by what I can only call his beauty, do I make these pictures."[15] Bloch was aware that in depicting the lynch scene he was deviating from his insistence on portraying Black people as "human beings" (rather than victims), and that he could no longer ignore the need to protest visually against lynching.

Living within the Black community may have directly inspired Bloch's presentation of the lynching as a crucifixion. The scene is constructed in two registers, echoing Renaissance compositions: the mob holding the rope surrounds the tree in the lower register, while in the upper, in the center of the composition, a crucified man with his head raised to heaven asks, "Why hast Thou forsaken me?"

In the following year Bloch painted a portrait of *The Prisoner* (1934), denouncing the Scottsboro trials.[16] This image was published as a lithograph in *The New Masses* in response to Langston Hughes's request to use it for raising money for the defense. Hughes's letter, which was sent to many artists including Bloch, indicates that Bloch was expected to join artists and intellectuals in their struggle: "We hope to show by this gesture that at least the artists, writers and intellectuals of this country do not want to stand by doing nothing while prejudice and hate gathers an upper hand."[17]

Bloch's paintings were enthusiastically received in the *Negro History Bulletin*, both his "psychological portraits of Negroes" and his politically engaged paintings: "These two pictures [*Lynching, The Prisoners*] spell out on canvas more effectively than any words or testimony the crushing pain and sorrow which the Negro has felt during his interracial associations in America."[18] Alain Locke, speaking specifically of Bloch's portraits, praised his depictions of "unconventional and little known aspects of Negro life and character."[19]

While Park ignored Bloch's Jewishness and his broader interest in African Americans, she did single out Louis Lozowick as "the Jewish artist to identify most closely with lynching." Lozowick, born in 1892 in the Ukraine, came to America in 1906 and became a member of the John Reed Club. In his lithograph *Lynching (Lynch Law)* (fig. 58, 1936) the hanged man is a self-portrait. It thus calls for a variation in the conception of lynching. The artist does not use the traditional attributes of the scene, but concentrates on the fragmentation of the lynched man's head viewed at the lower edge of the composition, separated from his body. Lozowick's is a symbolic image of mutilation rather than a portrayal of the act itself. His work thus differs from violent images such as that by Harry Sternberg, born in 1904 on the Lower East Side, the son of an immigrant peddler from Bessarabia. In Sternberg's ironically titled *Southern Holiday* (fig. 59, 1935), done in reaction to reading about southern atrocities that filled him "with anger and shame," the artist depicted an explicit castration of a hanged man, exposed and bleeding.[20]

If Sternberg exaggerated the physical degradation, Lozowick wished to do away with the physical body altogether. His concentration on the head is an artistic device to avoid exposing the artist's own body on the scaffold. Instead, the perspectival focus emphasizes the distorted features of the suffering head. He is doubly fragmented, both by the rope encircling his neck and by the picture's frame. The head endows the image with a spiritual connotation and at the same time brings the spectator into direct contact with its physical as well as spiritual suffering. There is a contrast between figure and background: while the head is clearly defined and highlighted, the lithograph technique is used to create an undefined background, suggestive rather than descriptive of Evil taking control. It is this expressive decontextualization that makes Lozowick's self-portrait into a universal image. The artist himself related the social and political climate in Europe and in the South to his lynch scene:

> It represents a lynching but it is a self portrait just the same. I cannot recall the special event or the immediate reason that may have prompted me to do the scene. The time was certainly turbulent. The depression was still on. Nazism was growing in Europe. The news from the South was disturbing. I was still under the impression of newspaper reports about a flood in Alabama where while white[s] were being rescued, blacks were callously left to drown. Whether that was the reason I could not tell. It could have been.[21]

If, as Margaret Vendryes pointed out, a lynching was a threat to every Black man, then it seems that this threat was equally real for Lozowick. The reference to his shock at learning about people drowning in the floods may explain the effect of a floating head conveyed by the lithograph. The personal sense of being lynched combines the artist's identification with the South and his concern for the prospects of people under Nazism in Europe. We have here a regard parallel to the one expressed in *The Crisis* cartoon of June 1934. Care for the "other" also implies caring for oneself and for one's own people.

Other lynch scenes done by Jewish-American artists include Philip Reisman's *South*

FIG. 56. Julius Bloch, *The Lynching* (1932), oil on canvas, 19 x 12 (48.3 x 30.5 cm.).
Collection of Whitney Museum of American Art.
Purchase 33.28. © 1966: Whitney Museum of American Art.

FIG. 57. Julius Bloch, *Horace Pippin* (1943), oil on canvas, 24 x 20 $^{1}/_{6}$.
Courtesy of the Museum of American Art of the Pennsylvania Academy of the Fine Arts,
Philadelphia. Bequest of the artist in memory of Emma and Nathan Bloch.

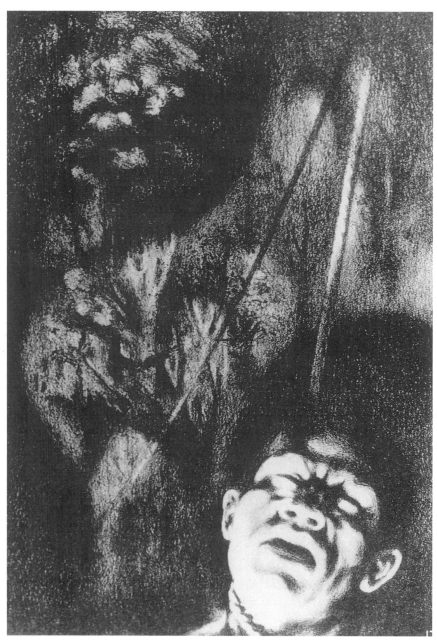

FIG. 58. Louis Lozowick, *Lynching (Lynch Law)* (1936),
lithograph, 10 $^5/_{16}$ x 7 $^5/_{16}$. Courtesy of Hirschl and Adler Gallery, New York.

FIG. 59. Harry Sternberg, *Southern Holiday* (1935),
lithograph, 21 3/4 x 15 3/4, private collection.

(1934), with the lynched man next to his praying wife and the Klansmen pointing toward them. Joseph Hirsch's *Lynch*, which was part of the ACA Gallery exhibition *A Tribute to Theodore Roosevelt* (1947), showed the weeping wife of a lynched man, contrasted with the unaware playful baby on her lap.

More often than painters, sculptors depicting lynch scenes concentrate on an individual image that acquires an iconic rather than a narrative quality. This can be exemplified by three works from the 1930s: Adolf Wolff's *The Lynch Law* (fig. 60, 1931), Aaron Goodelman's *Necklace* (fig. 61, 1933), and Seymour Lipton's *Lynched* (fig. 62, 1933). Being three dimensional, these images bring the viewer into a direct one-to-one relationship with the victim. At least in the case of these sculptors, there is no spectacle. Adolf Wolff, who was born in Brussels in 1883 and emigrated to America as a boy, was known as a revolutionary, his sculpture part of his activities in the John Reed Club. At the exhibition *Revolutionary Art in the Capitalist Countries*, held in Moscow in 1932, Wolff was represented with images of a worker, a coal miner on strike, a lynched Black man, and a sculpture of a Black woman standing erect with clenched fists. The works were purchased by the Soviet government.[22]

The two sculptures symbolizing the Black people thus present a contrast: the lynched victim, and the aspirations for the future implied by the Black woman's determined stance, echoing that of another sculpture by Wolff, *Arise Oppressed of the Earth* (c. 1931). Accordingly, whereas the woman is looking forward in an attitude typical of communist ideology, conveying hope for a better future, the hanged man's dignified elongated body is Christ-like. Furthermore, nature and the hanged man correspond, as the contorted tree and bent body are inseparable. It is through this fusion that the protagonist is associated with his Via Dolorosa, as cross bearer and crucified. Wolff's sculpture is in line with ideas expressed in his early poetry, such as "To Esther," addressed to his seven-year-old daughter:

> May your life and your death be the scourge of tyrants
> And the inspiration of those who fight for human freedom.[23]

Aaron Goodelman, who was born in 1890 in Bessarabia and emigrated to the United States in 1904, chose the intimate shape of a statuette (23 x 6 x 4 inches) to pay tribute to the victims of lynching.[24] As can be seen in the drawing for the sculpture, the original plan was to depict a hanging man in a very simplified frontal way, with a rope encircling his neck and his body attached to an elliptical wooden shape.[25] In the final sculpture the artist renounced the background altogether and left only the noose, giving the ironic title *Necklace* to the whole work. The emphasis here is on the upright pose of a rather effeminate naked young man, his body intact, his eyes drooping, suggesting an androgynous type of portrayal. The statuette carries a universalized meaning that includes both genders. Goodelman plays on the discrepancy between the beauty of the protagonist and his fate and on the painful contradiction between the poetic title *Neck-*

lace and the strangling noose. It is a double pun, since the artist is associating between the object of beauty and the object of torture, and yet endowing the image with beauty, ennobling it as if trying to redeem the lynched man. The miniature size of the sculpture suggests an intimate quality. By bringing the image close to the spectator, a kind of private icon is created.

The sculpture was also part of Goodelman's first one-man exhibition, at the Eighth Street Gallery in 1933. All the reviews of the show singled this work out. The *New York Sun* (November 17, 1933) pointed out the "subtly stylized figure of the black boy in the rather gruesome 'Necklace'. . . a result of indignant brooding over the Scottsboro and other similar cases." The article in *Art News* (November 28, 1933) drew attention to the back of the sculpture: "all the tragedy and youthful surrender are depicted in the frail back." The *New York World Telegraph* (November 29, 1933) emphasized Goodelman's social commitment: "The Bronze is alive with all of Goodelman's hatred of injustice and oppression."[26]

Seymour Lipton's first wood carving was dedicated to the theme of lynching. The review of his wooden sculptures at the ACA Gallery mentions *Lynched* as growing "out of his sympathy for the unfortunate and oppressed."[27] In this statuette (24 inches wide) the artist, born in New York in 1903, juxtaposed the flat rectangular shape of the base with the distorted three-dimensional lynched figure. It seems as if the lynching is perceived in terms of the tension between body and ground since the violent twist of the body has to adjust itself to the angularity of the flat board serving as a mattress. Does this mattress allude not just to lynching but to the long history of slavery? Or does it also, in its square format, metaphorically allude to the inability of Black people to fit into the procrustean bed of racist society? Lipton's figure is lying on the ground, and the viewer sees it from a number of perspectives, above, below, and sideways. The bound figure creates a zigzag shape and we see the arms, torso, thigh, and lower leg. The lifted leg may also be a censoring device, so that the image does not acquire a distinct sexual quality.

Roberta K. Tarbell compared Lipton's *Lynched* with the Gothic motif of the "broken necked" Madonna, "imposed, with good reasons, upon the hanged man."[28] Marlene Park associated the image with a "fetal position."[29] If indeed it is a fetus, it is a very ironic one for an artist who declared that the subject matter he deals with "is the world of good and evil" and that his images are "reconstructed from the data of actualities."[30]

The three sculptors discussed here share a left-wing ideological commitment. Their small-scale statues are a means to evoke the viewer's sympathies with Blacks and to serve as an attempt to fight racism. In this respect, all the artists we have looked at in the present chapter, Black and Jewish, adhered to similar social and political beliefs, conveyed in a direct and explicit artistic language. This type of political art uses strong images that are easy to read. It is meant to challenge and, hopefully, to change the status quo. The nonequivocal style is used both for the expression of dreams, wishes, and hopes, and for condemning the practice of lynching.

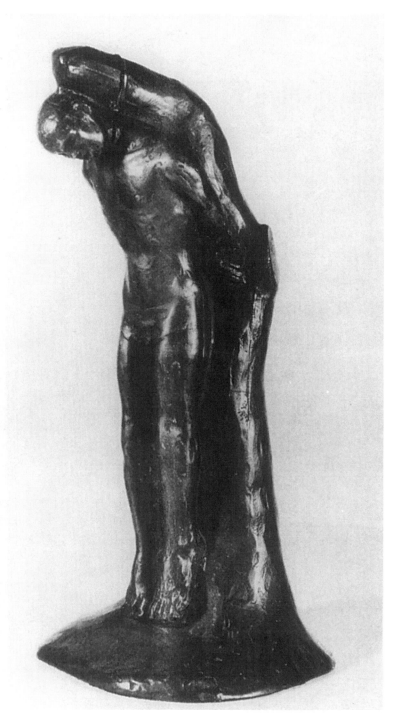

FIG. 60. Adolf Wolff, *The Lynch Law* (1931), bronze,
lost in Russia, perhaps Birobidjan.

FIG. 61. Aaron Goodelman, *The Necklace* (1933), bronze, 23 x 6 x 4.
Collection, The Jewish Museum, New York. © Museum purchase;
Kristie A. Jayne Fund with the cooperation of the Goodelman family. Photo
by John Parnell.

FIG. 62. Seymour Lipton, *Lynched* (1933), mahogany, length 24.
Collection, James R. Palmer, courtesy of James R. Palmer.

When we turn to later representations of lynching and Ku Klux Klan imagery, we can note a change in tone, manner, and approach. The role of lynch scenes in both Jewish- and African-American art becomes more complex and less direct. Take first the case of Philip Guston: "Like Babel with his Cossacks, I feel as if I have been living with the Klan. Riding around empty streets, sitting in their rooms smoking, looking at light bulbs . . . windows."[31]

This curious statement comes from Philip Guston, who in his intentionally "bad boy" paintings depicts Klan characters roaming the streets as well as inhabiting the artist's studio. Although the artistic source for the Klan images is in the art of the 1930s, mainly Gropper, Guston sets the tone for a different type of voice, getting away from the explicit style of nonequivocal social commitment discussed above. His 1970 exhibition at the Marlborough Gallery caused a sensation and prompted angry reactions from fellow painters to the type of imagery shown and to the artist's abandonment of his abstract style, thus "betraying" the Abstract Expressionists. By moving back to figuration, Guston broke away from the linear modernist discourse. However, to view the Klan imagery in a fuller context of his work, we have to take into account that Guston's beginnings were in a figurative style and a socially oriented frame of mind. Guston's art evolved in a dialectical rather than linear manner from figuration and social art, to abstraction and individualism, and from there back to figuration in a neo-expressionistic style. In contrast to his late style, which displays a perplexing tension between the comic and the macabre, in the 1930s Guston conveyed a direct message.

Francis V. O'Connor called Guston's early style "political humanism": a socially committed art that would reveal the causes and motives of social realities in plastic terms. In the *Conspirators* (from the early 1930s),[32] the artist moved from a narrative description in his drawing of the scene to a *pittura metafisica* mystification in the oil painting. The drawing has more than one focus. A hooded Klansman is contemplating a rope, made conspicuous by its disproportionately thick dimensions. The rope is rather puzzling, since the scene at the back already shows a lynched Black man hanging from a tree next to another lynched figure fastened to a cross, while a group of Klansmen are bunched together. The artist is obviously alluding to Christ's being crucified between two other condemned men. However, in the drawing there is only one additional hanged figure. If the scene is indeed related to the New Testament—Christ crucified between the good and bad thieves—the second hanged man is "missing." Hence, the heavy rope presumably suggests that another lynching is about to take place. The Christian iconography, with its association of eternity, implies a world in which lynching is an ongoing process: there will always be a "missing" human being.

In the final oil, which deviates from the drawing, Guston features an unholy "trinity": three Klan figures, hooded and shrouded, are huddled together, forming a mysterious triangle. We are led into the scene through the back of one man, with his two shadow images echoing each other. The artistic language used here suggests Giorgio de Chirico's manner. Both the Klansmen's shapes and the instruments of torture, which acquire a mysterious role and bear a resemblance to the work of the Italian artist. Thus, by avoiding the depiction of a concrete place and by decontextualizing the group through the artistic means of "estrangement," Guston refers to the Klansmen's most essential attribute: their lack of individuality, of particular personal human traits, the uniformity of their masked figures, which can be compared to the soulless mannequins in de Chirico.

Dore Ashton's study of Philip Guston cites another image from the early 1930s in which Klan imagery was inspired by Giorgio de Chirico. She elaborates on the response of Guston and his friends (Kadish, Harold Lehman) to the John Reed Club's call to depart from the practice of "art for art's sake." The theme chosen was the American Black in a "portable" mural shape. Guston depicted the flagellation of a Black man, a work done under the impact of the Scottsboro trial and liberal publications of the time. Stylistically, it is indebted to de Chirico's style of the 1920s. Yet the artist's worst premonitions came true when the murals were raided by members of the American Legion, who destroyed several of them and "took particular pleasure in using the eyes and the genitals of the black figures in the paintings for target figures."[33]

Ashton stresses the importance of *The Conspirators* within the later development of Guston's art: "[These were] not only . . . in the sense of a narrative content but, in a more complex sense, themes that embrace his dialogue with himself, his own past, the

past of the human race, and contemporary events. . . . The work of the 1970s is a characteristic Guston mixture of autobiography, myth, and art—the work of a meditative
temperament."[34]

And indeed, these insights are important for understanding the paradoxical nature
of Guston's late work in general and the Ku Klux Klan images in particular. In order to
grasp the reappearance of Guston's Klan imagery we have to take into account some
aspects of the artist's biography. Philip Guston was born in Montreal in 1913 to an
immigrant family who had escaped pogroms in Odessa in 1905. His father could not
adjust economically, and in 1919 the family moved to Los Angeles, where the elder
Guston worked as a junkman, driving a horse-wagon through the streets. When Philip
was ten or eleven years old, his father committed suicide. "It was my father," writes
Musa Meyer, Guston's daughter, "who found his father, the body hanging from a rope
thrown over the rafter of a shed."[35] The artist changed his name from Goldstein to Guston
in 1935, hiding his original name even from his daughter, who reports that she did not
know about the change until she was in college. Dore Ashton, who apparently knew
about it, was asked by Guston to avoid mentioning it in her book. Musa Meyer's specu-
lations about her father's motives shed light on the artist's problems with his Jewish
identity: "Many of his generation had changed their names. . . . But had my parents really
been that afraid of anti-Semitism? Was my father—heroic figure that he was to me
then—in some way ashamed of being Jewish? Had he wanted that badly to leave his
family behind? Or was he after something else entirely, a sort of assumed identity, like
the masked children in his paintings of the forties?"[36]

If we continue this line of thought, we may conjecture that the Klan figure with
whom the artist identifies is a follow-up on such an assumed persona. The most powerful visual coalescence between the artist and the Klan is expressed in *The Studio* (1969),
a painting dealing with the theme of the "double," where the artist wearing a Klan hood
is seen in the midst of painting a mirror image of himself on a canvas. This duplication
raises questions about the relationship between the identity of the artist and his
identification with the Klan. We are also confronting the power of art, symbolized by the
masquerader's hood, to transform reality, to create one's assumed identity. This artistic
device is reminiscent of Magritte's *The Human Condition I* (1933), in which the artist
tackles the problem of representation in art by the duplication on a canvas of a landscape
seen through a window. The aesthetic theoretical issue in Magritte becomes a personal
quest of identity in Guston. However, the question about the nature of Guston's choice
of masquerade remains: why did he choose to identify with this horrendous type of imagery, which as we have seen played a negative role in his early art? This is doubly puzzling
in light of the artist's past images of the Klan and his political activities during the civil
rights movement. Here he served as a chairman of the art committee of Artists for CORE
(Congress for Racial Equality), raising money for legal defense, scholarship, and education in the South.[37]

In the last stage of his career Guston specifically expressed his identification with the Klan:

> They are self-portraits. I perceive myself as being behind the hood. In the new series of "hoods" my attempt was really not to illustrate, to do pictures of the Ku Klux Klan, as I had done earlier. The idea of evil fascinates me, rather like Isaac Babel who had joined the Cossacks, lived with them and written stories about them. I almost tried to imagine that I was living with the Klan. What would it be like to be evil? to plan, to plot.[38]

As much as he is protesting, Guston is apparently hiding behind the hood. His self-identification with this type of imagery, implying identification with the aggressor, in fact conceals the artist's family history, revealing a sad aspect of Jewish immigration to America. Irvin Sandler recounts the traumatic experience Guston underwent as a ten-year-old child witnessing his father's suicide by hanging, "which he most likely identified with the lynchings perpetrated by the KKK."[39] Two aspects of the artist's history are conflated: his father's suicide by hanging and his own suppression of his origins by concealing his Jewish family name. By taking his own life due to his social and economic inadequacy, notwithstanding the hopes projected onto the new world in his flight from an Odessa pogrom, Leib Goldstein became his own Klansman.[40] In camouflaging his Jewish identity, the artist repeats his father's wish to be annihilated. Furthermore, by choosing a Klansman for his self-portrait, Guston identifies with his father's act but also carries on the burden of his guilt for his father's deed. His inability to be true to himself in American society recaptures his father's failure.

From this perspective, Guston's early work gains an additional dimension. Hence the ominous rope and the "missing" third man in the drawing for *The Conspirators* may also symbolize Guston's family history of self-lynching. It is here as well as in the flagellation scene that the artist intertwines African-American and Jewish history. Lynching, either committed by an external power (in the case of Black people) or through the socioethnic circumstances brought about by one's self, becomes here a sad meeting ground between Jews and African Americans. The quasi-humorous quality that some of his apparently comic Klan figures project is the artist's way of struggling with and banishing these evil spirits, as a way of neutralizing their power. The personal and the social meet.

African-American artists of the last third of the twentieth century typically approach the subject of lynching by stressing the complexity of viewing such an image. Pat Ward Williams, an African-American artist born in 1948 in Philadelphia to parents who were both teachers, brings a different, ambivalent, equivocal, contemporary tone to her *Accused/Blowtorch/Padlock* (fig. 63, 1986). Maurice Berger emphasizes "the irresponsibility of representation" as the central issue of this work. The image has also rightly been called "a modern classic of political art."[41] Here an actual photograph of a lynch scene encased in a window frame is incorporated in the work, surrounded by a series of

FIG. 63. Pat Ward Williams, *Accused/Blowtorch/Padlock* (1986),
mixed media, photograph, silkscreen. P.P.O.W. Gallery, New York.

questions that emerge as part of the experience of viewing the harrowing scene. Using a postmodernist style, she plays the simultaneous role of the creator of an image and the commentator on it in the discourse that it evokes, that is, both the artist and the critic. Moreover, it is a text that brings together the lynching of a Black man and the Jewish experience. Yet this analogy is brought up as a question rather than a direct statement. The text inscribed on a blackboard reads:

> There's something going on here. I didn't see it right away. I just saw he looked so helpless. He doesn't look lynched yet. What is that under his chin. How long had he been LOCKED to that tree? Can you be BLACK and look at this?

To be continued in two parallel lines with more questions:

> Who took this picture? Couldn't he just as easily let the man go? Did he take his camera home and then come back with a blowtorch? Where do you TORTURE someone? BURN off an ear? melt an eye? A screaming mouth. How can this photograph EXIST? WHO took this picture?

As for the analogy between Jews and Blacks:

> Life Magazine published this picture. Could Hitler show pics. of the Holocaust to keep the JEWS in line? Life answers—Page 141—no credit. Oh God, Somebody do something.

Pat Ward Williams's questions, handwritten and reproducing her own intonations, are multilayered: she interrogates the deed itself, the motivation of the photographer, the responsibility of the media, and the spectator's gaze. Furthermore, there is a correspondence between the fragmentation of the body through the very detailed verbal dissection and the fragmentation of the body reproduced next to broken body parts. In this respect, on the one hand she continues the visual tradition of denouncing lynching and on the other deliberately recapitulates the function of documentary photography by reproducing the image herself.

And how are we to account for the analogy between the Holocaust and the lynching image? Is she drawing on the similarity or on the difference in experience? Does she consider the historical fact that photographs of the Holocaust were not allowed to be taken nor shown publicly (as incriminating evidence) by Hitler? However, the main difference between expressions of the Holocaust and the Black experiences, as shown in the discussion of images in the 1930s and the art of Black artists in the third part of the twentieth century, is that early nonequivocal statements have been replaced by later questions. Moreover, the questions are asked without any intention of getting or giving a definite answer. However, whether Pat Ward Williams's questioning of Hitler's and the photographer's methods is ironic or not, and whether the African-American experience and the Holocaust are conceived by her as identical or not, the very fact that they are brought together in the text points to her determination to keep the histories of the two peoples together. In fact, the text is full of ironies, such as the very mention of the word "Life" vis-à-vis the ghastly image of the lynched man. And yet, in spite of her specific condemnation of *Life* magazine, the photographed image incorporated in her work was also published in Black magazines, such as the April 24, 1937, issue of *The Baltimore Afro-American*.

Pat Ward Williams's questioning of Jewish and Black history in relation to the Holocaust is also connected to other African-American artists' use of the term "Holocaust" for describing their own circumstances. This can be seen in Emilio Cruz's *Staff Meeting at the Holocaust* (1989), where frozen, wood-like Black figures are presented in line, stretching their necks in a submissive posture, as if waiting for their execution. The title of the work is macabre in its ambiguity: the human elongated figures look like staffs or poles, but the association with "meeting" suggests a group of people having a common business, a most terrible fate in this case.

Most of the Jewish artists discussed in chapters 2–3 who worked in the first half of the twentieth century modeled their aspirations, as well as their sense of injustice, on the image of the African American. On the psychological level their sense of introjection of the "other's" experience is opposed to the racial projections cited by Ginzburg, mentioned at the beginning of the present discussion on lynching. Moreover, the metaphorical level is transformed into a twinning relationship, to borrow Kohut's psychoanalytic terminology.[42] For Kohut, "twinning transference" means that I know that there is a similarity between myself and you, though I know the difference. The artist is using the metaphor of the other as a theme for art in order to search for his or her own ethnic identity. Rather than consciously exploring themselves, they explore others. But what actually happens in the process—identification with the other—means that through it the artists are looking at themselves. Hence, the Jewish artists' identification with the African Americans is their journey in search of their Jewishness. An African-American artist who went through a similar process was Henry Ossawa Tanner, who throughout his life searched for a Semitic type for his New Testament protagonists and who, as we saw at the beginning of chapter 1, was accused of devoting his life to Jewish biblical types rather than to "the Negro subject." But it was through his search for the "Jewish other" that he was looking for himself.

However, as we approach the end of the century, the matter-of-factness of the positive identification and the one-to-one correlation found in the earlier works of both African-American and Jewish-American artists is no longer taken for granted. A Jewish-American artist defining himself through the image of the Klansman and an African-American artist questioning the analogy between Blacks and Jews with regard to the Holocaust, as exemplified by the works of Philip Guston and Pat Ward Williams, respectively, bring a different, more skeptical tone to the mutual reflections. The complexity of the mutual gaze is heightened.

wonking Together
The civil Rights movement

Most of the Jewish-American artists presented in the previous chapter who were politically engaged in the Black cause during the anti-lynching campaign were equally committed to the struggle for freedom during the time of the civil rights movement. Ritualized bodily gestures were part of the language of protest and were echoed in the politically engaged art works of the period. The body language that was used by these artists to convey their position was diverse. Images depicting unified visions of the body occur next to fragmentary ones, and, depending on the circumstances, some images convey the sense of the threat to the body, or, as we shall see, even suggest its nonexistence.

As a matter of fact, Raphael Soyer's unified vision, which was discussed in chapter 2, should also be examined in the context of the civil rights movement. Whereas the lynching scenes depicted images of the fragmentation of the body, Soyer by way of reparation makes up for this through fusion. However, violent scenes between protesters and the police in the 1960s, which called for "physical" images, echo the brutality of lynching. Andy Warhol made multiple images of the Birmingham, Alabama, riots. The events also traumatized the Jewish-American artist Jack Levine, who was born in Boston in 1915, the son of immigrants from Lithuania: "I had seen a picture in the newspapers of a dog snarling and snapping at a group of blacks, and I had an image like that in my mind when I began painting *Birmingham*"[1] (fig. 64).

Unlike Warhol's version, in which the dog is seen attacking the African-American victim, Levine focuses on the police force at the moment before the actual attack. Since the victims are not depicted and the dogs are brought to the foreground of the painting, the spectators become part of the scene. Thus by placing the image in the viewer's own space, the artist reduces the distance between him or her and the actual event. This makes every viewer a potential target for the dog's snarl, and by bringing the threat closer to every spectator the artist evokes a universal sense of empathy with the actual African-American prey. Stylistically, the artist plays a double game, as images derived from contemporary photography are depicted in Rembrandtesque style. The contrast between the style, which employs Baroque highlighting, and the macabre content is an ironic way to intensify the depiction of the brutal event.

In response to the physical threat to the body, the language of symbolic gesture also assumed a role in the visual language of the 1960s and in its visual expressions. Hands became a central iconographic symbol of common anti-racist struggle. Large buttons, one and a half times the size of a silver dollar, were worn by the marchers of the August 28, 1963, March on Washington. The button, black on white, showed a White and Black hand clasped in friendship. The badge of the activists of the Freedom Summer in Mississippi featured a Black and a White handshake. Another variation appeared on the NAACP button of the Freedom Fighters (fig. 65), which showed Black and White hands breaking a chain. The June–July 1964 issue of *The Crisis* urged supporters to purchase these new buttons representing "Black and white together, breaking the chains of segregation and discrimination."

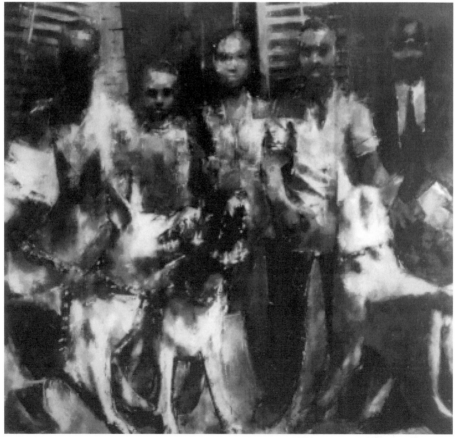

FIG. 64. Jack Levine, *Birmingham '63* (1963), oil on canvas, 71 x 75 $^1/_2$. Marjorie and Charles Benton collection, Evanston, Illinois. © Jack Levine/Licensed by VAGA, New York.

FIG. 65. *Freedom
Fighters* (button),
The Crisis,
(June–July 1964),
with permission.

Furthermore, Blacks and Whites held hands as part of the various marches and sit-ins, singing what was then the Marseillaise of the Black Revolution: "We shall overcome. . . . We'll walk hand in hand."[2] And Martin Luther King's famous "I have a dream" speech in the 1963 March on Washington described one part of his vision: "I have a dream that one day the state of Alabama . . . will be transformed into a situation where little black boys and black girls will be able to join hands with little white boys and white girls and walk together as sisters and brothers." Holding hands is a recurrent theme in the speech, which concluded with "black men and white men, Jews and Gentiles, Protestants and Catholics, will be able to join hands."[3] We are reminded of an earlier formulation of the encounter of hands, referring specifically to the link between the Black and the Jewish boy, in Langston Hughes's "You and I / offering hands / Being brothers / Being one, / Being America."

Hands as signifiers of meaning, detached from a complete body, became an iconic representation that focused on the importance of the symbolic gesture itself. The decontextualized hand acquires a universal significance. Whereas Raphael Soyer's maximalist vision of the White woman nursing her Black child is an image of complete bodily fusion, the handshake is merely the most basic and minimal form of physical encounter between people. However, when viewed in the context of the period and the history of discrimination in America, even the handshake was a taboo.[4] The dangers involved in such a basic act of human relationship were portrayed in African-American literature. The taboo on handshakes between Blacks and Whites was tragically explored

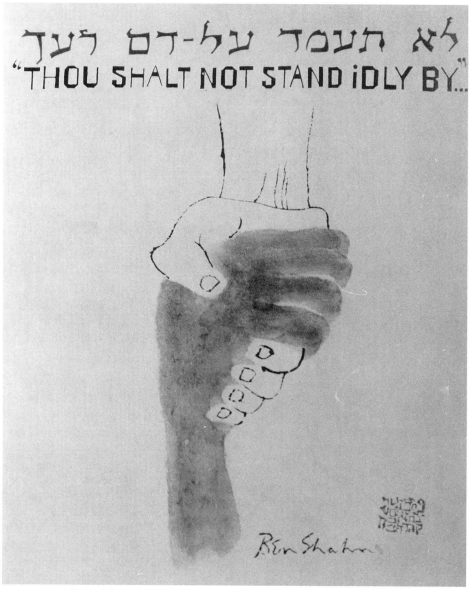

אל תעמד על-דם רעך

"THOU SHALT NOT STAND iDLY BY..."

FIG. 66. Ben Shahn, *Thou Shalt Not Stand Idly By* (1965), photo-offset lithograph in black and burnt siena, 22 X 16 3/4. © Estate of Ben Shahn/Licensed by VAGA, New York. Private collection, photograph, courtesy of Bernarda Ben Shahn.

in Richard Wright's novel *Native Son* (1940). In the novel, all hell breaks loose in the aftermath of a crossracial handshake brought about by Jan, a well-meaning White man, with Bigger, the new Black employee in a White family's service. The subtext of the handshake and its significance in the 1960s is illustrated in the following passage:

> Jan smiled broadly, then extended an open palm toward him. Bigger's entire body tightened with suspense and dread. . . . Bigger's right hand gripped the steering wheel and he wondered if he ought to shake hands with this white man. . . . Jan's hand was still extended. Bigger's right hand raised itself about three inches, then stopped in mid-air.
> "Come on and shake," Jan said.[5]

Bigger completely misunderstands the message of the extended hand and asks himself whether Jan and his girlfriend are laughing at him. As a matter of fact, it is a mutual misunderstanding: the well-meaning Whites are not aware that from Bigger's perspective they have broken a taboo, which once broken will lead to a tragic end. As if from the first touch all the tragic consequences ensue: Mary's murder, Bessie's murder, and Bigger's death sentence. A central part of the criminal investigation is devoted to the handshake:

> "Did you *shake hands* with that Negro?"
> "Yes."
> "Did you *offer* to shake hands with him?"
> "Yes, it is what any decent person. . . ."[6] [emphasis in original]

This taboo of the handshake is reiterated in John Oliver Killens's novel *Youngblood*, a landmark in social protest, which was written in 1954. James Baldwin and Saul Bellow commended the book in the pages of *The Crisis* (April 1966), Bellow calling Killens "a writer of great honesty. His talent is for solidity and for doing justice."[7] The image representing the book featured two raised hands—one White, one Black—as a blood transfusion unites them. However, in the book we also read that from the point of view of the Southerners, the White boss, "Young Cross Jr. too easy on niggers. They liable to git clean outa hand. I seen him shake a nigger's hand once."[8] And later, "Should he hold out his hands and say glad to meet you? White folks didn't shake Negroes' hands—not down here."[9]

In view of the powerful connotations of the handshake in the history of American race relationships, the iconography of the hands in the civil rights movement gains an amplified significance. Ben Shahn's *Thou Shalt Not Stand Idly By* (fig. 66, 1965) emerged from this heightened awareness.[10] It demonstrates Shahn's involvement with the visual language of the struggle, where badges and buttons, with multiracial hands playing a symbolic role, counteracted racist body language. The lithograph commemorates the tragic events of the 1964 Freedom Summer in Mississippi, which led to the murder of an African American and two Jewish students: James Earl Chaney, Andrew Goodman, and

Michael Henry Schwerner. This event, as Jonathan Kaufman points out, later became "the touchstone of black–Jewish cooperation in the civil rights movement."[11]

It is significant that Ben Shahn, who was born in Lithuania in 1898 and moved with his family to Brooklyn in 1906, commemorates the tragedy by turning to a biblical text. He adorned the page with both Hebrew and English inscriptions, and wrote out the letters of the Hebrew alphabet next to his signature. The text is from Leviticus 19:16, the meaning of which has been the focus of much interpretative controversy. Shahn reads the phrase as meaning that (White) conscientious people should not "stand idly by" while their Black fellowmen are suffering. Shahn's innovation is in extending this text to the political realm. He is moving beyond the traditionally envisaged individual rescue scene implied by the original text and addressed by Jewish commentaries, namely, "Your fellow drowning in the river." This traditional interpretation could be compared to Lozowick's lynch scene alluding to a drowning man. Shahn addresses the witnessing of bloodshed within one's political community and acting to prevent it not just through direct individual rescue but through political and civil action. Shahn's image, in which one hand is drawing up another, has its source in the midrashic interpretation of duty, that one ought to help a drowning man. The imagery in which a White hand pulls up a Black one represents a political reading of the text.

Shahn's use of a biblical text in the concrete context of the civil rights movement is in line with the use of rabbinical commentary among American rabbis in support of the alliance. It is also significant that talmudic discussions in the political context of the civil rights movement were acknowledged by African Americans. A case in point is an article by Rabbi Arthur Gilbert, published in *The Crisis* during the height of the struggle. The article deals with a talmudic debate concerning the question of which of two scriptural excerpts is superior: "These are the generations of Adam" (Genesis 5:1) or "Thou shalt love thy neighbor as thyself" (Leviticus 19:18). The first verse stresses the idea that all men derive from one man and therefore all men are equal. The second goes beyond the acknowledgment of equality in demanding self-sacrifice. This leads some rabbis to treat the second as superior to the first. However, other rabbis argue that since people often do not sufficiently love themselves, this second principle would not always assure one's responsibility to one's fellow being, and hence the first principle, that of human equality, is fundamental to the moral relationship.[12] The article applies the talmudic debate to the relations of Whites and Blacks in America and advocates equal justice rather than charity for Blacks. It is noteworthy that the article was published in the official journal of the NAACP and that Rabbi Arthur Gilbert and Ben Shahn, as well as Raphael Soyer, essentially shared a common approach to the biblical text, connecting it directly to the political struggle.

This is not the only case of deploying a biblical text in the service of the struggle against inequality in America. Shahn's application of such a text to the civil rights context appears in his mosaic mural at Temple Ohev Shalom in Nashville. Traditional Jewish symbols such as the ram's horn and the seven-branched menorah frame an image in which five multiracial heads are featured. The mosaic depicts the brotherhood of mankind, with an inscription in Hebrew based on Malachi 2:10: "Have we not all one father? Hath not one God created us? Why do we deal treacherously every man against his brother?" According to the artist:

> I have selected these lines because of their richness in contemporary meaning, because of their profound moral and humanistic implications. . . . I hope, rather, to present the ancient, celebrated and many-storied symbols of the Jewish people in such a way that the viewer may always find in them new meaning, so that so long as the mosaic exists it will constitute a sort of imperative, a pressing reminder of deeply rooted principle.[13]

Avram Kampf, artistic consultant to the temple project, emphasizes the social and Jewish sources of the mosaic, as well as Shahn's combination of Hebraic tradition and contemporary ideas in pursuit of "the equality of man and man's hope for redemption."[14] The importance of this imagery to our analysis of the hands in *Thou Shalt Not Stand Idly By* lies in the fact that the mosaic contains two different hands: the hand of God, the creative hand, the hand of compassion, which, according to the artist, "uplifts those that fall"; and the warning hand, raised against those who "deal treacherously against their brother."[15] Hence, the uplifting hand is a common theme relating the temple mosaic to the commemoration of the Mississippi tragedy.

In an interview following the murders of Chaney, Goodman, and Schwerner in Mississippi, Shahn related his awareness of social injustice to his early talmudic studies:

> I began as a student of Talmud when I was seven. And in discussing . . . the time the Temple was finished and the Ark was being brought into the Temple the Lord warned the Levites that it would be brought on and it would teeter on a pole that would be arranged between two oxen who would enter the Temple. And if it teetered no one was to touch it because it was the Lord's Ark and He wouldn't let it fall. And it teetered and one of the attendants of the Temple, a Levite, touched it and he was struck dead. And I immediately objected to my teacher about this injustice of God. . . . It is very instinctive to try to hold something that is teetering.

The direct impact of this lesson of the Bible on the seven-year-old Shahn was that he did not go back to school for some time, though later he "must have compromised" and gone back. Shahn sees this early experience as his first encounter with justice "on a very high level. . . . On a Lordly level, almost."[16] Shahn's moral crisis in reaction to this text clearly attests to his enormous sensitivity to justice. His politically conscious art is implied by his constant dialogue with talmudic texts.

Shahn's *Thou Shalt Not Stand Idly By* insists on the demand to lend help in the context of the events of the period. Let us bear in mind that the organizers of the Mississippi Summer project, which was part of the struggle to promote voter registration in the South, called for people from all parts of the country, Blacks and Whites, to join in. The depiction of supportive hands was Ben Shahn's response to this call.

However, the reception today of Shahn's image by those who view it out of its historical context is more critical. The handlift is perceived as paternalistic. Accordingly, the curators of the exhibition *Bridges and Boundaries*, where *Thou Shalt Not Stand Idly By* was displayed, argue, "While the positioning of the hands may be construed as paternalistic today, the composition aptly describes the situation in which some Blacks and some Jews found themselves during the civil rights movement."[17] Even in the context of the 1960s Shahn's vertical composition, in which the White hand lifts the Black one, differs from the horizontal body language stressing equality used by the NAACP and illustrated in *The Crisis*.

It is instructive to compare Shahn's treatment of the interracial hand contact with that of the American artist Thomas Hart Benton. In Benton's *Lincoln University Mural* (1954–55) we are faced with a much more conventionally perceived representation of the relationship between Whites and Blacks. According to Ezra Mendelsohn, the Blacks are kneeling and accepting largess from the imposing White president. Benton, of the "regional" White school, presents the viewer with a folkloristic image, far removed from the ideological statements of the Jewish-American artists, whose political radicalism he strongly deplored. Benton depicts African Americans as part of the American landscape: according to the picture their situation is not too bad; indeed it is seen to be improving. There is no cry for a radical change in this portrayal of Americana, in contrast with Shahn's image.[18]

Another context in which Shahn's handlift could be understood is the whole portfolio of lithographs he did in response to the events in Mississippi (1964). Whereas the handlift was a generalized statement done in a decontextualized vertical way, Shahn also commemorated the struggle in a horizontal composition, once more referring to a biblical text. The image *Psalm (133)* is a celebration of solidarity:

> Behold, how good and how pleasant it is for Brethren to dwell together in unity! It is like the precious ointment upon the head, that ran down upon the beard, even Aaron's beard; that went down to the skirts of his garments; As the dew of Hermon, and as the dew that descended upon the mountains of Zion: for there the Lord commanded the blessing, even life for evermore.

The text, from the King James translation, is visually symbolized by parallel images of two birds, black and white in a horizontal, egalitarian composition. The artist explained the significance he attributed to his illustration by saying that it is "a hopeless pleading to people to get together."[19] Shahn certainly designed his two dove-like birds in perfect innocence and good faith, but a "black bird"? Jim Crow and blackbirding are not far away. Was he completely unaware of the racist connotations, or did he wish to efface their impact?

The portfolio also includes specific portraits. There are two depictions of *Martin Luther King*. The first expresses an extrovert nature in which the whole face is centered around the power of the voice (fig. 67). The open mouth addresses the leader's rhetorical and charismatic powers, but it is also a recapitulation of the archetypal motif of the "primal cry" of the newborn (already encountered here in Epstein's sculpture) and the universal "Cry" (a leitmotif in Western art). King's words "We Shall Overcome" are the subject of another lithograph in which the text is inscribed above the head of the Black leader as a young man. Shahn also visualized African-American history through the portrayal of four stages in the life of Frederick Douglass (fig. 68), who emerged from slavery to become a spokesman of Blacks against slavery. Douglass described his amazing life in his 1845 autobiography, rewriting it ten years later as *My Bondage and My Freedom*, and revising and completing it in 1882 as *The Life and Times of Frederick Douglass*. Douglass was an author and editor and became the United States Minister to Haiti. The four stages recount the gradual emergence of a leader by tracing the subtle changes in hair and overall expression. The art of portraiture serves Shahn to show the evolution of an angry young man into a "lionized" and dignified elder statesman. The series was published by the Institute of Negro Arts and History in Washington, D.C.

Shahn also referred directly to the events in Mississippi by depicting the three men murdered there; hence in the portraits of James Chaney (fig. 69), Andrew Goodman (fig. 70), and Michael Schwerner (fig. 71) common humanness is represented side by side. The artist employs his refined line in delineating their individual characters; the images share a sense of freshness which is a tribute to their youth, vulnerability, and loss. Next to the quotations from the Bible and from Martin Luther King, Shahn paid tribute to a long list of civil rights martyrs in an image that evokes the sense of a commemorative wall. It includes a poem by Stephen Spender that lends the print its title: *I Think Continually of Those Who Were Truly Great*.[20]

To get a broader view of Shahn's involvement with the civil rights struggle, it is necessary to examine archival material containing many letters that document the artist's engagement with the Black cause. Consider the letters of acknowledgment he received for his support of the Southern Conference for Human Welfare, publishers of the *Southern Patriot*, written in late 1945. This progressive organization's main effort was to achieve fully functioning democracy in the South. Shahn was approached because of his posters designed on behalf of people oppressed by hunger, racism, or totalitarianism. The letter stresses the importance the organization attributed to assistance from other parts of the country so that the South would not be forgotten and people outside it would "make it known to Congress" that the South was not alone. Shahn is also requested to assist financially and morally.[21] A following letter acknowledges the artist's donation of money as well as "the great contribution you have made through the years to the struggle of justice."[22]

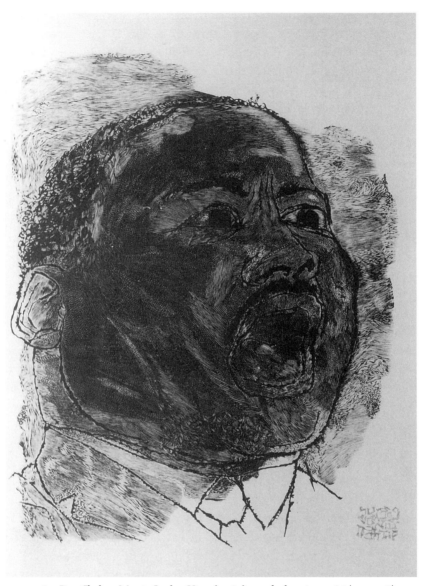

FIG. 67. Ben Shahn, *Martin Luther King* (1965), wash drawing, 26 $^1/_4$ x 10 $^1/_4$. Amon Carter Museum, Fort Worth. © Estate of Ben Shahn/Licensed by VAGA, New York. Photograph, courtesy of Bernarda Ben Shahn.

FREDERICK DOUGLASS

FIG. 68. Ben Shahn, *Frederick Douglass* (1965), photo-silkscreen, 22 x 16 5/8.
© Estate of Ben Shahn/Licensed by VAGA, New York. Ben Shahn.
Private collection, photograph, courtesy of Bernarda Ben Shahn.

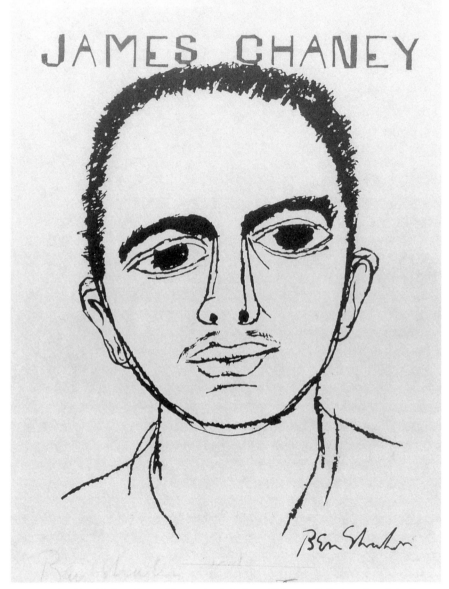

FIG. 69. Ben Shahn, *James Chaney* (1965), from "Human Relations Portfolio,"
serigraph, 22 x 16 7/8. © Estate of Ben Shahn/Licensed by VAGA, New York.
Private collection, photograph, courtesy of Bernarda Ben Shahn.

ANDREW GOODMAN

FIG. 70. Ben Shahn, *Andrew Goodman* (1965), from "Human Relations portfolio,"
serigraph, 22 x 16 7/8. © Estate of Ben Shahn/Licensed by VAGA, New York.
Private collection, photograph, courtesy of Bernarda Ben Shahn.

FIG. 71. Ben Shahn, *Michael Schwerner* (1965), from "Human Relations Portfolio,"
serigraph, 22 x 16 7/8. © Estate of Ben Shahn/Licensed by VAGA, New York.
Private collection, photograph, courtesy of Bernarda Ben Shahn.

In 1952 Shahn received a letter from J. Joseph of the National Council of the Arts, Sciences, and Professions in New York, asking him to express his indignation at the bombing and death of Harry T. Moore, state coordinator for the NAACP. The communication was also sent, among others, to the Jewish-American artists Peter Blume, Minna Harkavy, and Max Weber and the African-American artist Aaron Douglas.[23] Ben Shahn seems to recognize the helplessness of artists in these circumstances and asks for government action: "The recent horrifying incident of the murder through bombing of a Negro official of the NAACP in Florida is an addition to the field of the social investigation by painters. There have been sufficient examinations by artists. Now is the period for bold investigation under governmental sponsorship geared toward immediate cessation of this kind of blot on democracy."[24]

Throughout his career Shahn was asked on various occasions to illustrate projects related to Blacks. Thus, for instance, in 1949 he was approached by John Bartlow Martin to work on a common project called "The Mecca building." This was an elaborate building constructed at the time of the Columbian Exposition in the 1890s. "But since about 1910 it has served as a final stop for Negroes who can find no other place to live in Chicago." According to Martin, "they sleep on the floor, everywhere." The structure occupied more than one block. More people lived in this one building than in "the entire Chicago precincts." The letter concludes: "The place has a quality rarely found except for Dostoyevsky."[25] Ben Shahn created a series of drawings decrying the fact that a certain technological institution was evicting its residents because the owners were trying to tear the building down.[26]

Thanks to his reputation as an artist engaged in social matters and to his mastery of various artistic techniques (being a photographer, painter, and draftsman), Shahn was consulted on various projects. In 1954 he was asked by Milton Meltzer to help in a major enterprise, the publication of a pictorial history of the Black people in America, which was to be undertaken by Arna Bontemps, Langston Hughes, and Meltzer. The book was to use graphic material of every kind: drawings, paintings, posters, daguerreotypes, and photographs. Shahn's expertise is acknowledged by the editor: "I thought you might be able to suggest some sources of photos, beyond the usual ones of government agencies."[27]

It was in the same year that Shahn won an award for the design of a medallion of Martin Luther King.[28] In 1957 he also received the American Institute of Graphic Arts medal for his work, which "has expressed itself in trenchant appeal for human beings in bondage or hunger, suffering from race or totalitarian restrictions; in calls for social justice, in compassionate comment on sorrow, loneliness, or pride."[29] A year after he depicted Martin Luther King, the NAACP requested Shahn to draw a portrait of the executive secretary of the organization, Walter White. White was light-skinned enough to pass as a White man, allowing him to investigate lynching in the South with little difficulty.[30]

Shahn's archives also contain a newsletter sent to him by the Southern Conference

Educational Fund (SCEF), based in New Orleans. It is a call to the "un-American committee" to defend the South against bigots or to stay out of the South: "We are acutely aware . . . of a shocking amount of un-American activity in our Southern states . . . there are the bombings of the homes, schools, and houses of worship of not only Negroes, but also of our Jewish citizens."

The letter is an expression of concern that the investigating committee coming South will try to attach the "subversive" label to any liberal White Southerner "who dares to raise his voice in support of our democratic ideals."[31] A letter to Shahn and his wife from Eleanor Roosevelt shows that the artist was also concerned with activities in the South whose aim was "to build bridges between Negro and White Southerners and prevent the solidifying of the terrible wall that is increasingly separating these two groups."[32]

The editor of *Bandwagon* magazine wrote to Shahn in 1957, saying that "what we need . . . and we need badly, is a strong piece of editorial art on the civil rights issue." The editor sees the function of such a piece as "grabbing at the heart rather than the mind." The type of art he wished to see was influenced by a cartoon expressing a Southern viewpoint. Here two children—one Black and one White—beg for money from a White man and the White man gives money to the Black child. The caption of the image reads, "I can't help it if I am white, Sir." The editor asked Shahn to advise him on a counterexample to this image, which will also have an emotional appeal, though "from the other side of the coin."[33]

Shahn's alliance with the Black cause was not limited to America, as the letters written to him from South Africa indicate. In 1959 he was asked to support the Treason Trial Defense Fund for the trial of ninety-one anti-Apartheid leaders whose lives were at stake. Shahn was thanked for his continued help and asked whether he was willing to take part in an auction of international art works in Cape Town in support of the fund. The importance of the participation of American artists was expressed in both moral and financial terms: "Apart from the tremendous moral value of such support to the accused, original American work by internationally known artists would fetch considerable sums over here." Other Jewish-American artists are mentioned in the letter in the context of the auction are Saul Steinberg and William Gropper.[34] Another letter on this matter deals with the problems faced by Black protesters in South Africa: "The whole question for more than ten million Africans of whether any future protest any of them may take—voting being denied to them—will be legally declared 'treason' and subject them to the death penalty."[35] Shahn's participation was secured and acknowledged in a later dispatch that described the painting he sent to South Africa as "an excellent item," though without any specific reference to its title or subject matter.[36]

In the 1960s Ben Shahn backed the activities of SANE in support of CORE, the Congress of Racial Equality, which was trying "to keep the world from blowing up." The donations from supporters were needed for very basic and elementary things, since "someone had to pay the bus fare for those freedom riders" or the "lunch counter sit-ins."[37] Shahn was also engaged in activities in which Blacks and Whites expressed their views and artistic beliefs to each other. A symposium organized by the Department of Fine Arts at Hofstra College in Hempstead, New York, dealt with the topic of "Man's Image in the Arts of Today." The distinguished participants represented several arts: Ben Shahn, painter, Darius Milhaud, conductor-composer and James Baldwin, novelist.[38] Shahn was also appointed to be a member of the advisory board to bring the African diplomatic community in Washington, Howard University, and "White" Washington into inter-action. The main program for the future activities mentioned in the letter was the inten-tion of establishing a Museum of African and Western Art at Howard University, "showing the influence of the former upon the latter . . . something which could have no better location than at Howard."[39]

The last item in this archival survey is an announcement of the annual reception of the New York City Friends of the SCEF at which Martin Luther King was the principal speaker. The "distinguished persons" listed as the sponsors of the event included Leonard Bernstein, Langston Hughes, Jackie Robinson, and Shahn.[40]

Shahn's multifaceted engagement with joint activities also brought him to a close understanding of the art of the African-American artist Jacob Lawrence. Thus, for in-stance, in writing about the "responsible" art criticism of the 1960s, he singled out "Aline Louchheim of the *Times*, whose recent piece on Jacob Lawrence won instant recognition for a new and valuable orientation toward art."[41] As for Shahn's reception among Afri-can-American artists, *Thou Shalt Not Stand Idly By* was immediately accepted by Black civil rights artists. For example, Harlem-born Cliff Joseph said, "I admired Ben Shahn. He used to work against injustice. The style was used economically and consistently. He was making a statement in a direct line. He didn't overstate himself. Ben Shahn was a Jewish artist involved with the brotherhood of all races."

Joseph, who studied at the Pratt Institute, aligned with Shahn's commemoration of the death of the three students in Mississippi by means of hand imagery: "I used hands rather than faces in order to make a statement in a depersonalized way. Power itself without personal identity."[42] In his *Hands of Freedom* (fig. 72, 1965) the hands break the chains. There is a movement from left to right. In the first pair of hands, titled "Michael Schwerner" and "Justice," the chains are just beginning to crack. In the central pair, "Andrew Goodman" and "Equality," the two parts of the chain are separated. It is only in the third pair of hands, those of "James Chaney," that the chains are completely sev-ered. These hands overlap the second pair and are titled "Freedom." An upward move-ment is created from the first two White Jewish figures to the Black Chaney. Three moral values, the object of the joint struggle, are also presented in a hierarchy: from justice, through equality, to freedom. For White sympathizers, the liberation of the Blacks is a cause based on universal justice and equality; for the Blacks, it is the concern for their own freedom. Though the three students died together, the African-American artist

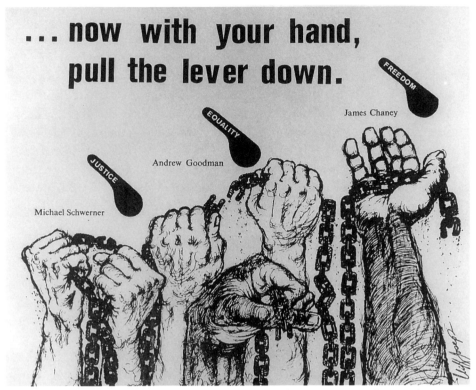

... now with your hand, pull the lever down.

FREEDOM

James Chaney

EQUALITY

Andrew Goodman

JUSTICE

Michael Schwerner

FIG. 72. Cliff Joseph, *Hands of Freedom* (1965), ink on paper, 14 x $^{1}/_{2}$ x 23 $^{1}/_{2}$.
Collection of the artist, courtesy of Cliff Joseph.

attributes the highest degree of symbolic significance to Chaney. As in Shahn's handlift, Cliff Joseph's image reveals that in spite of the common quest, competitive nuances are introduced in the respective images. For both, the hierarchical composition acquires a charged meaning. Whereas for Shahn it is a White hand on top, for Joseph it is the Black hands that are higher up.[43]

According to Joseph, the "chains represent denial of Justice, Equality and Freedom, that is what the civil rights movement was all about." As for the political activities of the period, he says: "As Blacks and Jews worked together, we were involved with the civil rights movement. I was involved in helping to work out things. Though I was not in the front lines I was supportive. We all had to be involved in that movement." Throughout his career Joseph believed that African-American artists could not dissociate themselves from political involvement: "As artists . . . we cannot separate ourselves from the political process which will decide our ultimate fate. Our work is political, regardless of pretensions of purity."[44]

Other artists responded to Ben Shahn's *Thou Shalt Not Stand Idly By*. While teaching at Howard University, Lila Oliver Asher acknowledged Shahn and the civil rights

FIG. 73. Lila Oliver Asher, *Homage to Ben Shahn* (1966), lithograph, 13 $^{1}/_{2}$ x 19 $^{1}/_{2}$. Collection of the artist, courtesy of Lila Oliver Asher.

movement in *Homage to Ben Shahn* (fig. 73, 1966).[45] The image was exhibited at the Studio Museum of Harlem (1974) and reproduced in *Jewish Currents* in the issue devoted to Black History Week (February 10–17). In her homage, Asher both copies and alters Shahn's image. Shahn's immaculate uplifting hand is tarnished by blood and the concise citation is expanded to a full quotation from Shahn: "'Thou shalt not stand idly by.' Is there nothing to weep about in this world any more? Is all our pity and anger to be reduced to a few tastefully arranged straight lines or petulant squirts from a tube held over the canvas?"

The complete quotation conveys the antimodernist rejection of art for art's sake and the artistic language of Abstract Expressionism. Rather than that, art should be engaged in a political cause, in support of those who suffer. The bleeding hand stands for the suffering of those who weep and show anger and pity for the plight of their fellow people. Asher's text is written in undulating lines in opposition to the straight lines of cool detached art. It thus visually complements the bleeding hand and the inner turmoil that the situation evokes.

Chaim Gross was another Jewish-American artist who supported the civil rights movement. His wife, Renee, noted, "Of course we went on the freedom marches. . . . Everybody went. . . . Every decent human being participated. . . . It was taken for granted that we'd join in."[46] Chapter 2 shows how in his early sculptures of the 1930s Gross was engaged with his positive vision of Blacks through the beauty of the Shulamit, the torso of the pregnant Black woman, and the Black woman's stride to a better life. I have also shown that his commemoration of his sister's death in the Holocaust used the African idiom. He had continuous contacts with African-American artists, as can be illustrated in a letter of acknowledgment from the African-American painter Hale Woodruff, who became famous through his mural of the *Amistad* mutiny mural (Talladega College in Alabama, 1938–39). Woodruff wrote from Spelman College in Atlanta: "I was delighted to receive the sculpture you so generously sent me. It's a grand piece and we are all so happy about it. I doubt that you could have sent anything we would like better."[47]

Gross expressed his sense of shock at the murder of Martin Luther King in a lithograph (fig. 74, 1968) that is a fusion of styles: documentary photography of King's portrait, repeated scenes from his funeral, the murder scene (the balcony and the inscription "Protest Meeting"), as well as the most famous line from King's speeches, "I have a dream." The lamentation is expressed by the juxtaposition of the documentary material with two imaginary birds. Two types of birds are depicted: birds of prey intertwined with snakes, suggesting evil and irrational disruptive forces, and a single bird on the right suggesting freedom. The broken glass of the framed drawn portrait conveys the sense of the violence perpetrated on the iconic figure.

Gross was consistent in his support for freedom for the Black people of America and also of Africa. In 1973 he was commissioned to design the United Nations' first-day stamp for the independence of Namibia (fig. 75). In this colorful print, African people behind bars are approached by a group of bright birds held by a liberating hand proclaiming freedom.

These images demonstrate that a number of artistic approaches were used by Jewish-American artists for expressing their sense of comradeship with African Americans on their road to freedom. Among them is a direct depiction of horror (Jack Levine), a symbolic gesture and portraits (Ben Shahn), and the contrast between documentary images and expressive visual comments (Chaim Gross). The same sense of working together is expressed in the work of the African-American artist Cliff Joseph, who greatly admired Shahn's artistic language of protest.

But the African-American artist whose work bears the closest resemblance to Ben Shahn's is Jacob Lawrence. Lawrence, who was born in 1917 in Atlantic City, New Jersey, and later moved with his family to Harlem, became the most systematic illustrator of African-American history. His graphic work includes the *Toussaint L'Ouverture* series (1937–38), the *Frederick Douglass* series (1938–39), the *Harriet Tubman* series (1938–40), the famous *Migration of the Negro* series (1940–41), and many other illustrations of the African-American experience.[48] There is an affinity between Lawrence's graphic style, in which the refined line is a central depictive tool in the service of social and political goals, and Ben Shahn's work. Milton Brown argues that Lawrence's notion of a series would seem to be the closest analogy to the Ben Shahn series of the early 1930s, the *Haggadah Illustrations* and *The Dreyfus Case* prints of 1931: "Both, inciden-

FIG. 74. Chaim Gross, *Martin Luther King* (1968), lithograph.
Courtesy of the Chaim Gross Studio Museum Collection, New York.

tally, inspired by Ben Shahn's concern with 'Jewishness' as Lawrence's *Toussaint* was by 'Blackness.'"[49] The two artists have influenced each other.

Shahn's graphic work *The Passion of Sacco and Vanzetti* (1931–32) condemning the suffering of two Italian workers charged with a crime and condemned to death in spite of demonstrations against the unfairness of their trials, had an impact on Lawrence's African-American history cycles as well as his artistic language. Lawrence's influence, in parallel, can be perceived in Shahn's 1965 portfolio. In his illustrations of Frederick Douglass, Shahn paid tribute not only to the great abolitionist but also to Lawrence's depiction of him.

Of the many African-American artists discussed in this book, Jacob Lawrence seems to have had the closest friendships with Jewish artists, as well as with Jewish gallery

FIG. 75. Chaim Gross, *Namibia*, a United Nations postage stamp, 1st Day Issue, October 1, 1973. Courtesy of the Chaim Gross Studio Museum Collection, New York.

owners. The importance of Edith Halpert as a patron for his art cannot be overestimated. Thus, for instance, the *Migration* series was first shown in Halpert's Downtown Gallery in New York in 1941; after the show Lawrence was asked to join the gallery. As a result of this exposure, half of this important series was bought by the Museum of Modern Art and the other half by the Phillips Memorial Gallery (later the Phillips Collection).[50] Halpert's exhibition *American Negro Art: 19th and 20th Centuries* included works by Henry O. Tanner, William Johnson, Horace Pippin, Romare Bearden, and Jacob Lawrence. Through the gallery Lawrence met Ben Shahn, Max Weber, and Jack Levine. While he was participating in the exhibition *Social Art Today* in 1946 at the ACA Gallery, owned by Herman Baron, he came to know Joseph Hirsch, Philip Evergood, and William Gropper.[51] Lawrence was awarded the first visiting artist fellowship at Brandeis University (1965), where he taught students in the art department.[52] In the 1960s his work was shown at the Terry Dintenfass Gallery, where he exhibited protest works related to civil rights activities in the South. His friend Jack Levine wrote to Lawrence after seeing the show: "I had a chance to see the paintings today. I thought they were wonderful. They have a profound drama which no one else can touch. An amazing epic style."[53]

In a symposium about the Black artist in America (1969), Romare Bearden commented that very little attention had been given to the cultural aspects of the civil rights struggle. He then raised the question as to the ways in which the "Black artist" related to the civil rights movement: "How does he, or his work, or his philosophy, relate to these pressing problems of the Black people in the country?" Jacob Lawrence conceived himself to be an artist who contributed to the struggle: "Well, I think you can relate in any number of ways, and the individual artist has to solve it in his own way. He may participate through the content of his works, or by donating a piece that has no specifically relevant content. I know that we all relate to the civil rights movement, and we all make contributions."[54]

One of the best-known images dedicated by Lawrence to the civil rights movement is his illustration for the cover of *Freedomways* (winter 1969), the quarterly review of the Freedom movement where a Christ-like, martyrlike image of a Black man appears, bleeding from one side. But the most pertinent image to the present study is *Praying Ministers* (fig. 76, 1962). Here clergy from various denominations, in the center of whom we see a rabbi wearing a talit, participate in a communal prayer "representing the many times clergymen of all faiths came together to pray for peace during this period of unrest."[55] It is significant that Lawrence portrays a positive image of fate-sharing in a communal prayer in which Jews participate. It seems also that this image can be seen as a metaphor for the artist's sense of working together in a self-referential way.

All the works discussed here share a manifest commitment to the civil rights movement. George Segal's *The Bus Riders* (fig. 77, 1964) carries more than a one-to-one relationship to the politics of the 1960s. Segal's sculptural environments of the period, containing white plaster figures placed within the setting of objects from everyday life, are imbued with ambiguity. It is a multilayered set of ambiguities: between figure and environment, between the actual identity of the protagonists and their unnatural white casting, and between the ghostly quality of the casts and reality. Directing our attention to the psychological ambivalences emerging from these dualities, Matthew Baigell has pointed out that "Segal seems purposely to leave unresolved these dualisms between reality and artifice in the figures and also in their environments."[56] The political dimension adds another layer to the intricate staging of Segal's environments.

In *The Bus Riders*, silence reigns, while tension is created between the "full" and the "empty": three white cast figures occupy the bus seats, while a fourth seat remains vacant, although a man is standing behind it. Such a setting raises questions: Why is he not sitting? And what is the significance of the empty seat? Is Segal alluding to the urban experience of alienation, where everybody is enclosed within themselves, making no eye contact? Is it out of choice that the man is standing? Or is he forced to do so? Are there

FIG. 76. Jacob Lawrence, *Praying Ministers* (1962), egg tempera on hardboard, 23 x 38. Spelman University, Atlanta Georgia. Courtesy of Jacob Lawrence.

sexual reasons preventing the man from sitting next to the young woman? Can the empty seat be addressed metaphorically, signifying that which is missing?

Though without analyzing *The Bus Riders'* components, Phyllis Tuchman aptly adds the political dimension to its perception. She takes into account that the sculpture was done when "the issue of riding in the back of the bus in the Deep South was constantly in the headlines."[57] From this angle, Segal's sculpture could be seen as tribute to the Montgomery bus boycott that began in December 1955, after a courageous woman, Rosa Parks, refused to move to the back of the bus. It was a two-part struggle consisting of Blacks boycotting segregated buses and then, in the beginning of the 1960s, of racially mixed groups of bus riders traveling together despite attacks by White mobs.[58]

Segal's enigmatic, apparitional sculpture can be compared to the two descriptive images exhibited in the Jewish Museum show relating to the same circumstances: Harvey Dinnerstein's *Walking Together* (1956) and Charles Alston's *Walking* (fig. 78, 1958). The two paintings portray Black marchers, Dinnerstein's with a realistic tinge, showing the crippled walking beside the healthy, and the African-American artist, Alston's, featuring marchers holding their heads high with pride. Segal does not deal with movement, but rather with a sense of frozen inactivity, creating suspense through his immobile white figures.

In relating Segal's image to the politics of bus segregation, how do we account for

FIG. 77. George Segal, *The Bus Riders* (1964), installation. Hirshhorn Museum and Sculpture Garden, Smithsonian Institute, Gift of Joseph H. Hirshhorn, 1966
© George Segal/Licensed by VAGA, New York. Courtesy of George Segal.

the whiteness of the figures, the artist's distancing device from reality in general and from the realities of the South in particular? It seems that in the white riders of the bus alluding to segregation, Segal is bringing the problem home—so close that the sitters are casts of his own family, the young woman in a summer dress being his wife. The artist is thus asking what it would feel like to be White and subjected to a discriminatory policy. What would it be like to be White and not be allowed to sit? However, the empty seat could both describe a situation and allude to the possibility of a different ending. It suggests another kind of scenario: the possibility that the man who is standing will eventually join the seated figures.

A later, politically engaged image by Segal, which in one aspect of its subtext alludes to Black history, is *The Sacrifice of Isaac (In Memory of May 4, 1970: Kent State)* (1970), at Princeton University. The sculpture differs from the traditional rendering of the scene in that Isaac is a young man, on his knees, with tied hands, and Abraham towers in front of him. Segal thus alludes to images of chained slaves on their knees as depicted, for instance, in Patrick Reason's frontispiece for Charles Andrews's *History of the African Free School* (1835). This work was reproduced in many books and periodicals sponsored

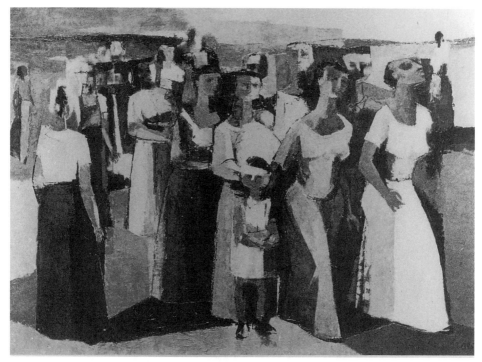

FIG. 78. Charles Alston, *Walking* (1958), oil on canvas, 48 x 68.
Collection Sydney Smith Gordon, courtesy of Sydney Smith Gordon.

by antislavery organizations, becoming a well-known icon.[59] In contrast to other works
(Rembrandt, Caravaggio) where Abraham aims at Isaac's throat as if in a sacrificial slaugh-
ter, Segal's Abraham aims at the heart. It is unclear whether the knife will stab the youth
or will be used for another purpose—to cut the captive's bonds and free him. Thus the
students' freedom struggle at Kent State, in its biblical guise of intergenerational struggle,
also alludes to the Black struggle for liberation. It can be seen as both the sacrifice of the
Blacks as well as their liberation.

Although supporting Martin Luther King, Segal, unlike other artists discussed here
(African American as well as Jewish), did not actively participate in demonstrations, nor
did he take part in other political activities. It is through his sculptures that he commented on political events, as well as on the human condition.[60] It seems that Linda
Nochlin's and Henry Millon's theoretical postulations regarding art in the service of
politics are applicable to Segal's *Bus Riders*: "In still other instances, the political intentions or the stipulated program of the work, although by no means completely hidden,
may seem at the outset to be veiled in ambiguity."[61]

We have seen how Cliff Joseph expressed his solidarity with Ben Shahn and with
Jewish participation in the political struggle of the 1960s. However, in his painting *Heirs
to the Kiss of Judas* (fig. 79, 1966), a different tone is heard, one that raises some ques-

tions. Whereas in Justice, Equality and Freedom the artist endowed the death of the three students with meaning (the breakers of the chains), the later image is highly pessimistic. Instead of joined hands, the body language of the white skeleton and the black shadow image is confrontational. Skeletal Third World children with protruding limbs emerge from the ground only to return to it in a cyclical pattern. The landscape is ominously desolate and bleak, suggesting Doomsday. It contains only mounds of paper money, and thirty pieces of silver at the base arranged as a cross and a Star of David. Moreover, the title also evokes somber allusions, referring to the betrayal of Judas. By using the word "Heirs," the artist is saying that the betrayal did not take place only in the past; it also belongs to the present. He expresses his anger and sadness at this continuing process of betrayal. The image has a sad sense of premonition.

How are we to understand this betrayal? Should it be read in the context of the artist's religious upbringing? Judas found a place in African-American spirituals, as in "Lord I want to be a Christian," where the contrast between Jesus and Judas is brought out:

> Lord, I want to be a Christian in my heart,
> Lord, I want to be more loving in my heart,
> Lord, I want to be more holy in my heart,
> I don't want to be like Judas in my heart
> Lord, I want to be like Jesus in my heart.[62]

FIG. 79. Cliff Joseph, *Heirs to the Kiss of Judas* (1966), oil on canvas. Collection of the artist, courtesy of Cliff Joseph.

Russell Adams, the coeditor of *CommonQuest*, described how his views of Jews were formulated as part of his religious upbringing. On the one hand there were the biblical Moses and Joshua; on the other, he describes Baptist ministers who portrayed the Jews "as guilty of some unforgivable transgression. Some ministers conflated the words 'Jews' and 'Judas Iscariot' and linked the former to the themes of rejection and betrayal."[63] In other words, Cliff Joseph's title is not unrelated to the way Judas features in Christian theology. And Joseph speculates on the place of biblical images in our lives, raising the question: "Do these biblical figures play a role in our lives? Some we look up to, like Jesus, some are evil, like Judas. However, Christ knew what was going to happen, so did Judas have an actual part to play?"

A second way of understanding the title is in nonspecific terms relating to the notion of betrayal per se without attributing it directly to the Jewish people. According to the artist, in spite of these allusions, the fact that there are thirty pieces of silver at the base of the mound, in a form that suggests a conflation of the Star of David and a cross, implies that it is a "joint" betrayal. It is the betrayal of the Black people by organized religions, the Judeo-Christian culture, in their fight over riches. According to the artist, the painting "has nothing to do with Judaism as well as everything to do with Judaism. It has nothing to do with Christianity and everything to do with Christianity. The basic needs of the Black community were not addressed by either."

Joseph brings the fate of Jews and Christians together in his painting *My Country Right and Wrong* (fig. 80, 1968) which was done in opposition to the Vietnam War, or more specifically to oppose the supporters of that war. The figures, blindfolded by the American flag, seem to wander around aimlessly in a landscape full of the bones of war victims. The bomb-clutching American eagle flies over the symbols of the organized religions, the cross and the Star of David, planted among the bones. Blinded by the force of patriotism, the figures are walking like automatons, unable to see reality. The American flag is flown upside down, conventionally representing extreme distress. The great irony is that the symbols of organized religion represent the cause of the war as well as its victims, since they are inserted into the ground as if in a graveyard. The artist sees the importance of protest art also as a way to deal with his feelings, his fears, his anger, when "acting out was diverted into art."[64] Unlike his civil rights images, in which Cliff Joseph expressed a positive vision of Jews and Blacks sharing a similar fate, in the second part of the 1960s he depicts Jews in negative contexts.

In *Why?*, Joseph wished to depict the authentic look of Jesus "with the features of a Jewish person in that part of the world where he came from." Jesus is conceived in political terms. Joseph's interpretation of "Why has thou forsaken me" takes Jesus as trying to change the social system of his time. He is asking, "Why have you not continued this work? Why did you not carry on the fight?"

Another African-American artist depicting his relations with Jews in an ambivalent way in the 1960s is David Hammons. Hammons, who was born in 1943 in Springfield, Illinois, has become one of the leading artists working today, always questioning prevail-

FIG. 80. Cliff Joseph, *My Country Right or Wrong* (1968), oil on masonite, 32 x 48.
Collection of the artist, courtesy of Cliff Joseph.

ing myths in his art. In the 1960s his vehicle was graphic art. The uniqueness of
Hammons's prints is that they are body prints. The artist used his own body on the
printing plate, smearing it with grease as a basis for his image. Thus he became "both the
creator of the object and the object of meaning."[65] Many of these body prints featured the
American flag. Whereas the Pop artist Jasper Johns questioned through his flags the
relationship between a flag and a work of art, African-American artists did not rest content with merely artistic questions. For Betty Saar, Faith Ringgold, and David Hammons
the flag signified the disparity between the American constitution and the status of African Americans.[66] Thus, these artists share an ironic staging of the flag in the context of
the American Dream. Some of Hammons's prints use the flag "as a symbol of America's
unkept promises to, and violence against, African Americans."[67]

One of these images is his self-portrait, *Rabbi* (fig. 81, 1960s). Hammons adapted
James Montgomery Flagg's representation of Uncle Sam, which was first used in World
War I recruiting posters and then again in World War II, with the caption *I Want You*.
Rather than Uncle Sam confronting the viewer with a pointing hand, Hammons's is a
self-portrait in profile. Here a number of realms are superimposed on one another: the
artist, the rabbi, the flag, and the traditional allusions to Uncle Sam. Hammons plays the
role of the rabbi, pointing with his finger and wearing the American flag. It is an ironic
portrayal which is built on contradictions: on the one hand the rabbi "is the one who
knows the difference between Good and Evil; he is a father beside your own father," to
quote the artist.[68] His pointing gesture indicates that he knows the truth and is telling us

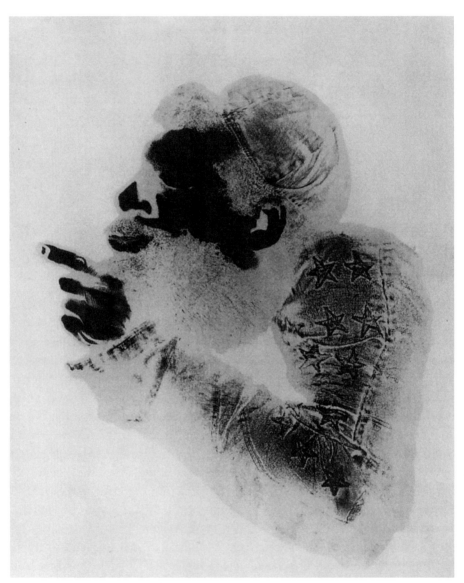

FIG. 81. David Hammons, *Rabbi* (1960's), silkscreen, 28 x 22.
Collection of the artist, courtesy of David Hammons.

what to do. And yet the American flag is sewn into his jacket: "On its face value, the flag represents equality and freedom for all. However, it represents equality and freedom for all except us," says Hammons. The rabbi wearing the flag becomes a means of highlighting this contradiction, an image of American patriotism and power, which at the same time suggests betrayal. However, Hammons is also engaged in self-irony, since he is the bearer of it all. Furthermore, in this self-portrait Hammons admits that he, like the rabbi, cannot do away with the American flag, which is an integral part of his art. By continuously reproducing it, though in an antimythical manner, he continues propagating the discourse about it.

David Hammons's ironic humor sheds light on the intricate link between Jewish and African Americans, especially in referring to Judaism in its religious aspect, where the rabbi's authority is conceived as an instrument of power. In this respect Hammons shares the ambivalence expressed by Cliff Joseph in his *Heirs to the Kiss of Judas*, both artists adding the skeptical note to the common quest of the 1960s. Addressing the issue of mutual religious efforts in their art, they depart from the positive image of Rabbi Wise done by Henry Tanner and from the image of mutual sharing of grief in Jacob Lawrence's *Praying Ministers*.

The rabbi thus becomes the representative of the Jewish people to the African-American artists discussed here. This is also true in the work of Benny Andrews, whose interest in images of rabbis and scholars extended beyond the 1960s. Andrews's paintings, in which he expressed an interest in capturing the essence of the Jewish people, also centered around religious representations. In a sympathetic depiction of a *Young Rabbi* (1964) surrounded by a field of flowers, Andrews combines his memories of the rural South with his encounters in New York. The Jewish community of the Lower East Side epitomized for the artist a focused group of people who did not belong to the mainstream, people with whom he could identify. According to Andrews, whose genetic roots are entangled deep in the southern soil (his grandmother was Black and his grandfather White), his background set him apart from people who belonged to mainstream society.

When he came to New York after completing his BFA at the Art Institute of Chicago in 1958, where Jack Levine became his admired model, Andrews became fascinated with Jewish traditions and, as an artist, in Jewish ceremonial art. A rabbi taught him the significance of Passover, and he drew the analogy between the Black and the Jewish fate symbolized by the Exodus in his painting titled, in Hebrew, *The Seder* (fig. 82, 1960). Here the various symbols of the Exodus appear: wine, matzah, the traditional *seder* plate, and a seven-branched candelabrum express Andrews's fascination with the feast of freedom's rituals.

In *America Series* (1991), a multifaceted collage of a broad vista of American types, Benny Andrews included two characters who to him were typical of Jewish life, The Scholar and *The Student* (fig. 83). It is noteworthy that among other types in the series—the homeless, rural land workers, members of the Ku Klux Klan—Andrews finds the

FIG. 82. Benny Andrews, *The Seder* (1960), oil and collage on canvas, 81 x 51. Collection of the artist, courtesy of Benny Andrews.

FIG. 83. Benny Andrews, *The Student* (1991), oil and collage on paper, 39 $^1/_2$ x 27 $^1/_2$. Collection of the artist, courtesy of Benny Andrews.

traditional religious studies and the importance of the Book as the most characteristic attributes of the Jewish people. According to Joanne Silver: "By selecting the materials he does, Andrews is making a larger political point about the commonality of experience. A bearded Jewish scholar might treasure a library of sparkling cloth-bound books, while the figure of 'Poverty' clutches at food with arms clad in dark and ragged fabric. The hunger—for knowledge or food—links these quite different individuals."[69]

The 1960s, the golden age of the common struggle of Jews and Blacks in the civil rights movement, produced also the first seeds of discord, ambivalence, and suspicion. This trend had its roots in the general political and social scene, such as the emergence of the movement of Black Power. Black artists also raised questions and used irony as a means of conveying their distancing positions. However, as shown by Benny Andrews's continued affirmative representation of Jewish scholars, which went beyond the 1960s, the voices relating to the representation of Jews by African-American artists are multiple. However, among the Jewish-American artists of the 1960s discussed here, only one tone prevailed, that of identification with the civil rights movement.

CHAPTER 5

"Hot" versus "cool"
Involvement and Detachment

When I said earlier that I was sorry I wasn't born a Negro, I was talking about a natural advantage I would enjoy in relation to jazz.[1]

Because of some of these people [Blacks], I think I've become sensitized, enriched and broadened.[2]

Many of the Jewish-American artists dealt with so far in this study knew each other quite well. Some were friends who shared political and artistic interests. Larry Rivers, born in 1923 in the Bronx as Yitzroch Loiza Grossberg to a Jewish immigrant family, does not come from this artistic milieu. He belonged to the next generation of artists, likely to be found in the Cedar bar, where the Abstract Expressionists had their drinking sprees and exchanged aesthetic polemics. Rivers is not easily defined artistically. Never content with the modernist belief in an either/or division of abstraction and figuration, he combines painterliness (the "touch" of Abstract Expressionism) with the mass imagery of Pop (pinups, photos, print, mixed media). His antimythical approach to subject matter is that of "irreverence in attitude and execution," to quote John Wilmerding.[3] More of an individualist, Larry Rivers's engrossment with African-American culture does not arise from ties with other Jewish-American artists carrying a social banner. He does not fit into any easy categorization, since he does not defer to any defined group of American artists or style.

Rivers's autobiographical style and his wish to become part of the African-American experience itself has led critics to consider him an "enfant terrible," painter, collagist, poet, imp, clown, joker, as well as a serious artist, and at times as a combination of these attributes and more. Rivers is an artist whose fluctuating moods are reflected in his involvement with the rendition of African Americans: "He was blessed (and afterwards dogged) by the circumstance of being everybody's idea of a hipster from the Bronx."[4]

Another critic, with an overview of Rivers's involvement with African Americans, evaluates this engagement more precisely, in moral terms: "He has established himself as the painterly conscience of an African assignment he has given himself."[5] The difficulty in pinning down Rivers's artistic stance as related to Blacks is due to his wavering between identification with and sincere admiration of Blacks, to the point of expressing envy of their creative powers, a serious appraisal of their history, and a demystifying, humorous stance. His attitude to African Americans stemmed from direct and intimate contact, not merely from ideological concern: "I also think that my experience in jazz, the number of black guys who have filtered through my life from time to time, gave me some ideas. Whatever I would do on this subject would not just be an interesting idea. . . . It came out of the fabric of my life."[6]

Haya Friedberg has convincingly shown that Larry Rivers's identification with Blacks, his positive homosexual self-image, and his musical interests as a jazz player were his way of breaking away from his stifling and restrictive Jewish background. Experiencing himself as an "other" drew him closer to the Black community, which was perceived as the "other" in American society.[7]

Some Jewish-American artists have expressed a special appreciation of Africa. As noted in chapter 2 Philip Evergood evaluated African culture as higher than American. Chaim Gross was influenced by African art, became an important collector of it, and also traveled to Africa. Rivers went a stage further than his predecessors; he attempted the impossible task of experiencing Africa in the same way that African Americans do. He made numerous images of the continent. In his longing for it, he shares the Black quest, replacing the longing for "Zion" by the craving for Africa. His *Africa I* and *Africa II* (1963) express his wish to become part of that land by leaving his artistic footprints on it. His map of Africa consists of patches of colors that deviate intentionally from the traditional map coloration. Thus, with his own choice of colors he becomes one with the land as he privately maps the Black continent. And yet, as always with Larry Rivers, irony and humor serve as a distancing device, perhaps to both discard and disguise his infatuation with Africa, as in his *Throw-Away Dress: New York to Nairobi* (1967). In various works he swings back and forth in alternating moods that affect the craved-for image. In his *African Continent and African* (fig. 84, 1969) he is shying away from a throw-away image and toward a permanent one. Now the image is serious; it becomes an anticolonial statement in the shape of an Africa anthropomorphically delineated and thus fused with the African. The photograph of the head of an African woman, seen in parallel to the map, stresses the correspondence between Africa and its people. Here the relationship between image and title could be interpreted as self-referential: the artist's self-awareness of the futility of his own efforts to become part of a continent in which geographical location and inhabitants are inseparable. Being left out, in an outsider's position, he can never really belong.

FIG. 84. Larry Rivers, *African Continent and African* (1969), mixed media, 45 x 36. Menil Foundation, Houston. © Larry Rivers/Licensed by VAGA, New York.

Images of Africa in Rivers's art derived from his 1967 trip to Africa with the filmmaker Pierre Gaisseau, who had made a documentary about New Guinea called *The Sky Above, The Mud Below*. Once in Africa Rivers was attracted to the beauty of the Ethiopians, and he and Gaisseau filmed the Black Jews, who were "reading from the Hebrew books I used on Saturdays in the synagogue." He also explored Kenya. In Benin the pair filmed the king's palace, and later they were imprisoned in Lagos, suspected of spying because they had a map of Africa. This somewhat comic finish is written up in Rivers's diary. He describes his ordeal in a mock-heroic tone ("Doesn't he [the security guard] recognize how much I love black people?"). The tone is also a means of overcoming the disillusion he felt in confronting his dream land. He thus plays the role of many a traveler confronting illusions. In the end, however, the documentary, called *Africa and I*, won the 1970 Chicago Documentary Festival prize.[8]

Another multifaceted and important encounter in Rivers's self-quest, in which he experienced identification and disillusionment, was with the poet and playwright LeRoi Jones/ Amiri Baraka. Their relationship, which began warmly and later turned bitter, revolved around the identity metamorphosis that LeRoi Jones underwent, culminating in a name change, a complete reversal in ideological commitments and a need "to purge himself of his white/Jewish/Western self,"[9] a symbolic evaluation of Jones's cultural engagement at the time. In a way, this particular case also sheds light on the larger issue of the relationships between some African Americans and some American Jews. Due to the prominence of the two protagonists, their artistic cooperation, disillusionment, and break-up, a short detour about the way each perceived the other will be useful for the analysis of their artistic collaboration and Rivers's various portraits of Jones / Baraka.

Rivers is mentioned in Jones's autobiography as part of the group hanging around the old Cedar Tavern on University Place, where the Abstract Expressionists (Jackson Pollock, Franz Kline, Philip Guston, and others) used to meet. There were fights among the drunken artists about "genius": "the torture of genius, genius unappreciated, genius assaulted by philistines." It was through that circle that Jones came to know the Black Mountain school of poets.[10] As for the artistic closeness between Blacks and Jews, the poet ironically describes the days in which Blacks and Jews would read Ezra Pound and would "look at all the 'kikes' and 'niggers' in his work, gloss it, look over it, justify it."[11]

Both Rivers and Jones described the incident that was a breaking point in their friendship, although both indicate that some positive feelings remained. Rivers wrote a condensed and telescoped recapitulation of the development of their contact in his autobiography: "For years LeRoi and I were friends. Up to a certain point our friendship was very warm, sometimes druggy, but always full of jokes, full of unserious discussions of cultural and political affairs. His laugh was part of his speech, and I always liked seeing him."

He goes on to describe an art symposium at the Village Vanguard, in which he, Jones, and the jazz saxophonist Archie Shepp participated:

Soon things began to get wild. LeRoi told me I was making art for a bunch of uptown fags. Archie brought up the twelve million blacks in the Congo anni- hilated by slavery and the Belgians. I began to make an allusion to the Holo- caust. . . . Archie pointed his finger at me and shouted, "There you go again, always bringing up the fucking Jews." He couldn't talk about *his* pain with- out Jews bringing up theirs! . . . LeRoi's and Archie's responses to the ques- tions amounted to: There's only one kind of white—Whitey, who hates Negroes.

In response to a point made by the audience about the two Jewish civil rights workers who were murdered in Mississippi alongside a Black, Jones said: "I can't worry about the two Jewish boys. I have my own to bury." The consequence of this traumatic encounter, according to Rivers's testimony, was that the two became estranged and did not see each other for twenty years.[12]

Jones also describes this incident quite elaborately in his memoirs, and it is inter- esting to compare perspectives:

We were discussing racial problems in the U.S., and Larry, I guess, because we had been friends and had had a lot of laughs together, did not feel particu- larly threatened by me or Archie, both of whom he had sopped up innumer- able alcohol with. Larry was even an old scag man from way back when he was an uptight young Jew looking to play the alto like Charlie Parker.

It is interesting that there is no mention here of the murdered Blacks in the Congo, the Holocaust, or the civil rights movement. Jones stresses that he "perhaps too cruelly" referred to Rivers as an artist who worked for "rich faggots" and was "part of the dying shit just like them."[13]

The dispute between the two reflects a change in the attitude of some Blacks and some Jews in the evaluation of suffering. Whereas suffering often served as a common denominator for both communities, at a certain stage suffering became an object of ri- valry, each group trying to monopolize it. Suffering turned into a dividing force once each community claimed to have been subject to a unique suffering. Such an attitude naturally reduces the capacity to sympathize with the suffering of others.

Amiri Baraka sounds apologetic as he looks back at this incident. Rivers himself has a similar tone when he admits from a later perspective that it was a period of upheaval for Jones, a period in which he opened a Black theater, divorced his White (Jewish) wife, and decided to devote his life to "his people." It is noteworthy that later, when Rivers himself became engaged with "his people," in his exhibition *The History of the Matzah: The Story of the Jews* at the Jewish Museum (1984), he invited Jones to the show, and Jones came. The two seem to be talking to each other through the pages of their autobi- ographies in a partly conciliatory manner. Parallel to Jones's apologetic tone, Rivers writes about Jones's book: "I read it and liked it and felt a great deal of empathy."[14]

In 1964, when the two were still collaborating, Rivers was asked by Jones to do the sets for two of his plays, *The Slave* and *The Toilet*, performed consecutively on the same evening. Both plays stage racial confrontations. The first, conceived as "A Fable in a Prologue and Two Acts," was first presented at the St. Mark Playhouse, New York City, in December 1964, with designs by Rivers. It is the story of a triangle that includes Walker Vessels, a Black leader, his White ex-wife, Grace, and her present husband, Easley, also White, a professor of literature. The original couple have separated because of Walker's commitments as a leader of his community. The play, in which the racial tensions between the three are played out, ends with Walker killing Easley and with the death of Grace in a racial bombing. The fate of Walker's and Grace's two daughters is ambiguous: there is a discrepancy between the text, which states repeatedly, "They're dead," and a child who is heard crying in the midst of the explosions. Since it remains unclear whether the children are alive or dead, there is no indication whether there is any hope for the future of mixed races. The racial conflict in the play is sharply phrased in the following dialogue:

> GRACE: Walker, you were preaching the murder of all white people. Walker, I was, am, white. What do you think was going through my mind every time you were at some rally or meeting whose sole purpose was to bring about the destruction of white people?
>
> WALKER: Oh, Goddamn it, Grace, are you so stupid? You were my wife. . . . You mean because I loved you and was married to you . . . had had children by you, I wasn't supposed to say the things I felt. I was crying out against three hundred years of oppression; not against individuals.[15]

There is an obvious autobiographical dimension in the play, which was written in a transitional period leading to the playwright's break with his former self. This meant moving uptown, changing his name, and separating from his White Jewish wife as part of acquiring the new identity of a Black activist. There is tension in the play between the title (*Slave*) and the exaggerated activism of the Black leader. Thus, LeRoi Jones is engaged here in ironic self-awareness, which makes his hero "the eternal entertainer, the poet, the 'slave' unable to liberate either himself or others."[16]

The Toilet is a play about homosexuality and race, set in the dirty, foul-smelling latrine of a boy's school. It presents the aggressiveness of a group of Black boys toward a homosexual White boy, James Karolis. James sends a love letter to a Black boy, a gang leader by the name of Ray Foots. The play stages ambivalences: the two protagonists fight each other in front of the other boys, and as Karolis is winning, the group attacks him. He is badly battered, his head stuck into a urinal. And yet according to the stage instructions, the play ends with Foots staring at Karolis; Foots "then runs and kneels before the body, weeping and cradling the head in his arm."[17]

Rivers recounts that he made "pretty *moderne* [sic] stodgy pieces of furniture" for

The Slave with his own hands.[18] By doing the scenery himself rather than letting others carry out his designs, Rivers demonstrated the degree of his involvement and commitment to Jones's play. He was also engaged in other practical aspects of the production, such as how to prevent the books from toppling over in Easley's bombed apartment. The setting for the two plays differs in essence: *The Slave* places the participants in middle-class respectability, which is eventually shattered. *The Toilet* contains a series of rectangular wooden urinals painted porcelain white and one closed booth. The graffiti Rivers scribbled on the wall across the urinal were partly removed following objections from the Black actors.

Rivers considered *The Toilet* to be "a brutal and beautiful play."[19] However, in the proposed poster for the two shows he played with a number of levels. The design is a condensation of the scheme of the two plays: the playwright's portrait as a partly black, partly white face titled, "Le roi jones" (spelling it in the French way, to denote a king) crowns the poster. A triangle symbolizes the relationships in *The Slave*, and a set of urinal stands for *The Toilet*. However, Rivers added his own tongue-in-cheek perspective. By drawing connecting lines between the two titles and the author's name, the text is made to read: "le roi jones the slave toilet."[20] In the poster Rivers moves from Jones's aggrandizement to his invalidation. The playwright could not have missed the point.

It is obvious that the two plays were significant to the relationship of the writer and the stage designer. Their cooperation was based on friendship and artistic understanding, and originally on a mutual curiosity toward "the other." However, the text is heavily charged, advocating the murder of all White people. Hence the dialogue between Grace and Walker quoted above is also relevant to the relationship between LeRoi Jones and Larry Rivers. Rivers reacted to the plays in a number of ways that convey the complexity of the situation. He designed and executed the settings for the plays wholeheartedly. He expressed admiration for the *Toilet*. He grasped and addressed the ambivalence in the plays—as for instance the embrace in the final scene of *The Toilet*—through the double-faced, partly Black, partly White portrait of "le roi jones." In this respect he drew a direct line between the ambivalent race relations in the plays and the playwright himself, thus indicating Jones's autobiographical involvement. However, Rivers could not refrain from his own response to Jones's provocative text. Using counterprovocation through the irony of the poster, the artist made his own comment on an already charged situation. *The Toilet* is also relevant to Rivers's homosexual encounters, many of which are described in his memoirs. According to Rivers: "When I began playing saxophone and got hung up on jazz and it became clear who the greatest jazz musicians were, again I was envious, and at the same time madly attracted to blacks."[21]

However, in spite of their breakup, Rivers did not refrain from depicting Amiri Baraka. In fact he tried to capture the newly emerged personality of the Black leader, as can be seen in the portrait *Imamu Baraka Reading (LeRoi Jones)* (fig. 85). This image, which was part of the *Some American History* exhibition held in 1970, is a frontal portrait

FIG. 85. Larry Rivers, *Imamu Baraka Reading (LeRoi Jones)* (1970),
oil and charcoal on canvas, 36 $^{1}/_{4}$ x 26. Menil Foundation, Houston.
© Larry Rivers/Licensed by VAGA, New York.

in which the protagonist appears in African dress, pronouncing his message. Unlike his earlier portraits of Jones, where Rivers wished to present the conflict of a man torn between the Black and White worlds, *Imamu* is an image of a cultural leader, conveying a sense of wholeness. Furthermore, the vocal aspect of the exhibition was especially prominent, given its use of audio recordings; thus, Jones also became essentially "the voice" of the exhibition. It seems that in a sense, this portrait became Rivers's token of reconciliation, his acceptance of the metamorphosis that had occurred, which as noted had an impact on himself as well. And yet, as always with Rivers, there is another tone: by juxtaposing the Black leader and his White delineated shadow with "RED" and "BLUE," he employs a racially neutralizing device.

The sexual dimension in the designs for *The Toilet* was by no means exceptional. One of Rivers's ways of addressing sexual issues in a racial context is through the use of fragmented body parts. Consider his fetishized *America's No. 1 Problem* (fig. 86, 1969), in which the artist problematizes through seemingly conceptual "cool" language a "hot" issue of male virile superiority. The image consists of two detached male organs: one pink, one black, set one above the other above a ruler, alluding to measurement. The artist is amusing himself with the viewer, who is asked through the compositional arrangement to compare the sizes of the two organs, only to find that they are identical. Yet a competitive mood is suggested in the horizontal stratification, the pink being placed above the black. At the same time, by using pink rather than white Rivers is perceiving the "White" body from an ironic perspective. By questioning the whiteness of Whites through pink, he is questioning simplistic color assumptions. He is also playing with the halo effect surrounding the detached member, ironically representing *pars pro toto*.

This provocative, "rather scurrilous, electrified construction," to use Sam Hunter's words,[22] is also an acknowledgment of Frantz Fanon's analysis in his classical text *Black Skin White Masks*. This source of influence on Rivers has been overlooked by critics. However, the artist himself mentions Fanon in remarking that his construction *Lampman Loves It* "could look like a reference to the simple myth of a Black man's virility in a sexual situation with a white woman."[23] *America's No. 1 Problem* seems to be Rivers's adaptation into the visual dimension of Fanon's text:

> One is no longer aware of the Negro but only of a penis; the Negro is eclipsed. He is turned into a penis. He *is* a penis. It is easy to imagine what such descriptions can stimulate in a young girl in Lyon. Horror? Lust? Not indifference in any case. Now, what is the truth? The average length of the penis among the black man of Africa, Dr. Pales says, rarely exceeds 120 millimeters (4.6244 inches). Testut, in his *Traité d'anatomie humaine*, offers the same figure for the European. But these are facts that persuade no one. The white man is convinced that the Negro is a beast.[24]

Fanon's sarcastic comments on so-called scientific investigations of measurements in the

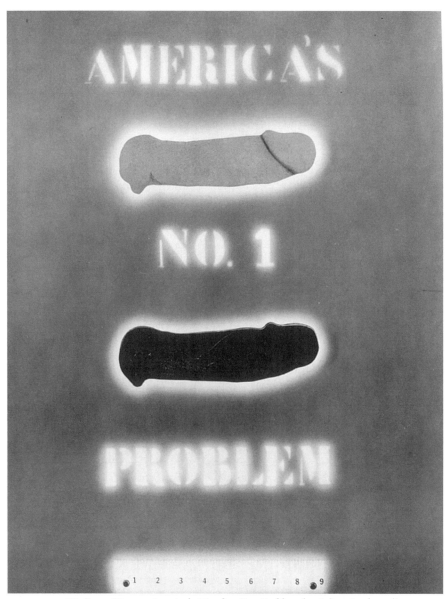

FIG. 86. Larry Rivers, *America's Number One Problem* (1969), mixed media construction, 26 $^1/_2$ x 20 $^1/_2$ construction. Collection R. Tobin, St. Antonio. © Larry Rivers/Licensed by VAGA, New York.

French context are transferred in Rivers to the American scene. Rivers agrees with Fanon's psychoanalytic analysis, which links White people's sexual inferiority complex with lynching. He takes up Fanon's question: "Is the lynching of the Negro not a sexual revenge? We know how much of sexuality there is in all cruelties, tortures, beatings."[25] Rivers dramatizes this issue in his *Caucasian Woman Sprawled on a Bed and Eight figures of Hanged Men on Four Rectangular Boxes* (fig. 87, 1970). At a time when lynching had ceased to be an issue and a subject in protest art, he looks back to the period when lynching was a harsh reality and deals with it in a most blunt and direct manner. The narrative title with its technical instructions are ironic distancing devices, enhancing the horror.

Since this construction was part of the exhibition *Some American History* (commissioned by the Menil Foundation, Houston, in 1971) a discussion of the reception of the exhibition and its main raison d'être as presented in the catalogue essay should precede the analysis of this work, as well as of the other exhibits. According to the museum's press release, Rivers, in collaboration with six Black artists (Ellsworthy Ausby, Frank Bowling, Peter Bradley, Daniel LaRue Johnson, Joe Overstreet, and William Williams), was engaged in a two-year preparation for an exhibition about the Black experience in the United States. This was a combined venture by Rivers and African-American artists of his choice, "whose work he knows and admires" and who were willing to work together on Black subject matters.[26] The monumental show consisted of about twenty large constructions, as well as paintings, drawings, and collages. It concretized the Black experience through the use of documentary material and through an appeal to the senses of sight and sound. Multi-media installations with sound effects were scattered all over the exhibition space. These included excerpts from the speeches of W.E.B. Du Bois, Marcus Garvey, and Malcolm X, and various taped episodes.

This enterprise shows that although Rivers never placed his art at the service of any organized political movement, he was willing to be part of an African-American group. A White artist, curating an African-American show in which he was the main figure, was bound to evoke varied responses. And indeed much criticism of this combined venture was ambivalent. The critic Dale McConathy, for instance, writes in appreciation of the notion that the exhibition lifts Blacks from their "facelessness," "neglect," and "invisibility." It seems that for McConathy, Rivers's task was to redeem Blacks from the fate described by Ralph Ellison's classic depiction of the Black experience:

> I am an invisible man. . . . I am invisible, understand, simply because people refuse to see me. Like the bodiless heads you see sometimes in circus sideshows, it is as though I have been surrounded by mirrors of hard, distorting glass. When they approach me they see only my surroundings, themselves, or figments of their imagination—indeed everything and anything except me.[27]

In this respect, McConathy's appreciation of Rivers's small, tender drawings, "brown

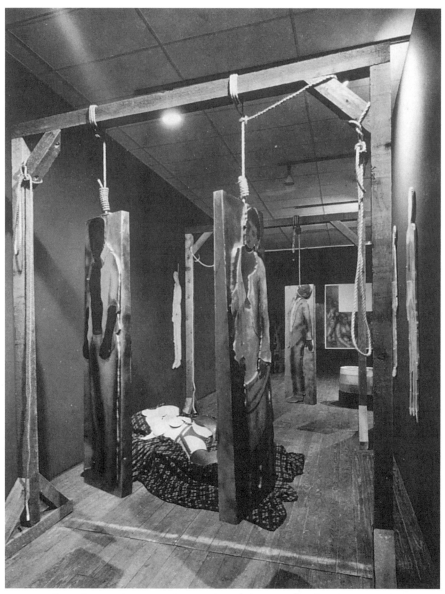

FIG. 87. Larry Rivers, *Caucasian Woman Sprawled on a Bed and Eight Figures of Hanged Men on Four Rectangular Boxes* (1970), construction, 72 x 17 x 5. Menil Foundation, Houston. © Larry Rivers/Licensed by VAGA, New York.

tempera sprayed on silver foil, with the marvelous glistening effect of black flesh," admits the artist's ability to make up for Black invisibility. And yet, on the other hand, the same critic evaluates the exhibition as being "another form of neo-colonialism, patronage for the sake of containment,"[28] thus undermining his previous judgment. In this almost impossible, self-imposed situation, it is not surprising that some of the reviews were rather blunt, posing provocative questions such as "Can 'whitey' understand?"[29] Rivers himself was fully aware of his paradoxical task, admitting, "When you work with black artists and you're white and in the 'control' role, well, it had a lot of tension. It was like a model of the rest of society, but more intense."[30]

And yet, when reviewing the reception of the *Some American History* exhibition, we can see that there is a sense in which Rivers comes closer to African-American artists than does any other Jewish-American artist discussed in this book. No artist other than Rivers was perceived by an African-American critic to be doing the type of art that could pass as Black: "There's a white boy going around here making black art. The first time I saw some of his work I thought he was black. Beautiful black girls that he paints. A hungry child in the streets of Harlem. A tall black man blowing a soprano saxophone while riding on a warm train way, way outta sight. Then it blew my mind when I found out this dude was white. *Black art, black art, black art.*"[31]

Furthermore, the African-American artist Frank Bowling, who also participated in the exhibition, evaluated it at a distance of twenty years: "The most courageous if not, as it turned out, the most sensitive attempt to put flesh on the bare bones of the contro-versy about the position of Black artists (painters and sculptors) on the American scene was, of course, by a white artist, Larry Rivers."[32]

However, either due to familiarity breeding contempt, or for reasons of competi-tion (after all, Rivers had by far the greatest number of the works in the show), this mutual enterprise was severely attacked by the very critics who praised Rivers's capabil-ity to create Black art. Walter Jones called Rivers the "Great White Father Larry Ocean," blaming him for dominating the show and for making considerably more money than the African-American artists.[33] And Bowling pointed out that Rivers "took upon him-self, rightly, to make most of the pieces."[34] Since the controversy broke out even before the show opened, Charles Childs, the African-American author of the catalogue essay, was able to remark that "the idea of having a white artist comment on black subject matter, on first glance, seems unacceptable." However, Childs rejected the separatist notion according to which "in the turbulent dialectic of black people's drive to affirm their own cultural identity," only Blacks can interpret Blackness.[35] The title he chose for his article picks up Walter Jones's reproachful tone and turns its negative connotations into positive ones. Thus, the negative "White Father Larry Ocean" becomes "Larry Ocean Swims the Nile, Mississippi and other Rivers," a positive depiction. The latter title captures Rivers's continuous involvement with Africa and his travels there (accord-ing to Childs, Rivers traveled 10,000 miles throughout Africa). Rivers is described as "a seasoned traveler, not a first time tourist,"[36] as reflected in the various maps of Africa, a recurrent theme in his art.

Childs, who appreciated Rivers's sense of intimacy with the Black community, wished to reward him in a parallel way. The title of his article thus alludes to Langston Hughes' "The Negro Speaks of Rivers," where the rivers celebrated are the Euphrates, the Nile, and the Mississippi. The river in Hughes's poem becomes a metaphor for the depth of Black experience:

> I have known rivers:
> I've known rivers ancient as the world and older than the
> flow of human blood in human veins.
> My soul has grown deep like the rivers.[37]

By associating Larry Rivers with these lines, Childs makes the artist part of the African-American world. Furthermore, Childs sees Rivers's merit as "being neither lily white nor lamp black, but between the two worlds."[38] Rivers's curiosity about the vitality of another culture and his wish "to leap over walls, especially those that separate men from one another" are also characteristics that make him eligible to deal with Black culture. He is conceived as going beyond identification based on a compassionate liberal position, bringing into the theme his "intimacy" with this community.

Moreover, Childs's presentation of Rivers is in the context of his Jewish (rather than merely White) identity. Rivers becomes the embodiment of Norman Mailer's "white-negro," one who could not become a "'square' Bar-Mitzvah-type." In a way Childs's attitude to Rivers's rebellion against his Jewish family is more polite than the artist's. For Childs, Rivers's gravitating toward the hipster type, away from his family, did not stem "out of disrespect for his own Jewishness, but, . . . because of his insatiable curiosity concerning the world around him." The artist himself is more terse in his evaluation of his Jewish background. As a way of circumventing the need to deal directly with Rivers's Jewishness, Childs quotes the artist himself on this matter. Rivers's memories of his father's attitude to "the black guys working for him" are in no way flattering. He is described as someone who would pay peanuts to his workers. As for his mother, Rivers commented: "Once all hell broke loose because my sister brought this black guy home. My mother made a fuss and it struck me as the biggest contradiction in the world that a Jewish lady should make a fuss, since that was precisely the kind of shit we put Hitler down for."[39]

There is another perspective in Childs's analysis that connects Larry Rivers's art to his Jewishness, namely, his tendency toward wit and humor: "In Jewish wit, it is the ability . . . to laugh at oneself sympathetically." Childs draws an analogy between the Jewish "schlemiel" and Langston Hughes's character "Simple," who analyzes "the futility and irony that come from carrying an oppressor's burden."[40]

As can be seen here, Childs chose to answer the question raised by the museum's

press release—"Why Larry Rivers for an exhibition about blacks?" by accentuating the
artist's biographical background with a special emphasis on his Jewishness and on his
many-sided ties with African Americans. These are used as assets, a sort of "alibi" that
could legitimize Rivers's part in the project. For Houston critic Eleanor Freed, his cre-
dentials include many witty works, "blasting the stupidity and inequity of society."[41]

The exhibition included works dealing with lynching, Africa, the Middle Passage,
slavery, contemporary America, and portrayals of African-American leaders. Rivers's pieces
were monumental: *The Slave Ship* (fig. 88) was 22 feet long, 13.5 feet high; *The Ghetto
Stoop* was 10.5 feet high. The ship, made of plywood and plexiglass, confronted the viewer
on entering the roofed gallery. Dark silhouettes of shackled figures were painted on panels in the holds of the ship. By its sheer size, Rivers may have tried to allude to another
play by Amiri Baraka, *The Slave Ship*, written after the author called for an "anti-West-
ern" theater in his post-1965 manifesto. In this play the entire theater is transformed
into a slave ship, the passengers journeying from enslavement to contemporary revolution, to a spiritual reascendancy. Baraka refrained from using a traditional plot, preferring a "historical pageant" of ritualistic effects of sound and dance. At the end of the play
the cast circulates among the audience, asking, "When will we rise up?"[42] Analogously,
Rivers wished the viewer to be exposed to the slave ship by concretizing the image through
a large, three-dimensional construction rather than a two-dimensional painted image.

However, Rivers's ship diverges from historical representations of the theme, as
can be seen in *A Pictorial History of the Negro in America*, where the diagram indicates that
slaves were not allowed more than a foot and half each, and were hence "crammed together like herrings in a barrel," to use W.E.B. Du Bois's comparison.[43] Hence, there is
a contradictory element in Rivers's spacious and even appealing slave ship, endowed
with "a kind of grace and beauty."[44] It seems that Rivers wished to compensate artistically for the most traumatic event in Black history. He did not want to engage in a
degrading representation and thus replaced the human "cargo" found in most illustrations of the Middle Passage with a more individualistic portrayal of human beings who
are intact with the beauty of their skin enhanced. Rather than visualizing the horror, the
historical sense of the event is transmitted vocally by a tape containing recitations from a
slave's diary, a simple telling of a day's atrocities.

Rivers's construction of the slave ship had a counterpart in an image by Frank
Bowling, who took the charged name *Middle Passage* (fig. 89) for his title. The Middle
Passage was so called because it was the second stage of a slave ship's trifold journey—from
an American or European port to Africa, then to the West Indies, and finally back to the
point of departure.[45]

Bowling wished to make the point that for him this choice was autobiographical,
an act of identifying with the Black history of slavery ("I am a product of the middle
passage"). Moreover, he also sees his paintings in terms of overcoming this history, since
these images were not brought together "because" of "that terrible crossing, but rather

FIG. 88. Larry Rivers, *A Slave Ship* (1970), construction, 13/6 x 22 x 4/6.
The Menil Foundation, Houston. © Larry Rivers/Licensed by VAGA, New York.

in spite of it."[46] Here we do not have a concrete depiction but rather a sophisticated palimpsest oil on canvas that brings the cartography of Guyana (of which Bowling is a native), Africa, and North America together into a personal framework, in which Bowling's symbolic figures emerge wraithlike from the misty, colorful background.

Later, in the 1980s, other African-American artists portrayed the Middle Passage in their work. Richard Hunt similarly wished to connect his own history with that of the matrix of the African-American experience in the commissioned model for a *Middle Passage Monument* (1985). His sculpture is cast in bronze. The ship is fragmented, a wreck raised from the depths of the sea (echoing the Romantic notion of the wreck as a monument, e.g., Caspar David Friedrich's *Wreck of Hope*).[47] Howardena Pindell, in her *Autobiography: Water/Ancestors/Middle Passage/Family Ghosts* (1988) created a highly textured surface in blue on stitched canvas associated with the water of the passage. This original marinescape shows the ship as seen from underneath while the artist's image floats in the water, suggesting her personal identification with the theme of death by drowning, but also the possibility of rebirth through the creative process.

The African-American artists described here who have depicted the sea voyage are

FIG. 89. Frank Bowling, *Middle Passage* (1970), oil on canvas, 122 x 122. Courtesy of The Menil Foundation, Houston.

all engaged with the theme in an autobiographical way. They use the charged term "Middle Passage"; Larry Rivers, the outsider, used the more factual "Slave Ship." Whereas Frank Bowling and Howardena Pindell interweave their interiorized knowledge into their work, Rivers refers more directly and objectively to recorded texts. It is remarkable that the exhibition *Some American History* highlights this topic as presented by both an African-American artist and a Jewish-American artist in the sophisticated artistic language of the 1970s.

Another monumental wooden construction by Rivers in the show, *The Ghetto Stoop*, bringing together sight and sound, is a scene showing a once-dignified architectural fa-cade that has undergone a metamorphosis into a dead-end disaster. The process is em-bodied by a taped reenactment of the menacing episode in the opening scene of Richard Wright's *Native Son*. Here the first sounds in the book, the onomatopoeic "Brrrrrriiiiiiiiiiiiiiiiiiiinng" of the alarm clock alert our senses to the sinister rat-killing scene into which Bigger plunges when he wakes up. Wright's version of the plague (preceding that of Albert Camus) was influenced by his memory of Chicago neighborhoods overrun with rats, and by the stories he had read about "Negro children being bitten by rats in their beds."[48] Characteristically, Rivers chose one of the most chilling scenes in African-American literature, one that even its author wished he could have done without. Overpowered by the reality and metaphorical meaning of rats, Wright wrote in his later introduction: "But the rat would not leave me; he presented himself in many attractive guises."[49] Rivers recaptures the horrors of this image.

The tone of Rivers's work varies. He moves from a wish to record as a historian to ironic humor. In his lynch construction he incorporates drawings based on actual cases in Mississippi, Florida, and Indiana. As the drawings indicate, the installation is based on research into the history of lynching. One of Rivers's sources is Ralph Ginzburg's *100 Years of Lynchings*, a book that contains newspaper accounts in a straightforward and unforgettable presentation of the history of the subject.[50] In a wish to preserve the documentary style, parts of newspaper clippings were incorporated in the exhibition text, as well as in the installation, citing Ginzburg as a source. A case in point is *The Montgomery Advertiser* of April 10, 1912: "Tom Miles, a negro, aged 29, was hanged to a tree here and his body filled with bullets today. He had been tried in police court yesterday on a charge of writing insulting notes to a white girl, employed in a department store, but was acquitted for lack of proof."[51]

Ginzburg's text contains the title "Lynched after acquittal"; Rivers omits this, letting the text speak for itself. In his presentation of lynching, Rivers differs from the lynch scenes studied in chapter 3, which were either graphic works, paintings, or sculptures, most images varying from one protagonist to four. His wooden construction becomes a dramatic spectacle, with as many as eight lynched people hanging from actual ropes. The larger number of participants is a way of summing up lynching history. The eight hanged men next to the eroticized woman also evoke memories of the Scottsboro trials in which, though eventually not sentenced to death, nine young men were imprisoned for many years. One of the women who accused them turned out to be a prostitute. Rivers's white-pink semi-nude blonde woman sprawled on a bed becomes an allusionary piece of erotica. It is here that we sense that the artist is pulled into two contrary directions. While documenting lynching, he seems at the same time to be enjoying the pornographic pose, which in a way undermines his concern about the cruelty of the act. The viewer is caught between the two parts of the scene, since the viewer's space is continuous with the spaces of both the hanged men and the woman. The whole scene is on the verge of offensiveness in its blunt three-dimensional realism, conveying in a particularly immediate manner the horror of the history of lynching. In addition, the work, and Rivers's comment on it, are rather sexist:

> The idea was a blockbuster. . . . It grew out of a SNCC picture I had seen
> showing a lynching and a lot of white guys standing around smiling. At first
> I wanted to reproduce that situation. . . . James Haskins, the black writer who

wrote *Diary of a Harlem Schoolteacher*, stopped by and looked behind each of the figures. He said, "Oh, I thought there would be a white chick on the reverse side." I took this to mean the idea was incomplete without the chick, so I put her on the floor underneath the figures, to emphasize the sexual inference under the issue of race in the country.[52]

In contrast, the relationship between sexuality and race is treated with intelligence and sensitivity in the most significant image in the exhibition, which has become a "classic": *Black Olympia*, or, as the artist originally called it, *I Like Olympia in Black Face* (fig. 90). This is a painted wooden construction of a dual nature. Rivers's conception of art about art as applied here is not just an antimythical response to Manet's masterpiece (itself an adaptation of Titian's *Venus of Urbino*), it is also a statement about the social stratification of Western society, in which traditionally the Black is the slave or servant. Rivers's is a double image, the back scene preserving Manet's hierarchy, the front reversing it, thus reversing the mistress-servant relation. It is through doubling and inverting that our modes of perceptions are questioned. Rivers is not only reversing the relationship but also the mode of representation: Manet's "cool" beautiful curve of the unattainable elegant Olympia is here blurred, and part of the body is wiped out, suggesting a more mundane, down-to-earth treatment. All figures (except for the black cat) are one-eyed, a leitmotif in Rivers's art signifying the one-sidedness of perception and vision. In the context of the relationship between the races, does the artist mean to say that both White and Black people have been one-sided in viewing the other? In this case, the dual setting of the scenes serves as a corrective device. The two scenes complement each other, creating a unity.

And yet, since the image is based on mimicry, a tongue-in-cheek tone is part of it. The black cat becomes white. Nonetheless, and in spite of Rivers's continuous sense of playfulness, the role reversal and doubling device also represent the lines he himself tried to cross between the two cultures of a man who, as quoted above, said: "I was sorry I wasn't born a Negro."

It is therefore noteworthy that Rivers's challenging image is one of the few works by White artists included in a recently published book, *Black Art and Culture in the 20th Century*. Here, Richard Powell sees this "*tableau vivant* burlesque of *Olympia*" as "a historic detour in black cultural representations of American Art." Rivers's image is conceived in terms of "sympathetic representations" of Blacks in American art, which Powell remarks are not too common. Furthermore, in spite of its "tongue in cheek witticism, it is also fearlessly ventured into a forbidden territory of black erotica that very few artists in the U.S.A. dared to enter."[53] Through this construction Rivers challenged what were the conventional stereotypical notions of beauty, and, although not part of the group of socially engaged artists, he added another layer to the Jewish-American artists (dealt with in chapter 2) who were fascinated by the beauty of the Black woman, symbolized by the Shulamit in the Song of Songs.

FIG. 90. Larry Rivers, *I Like Olympia in Black Face* (1970), painted construction, 41 x 78 x 33 7/8. Musée National d'Art Moderne, Centre Georges Pompidou. © Larry Rivers/Licensed by VAGA, New York.

Not only did Rivers dare to interfere with social hierarchies and engage in Black erotica; he raised questions and introduced a direct involvement with the issue of color in a racial context into art. There are different allusions in the two titles of the painting, the abridged one, *Black Olympia*, and *I Like Olympia in Black Face*, which puts a typically narcissistic emphasis on the first person, directing our attention to Rivers's own fantasies. Further, "Black Face" places the image in the context of the theatrical tradition of the minstrel shows, in which blackfaced White actors and musicians played Black people; the most famous of these was the Jewish singer and actor Al Jolson. Rivers acknowledged this genre in the context of his Olympia, calling it "corny minstrelization."[54] There is an obvious racist component in these acts of mimicry, provoking laughter by exaggerating the features, body language, and habits of Black people. However, the color reversal, like carnival cross-dressing, is also an attempt to be that "other" of whom one is making fun. In other words, the burlesque aspect is a defense mechanism and disguise against the embarrassment of admitting the urge to cross the boundaries. In fact, crossing the boundaries is exactly what Larry Rivers tried to do throughout his artistic career in relation to Blacks, so that in this respect *I like Olympia in Black Face* can also be seen as a personal statement in a self-referential tone encapsulating this process.

Rivers's image can be compared to earlier versions of works by Jewish-American artists dealing with "black face" staging. Ben Shahn's *May 5* (fig. 91, 1949) is an earlier, milder version of the theme. Shahn's is also an early instance of art about art. The image

FIG. 91. Ben Shahn, *May 5* (1949), tempera, 24 x 30. Collection Mr. and Mrs. Kook, New York. © Estate of Ben Shahn/Licensed by VAGA, New York, construction, Vaga, New York. Courtesy of Bernarda Ben Shahn.

is a depiction of a depiction, namely, a reproduction of a billboard of blackfaced figures with an inscription reassuring the audience that the actors will not be Blacks but rather White people with Black faces. Shahn's satirical note is conveyed by his appropriation of the racist billboard in a seemingly detached way, and letting the viewers see for themselves the racist component of the billboard. As James Thrall Soby said, it is "a satirical point of view made quietly."[55] In comparison to Shahn, Rivers's is a very noisy tone.

A more complicated case is that of the ambivalence projected in the paintings of Florine Stettheimer. The artist, who was born in 1871 in Germany to a well-to-do German-Jewish family that emigrated to America in 1890, painted her own variation of Olympia in *Soirée* (1917–19). While Barbara Bloemink, the author of a recent monograph on the artist, correctly interprets Olympia as a self-portrait, she does not discuss the transformation of the Black servant. For Florine Stettheimer, the Black woman is no longer a bustling maid bringing in flowers, but a contemplative frontally seated woman, her features echoing those of Olympia and hence those of the artist herself. Rather than an active participant, she becomes a lady in waiting. Bearing the artist's features, she becomes her complementary mirror image.

Stettheimer's stage settings and costumes designed for the opera *Four Saints in Three Acts* (c.1928–34), with a libretto by Gertrude Stein and music by Virgil Thompson, express less egalitarian tendencies. The context for Stettheimer's involvement in this opera, as shown by Barbara Bloemink, was her friendship with Carl Van Vechten, one of the White (and now often criticized) patrons of the Harlem Renaissance, author of a controversial novel dedicated to the Stettheimer sisters, with the unlikely title *Nigger Heaven* (1926). It was Van Vechten who took Virgil Thompson to the Lyric Theater to see Hal Johnson's choral play *Run, Little Chillun*, which was performed by Black singers. According to Bloemink, Thompson declared: "I am going to have *Four Saints* sung by Negroes. They alone possess the dignity and poise, the lack of self-consciousness that proper interpretation of the opera demands."[56]

However, in spite of Stettheimer's involvement with Carl Van Vechten's interests and the Harlem Renaissance and her own version of Olympia, an analysis of the data that Bloemink provides shows Stettheimer's racial prejudices, of which she was probably not fully aware. It is relevant to a discussion of Larry Rivers's *I like Olympia in Black Face*, because it also has to do with the colors of the faces of the actors in the opera. According to Stettheimer's biographer, the artist "became concerned that the actors' varying shades of brown skin might prove distracting." She therefore wished to paint the faces of the chorus in white or silver. When this idea was rejected, the participants agreed to cover their faces with "a tannish-brown stage makeup."[57] Behind her general progressive views, Stettheimer harbored some old conservative biases. It seems that she was obtuse to the richness of the variety of Black skin color and that the problem she had with its various shades was only a displacement of her prejudices.

It is noteworthy that this attitude is exceptional and that no other Jewish-American artists discussed in this book expressed such ideas in their art. Stettheimer also differs from the other artists presented here in that she is the only one who came from a well-off German-Jewish background. This spared her the typical immigrant experience of the Lower East Side or other such immigrant neighborhood that received the Jewish working class arriving in America from Eastern Europe, Rivers's family included. Coming from an upper-middle-class background, she did not share their socialist beliefs and political struggles.

Rivers expressed his craving for color reversal through the image of Olympia. Later, African-American artists staged color-reversals as part of transformations in which they themselves play a central role. Thus, in a video *Free, White and Twenty One* (1980), Howardena Pindell plays with a White persona, as she wraps and unwraps her face with a white bandage, blond wig and dark glasses. The peeling of the bandage associated with skin-peeling implies a lot of pain, which is voiced in the dual narrative: the African-American narrator tells of racial atrocities, the White dismisses them. Later on, in the 1980s, David Hammons pursued the line of color-reversal in his ten-foot-high metal cutout *How Ya Like Me Now?* (1988), where Jesse Jackson's portrait is featured in white face, corny blond wig, and blue eyes. The title is a line from a rap song by Kool Moe Dee.

There is a double irony involved here; when the work was installed in a public space in Washington it evoked rage in Black spectators. Though intended to ridicule racism, it was vandalized with sledge hammers by indignant Blacks. Hammons's image of Jackson is now ringed by a fence.[58]

Whereas Jewish-American artists discussed in previous chapters depicted Martin Luther King next to Frederick Douglass, Rivers's Menil show contained a construction of portraits of Douglass next to Malcolm X. The title of this four-foot high, three-dimensional representation of a book is quite extravagant: *Black Table: Portraits of Malcolm X and Frederick Douglass and Books by Black Authors for Reading*. It is a talking book coming alive through a recorded reading of speeches by the two protagonists. Malcolm X was the more militant African-American leader, opposing Martin Luther King's advocacy of non-violence. He joined the Nation of Islam in 1952, but later separated from it and changed his surname from "Little" to "X" to symbolize the unknown name of his African ancestors. But in so doing, he also made a dramatic gesture of defiance, both of racism in America and of the belief that Americans can work together to undo it. During a period in which many Jewish people gave a cold shoulder to the Black cause due to pronouncements by Nation of Islam and of Black Power members, Rivers monumentalized Malcolm X.

The source for the image is a photograph by Robert L. Haggins, *Malcolm X Speaking at a Meeting of the Organization of Afro-American Unity* (1964), in which Malcolm X, the speaker, points emphatically at the audience. Rivers dramatized this act further in a three-dimensional construction where the pointing hand projects from the cover of the book. By incorporating this image in his show, Rivers was a precursor of the Walker Art Center exhibition *Malcolm X: Man, Ideal, Icon* (1992). The talking book was included in this later enterprise. There the three-dimensional image also served as a metaphor for the aims of the exhibition. According to the curator, Kellie Jones, the intention was to create a context that would provide "a three-dimensional understanding of Malcolm X. Three years in the making, the exhibition reflects the ways in which black people have been discussing Malcolm X since the mid-'80s."[59] By being included in the show, Rivers is accepted as one of the Black people.

The catalogue states: "Larry Rivers muses on the continuum of African-American struggle from the 19th century to the 20th."[60] Critics reviewing the show also took it for granted that Rivers was part of the African-American group. Thus, in his analysis of early examples of Black artists visualizing Malcolm X, Darrell Moore places Rivers's image together with Elizabeth Catlett's *Malcolm X Speaks for Us* (1969), in which the leader becomes "someone from whom we can gain hope," and Vincent Smith's *For My People* (1965), with the "sorrowful feel" of the contrast between the speaker and his audience. Rivers's construction is seen thus: "An enlarged reproduction of an angry Malcolm X with finger pointing toward the air is pasted onto one side of the object, which is stenciled with 'X's.'. . . Black-authored books about the Black struggle for freedom hang off the sides, chained to the larger book. *Rivers's obvious symbolic imagery creates a call for Blacks to inform themselves and take action*."[61]

The images of African Americans by Larry Rivers that I have selected here clearly demonstrate how entangled and multilayered is his involvement with Black culture. This type of "hot" immersion can be compared with the "cool" detached art of the super-realists, as in the portrayals of Blacks by Philip Pearlstein and Alex Katz. These two types of artistic involvement ("hot" versus "cool"), though both reintroducing the figurative to American art, are poles apart, the first wishing to actually become the "other," while the second remains aloof at an exploratory distance. In its relation to subject matter, the art of super-realism claims to be neutral and disengaged, "giving primacy to style over subject matter."[62] This idea is stylistically expressed by the cool filters through which the figures and their surroundings are depicted, super-realism ultimately conveying a detachment from reality. This cool artistic language, though centering on the human figure, aims at neutralizing the narrative framework within which the figurative has traditionally been conceived in Western art. And yet, it is this discrepancy between form and content that is evocative. Notwithstanding, or perhaps because of this, these artists arouse the viewers' curiosity as to the *choice* of their imagery.

Philip Pearlstein, born in 1924 in Pittsburgh to immigrant parents from Eastern Europe, depicts multiracial images of enlarged, cropped nudes in a detached disposition, never touching each other. They are similar to his nude portrayals that are not multiracial. The artist, in spite of his aloof pose and contention that art should have "no political content," is willing to admit, "I don't know any other artist who as early as the sixties put black and white nudes together."[63]

Alex Katz, born in Brooklyn in 1927 to parents who emigrated from Odessa, portrays *Vincent and Tony* (fig. 92, 1969), one of the most intriguing paintings in the context of our discussion. A dual horizontal composition delineates the busts of two teenagers, one next to the other. The two seem to be squeezed into the foreground, their hair cropped by the frame. The compression of the two boys is enhanced vis-à-vis the wide expanse of the landscape space in the background. The two middle-class boys, one Black (Tony) the other White (Vincent), share the same space, posture, facial features as well as the full roundedness of their lips. They are both in a contemplative mood with a similar melancholy, "sulky" expression. Tony's features get a special emphasis through the glasses he is wearing, which endow him with a heightened sense of sight and an intellectual look. Though their shoulders are touching, they do not address each other. In the tradition of American art following Hopper, there is tension here between closeness and aloofness, proximity and detachment.

How are we to understand this picture? Can we rest content with a formal interpretation, ignoring content, especially in the light of the long historical tradition of the double portrait? And if we do not, is the artist trying to make a social or racial point in his picture? To put it in a current frame of discourse we may ask, is Alex Katz color-conscious or is he color-blind? An interview with the artist enables us to further examine these issues:

FIG. 92. Alex Katz, *Vincent and Tony* (1969), oil on canvas, 72 $^1/_2$ x 120 $^1/_2$. The Art Institute of Chicago. © Alex Katz/ Licensed by VAGA, New York, Marlborough Gallery. Photograph © 1997, The Art Institute of Chicago. All Rights Reserved.

> Vincent is my son, and Tony was his friend at school. They both went to the same school, Downtown Community school. It was a progressive school, where people learned to get along with one another. People from various backgrounds, races, and creeds. They were friends, Vincent and Tony. I am painting my physical and social environment. Tony was part of it. It's my social world. He is no better, no worse than anyone else. The contrast of their skin looks terrific. Each one enhances that of the other. They both look cool, contained, they think before they talk!

As for his social involvement, Katz wished to emphasize that he does not belong to the socially committed artists: "I don't have a social message. I am not trying to make the world look better."[64] And yet, by taking for granted the coexistence of the two boys, Alex Katz *is* making the world look better. In other words, taking it for granted is the strongest manifestation of a message. If for Lucienne Bloch during the 1930s, a multiracial playground was conceived as part of a vision, for Alex Katz at the end of the 1960s it is an accomplished fact involving no sentimentality, since Tony is no better and no worse than Vincent.

postmodernism
Addressing Racial and Ethnic stereotyping

The tradition of incorporating verbal texts in works of visual art goes back a long way. However, the combination of word and image has acquired a special significance in postmodern art in general and in politically oriented art in particular. Word and image are powerful complements, potentially transcending the traditional relationship of simple reference or illustration. The association of the two broadens the means by which the artist appeals for the spectator's attention and awareness: the sensual is united with the intellectual in an integrated aesthetic experience.

Word and image are often used as contrasts, as competing perspectives that deliberately create inner tensions in the interpretation of the work of art. The combination is thus a typically postmodern stylistic device, heightening the sense of irony and skepticism, enabling critical detachment and enhancing self-awareness.

The use of verbal texts is typically effective in works of art that are politically engaged. Words are close to the medium of politics: they refer to the same discourse as that of political rhetoric. In postmodern art they acquire a distinct visual presence. Words can be used to deliver a sharp, well-defined message, not necessarily simple or unambiguous. In juxtaposition with visual images, the overall effect of a work of art is forcefully amplified.

Naturally, for artists of the last two or three decades who deal with ethnic and racial issues, the use of this association of text and image has been very central. It has served them well in their efforts to deal with these sensitive issues in a more sophisticated and complex way, combining a socially committed attitude with a critical awareness of the limits and dangers involved in these commitments. We have seen in previous chapters (as in the case of the "engaged" type of artist, such as Ben Shahn, Raphael Soyer, and Cliff Joseph) that their use of texts was illustrative, maintaining closer referential relationship to the image. The artists who will be discussed in the present chapter exemplify what was referred to in the introduction as the "engaged/disengaged" position.

Language and visual image are played against each other in a manner that is at times highly involved and passionate, yet at times reflective and ironical.

The artists discussed in the present chapter—Jonathan Borofsky, Jean-Michel Basquiat, Adrian Piper, Art Spiegelman, and Barbara Kruger—all use word and image in addressing racial stereotypes. It is through these that the investigation of Jewish-American artists' attitudes to African Americans and the relation of African-American art to Jews can be continued.

Jonathan Borofsky, born in 1942 in Boston, is a second-generation American of a middle-class Jewish family whose grandparents immigrated from Eastern Europe. His mother is an architect and painter and his father a musician and piano teacher. An encounter between the artist himself and images of Blacks is a recurring theme in his work. Many of Borofsky's mixed-media installations consist of dream texts combined with visual illustrations, juxtaposing word and image.[1] In contrast to many of the artists examined in previous chapters of this book, Borofsky delves into his inner world, viewing external reality from an internal perspective. He grants the psychological dimension priority over the sociopolitical: "What goes on inside me is not different from what goes on outside. My starting point is my internal world. I look outside from this perspective."[2] Following Jung's ideas, the artist draws an analogy between the dark repressed side of the individual personality, the dark unknown within ourselves, and the repressed segments of our culture that in his case are personified in dreams by images of Black men. In his installations, as well as in his reflections about them, Borofsky studies that part of himself that is repressed, as a means of liberating himself and society in general.

Following a Jungian analysis, the artist acknowledges the importance to him of Jung's writings, and in particular *Man and his Symbols*,[3] which addresses issues of artistic creativity and the archetypal aspect of dream imagery. Jung himself illustrated his dreams as part of his self-analysis, and he and his followers advocate dream illustration as an integral part of their theory and practice, in order to expose ambivalences and eventually to be able to reconcile opposites. Some of Borofsky's dreams evince such characteristics: they are constructed around a central opposition between Blacks and Whites. The narrative contains a moment of surprise, leading to color reversals, and at times the dream ends with an open question. In this way the artist explores his affects and attitudes; he confronts his wishes, his fears, and his intricate, ambivalent stance toward the images he depicts. In Jungian terminology, Borofsky's dreams comply with the definition of "Enantiodromia," namely "running counter to." The term was extrapolated from Heraclitus's philosophy, where it is used to "designate the play of opposites in the course of events—the view that everything that exists turns into its opposite." This quotation from Heraclitus is explained by Jung as "the emergence of the unconscious opposite in the course of time" occurring "when an extreme, one-sided tendency dominates conscious life; in time an equally powerful counterposition is built up which first inhibits the conscious performance and subsequently breaks through the conscious control."[4]

Dream #1 (1972–73) contains six panels whose meaning can be interpreted only by reading the text in combination with the images. Among the most significant scenes: "I'm walking the streets of some strange town with my mother," (fig. 93) and "I hustle with mother and a huge crowd into a supermarket for protection . . . *at 1,944,821*" (fig. 94). This is a typical nightmare in which the artist regresses to childhood dependency in order eventually to relate the past to the present. The images accompanying the text are also rendered in childlike stylistic language. As the dream continues, the boy (the artist) and his mother are confronted by a group of gangsters: "Suddenly there are gun noises and rushes of different people. Little 14 year old 'minority' (black and Puerto Rican) gangsters are shooting at each other but also any one else they feel like" (fig. 95).

The colorful images of the first scene change in the gangster scene to stick-figures standing for "minority" people. In the next scene the confrontation of the hero and his mother with the gangsters is built around an element of surprise reversal, as the dream reflects a state of "enantiodromia":

> In the back alley we start running—run into several gangsters—they menace us with their guns. I plead for mercy as we slowly pull back from them. A thought crosses my mind—if they are going to shoot one of us, who would I rather it be?—my mother! I saw one of the gangsters' faces clearly— he was the one I was pleading with and was about 12 years old, very clean whiteish [*sic!*] baby face, possibly of some Spanish extraction—(maybe he's me) (fig. 96).

In this scene a color metamorphosis takes place, as the hero discovers that the gangster (featured as black in the previous scene) turns out to have a white face. This is also expressed in the visual dimension: whereas the previous scene included black figures only, in the present scene one of the gangsters has a white face. Furthermore, Borofsky's

FIG.S 93 and 94. Jonathan Borofsky, *Dream #1* (1972–73), oil on canvas, 48 x 60. Collection of the artist, courtesy of Jonathan Borofsky.

confrontation with the white-faced gangster leads him to identify with the latter: "(maybe he's me)." In dream imagery color is not fixed; it can change or contain both colors. As in alchemical processes, the metamorphosis is from black (*nigredo*) to white (*albedo*). The creative power of the dream, which in Borofsky's case begets hybrid color combinations, symbolizes both the wish but also the fear of the wish, to annul the color divisions of mankind.

On the external sociopolitical level, Borofsky's dream starts in a racially stereotypical way ("minority" equals gangsters). However, as the dream progresses, he deconstructs racial stereotypes. He moves from the Black gangsters to the White, from the group identity to the individual (the white-faced gangster), and from the other individual to himself ("maybe he's me"). The moment of self-awareness that the gangster is White and that he could have been that gangster deconstructs racial projections. Borofsky is expressing the thought that being a gangster is an internal state in which he himself is the criminal (after all, in the dream he was willing to let his mother be murdered). According to Jung, figures we dream about are symbolic manifestations of our inner state. By internalizing the images of the gangsters, and by admitting that he himself could be one, the artist both faces his own stereotypes about "minorities" and overcomes racial prejudices, realizing that one has to face one's own criminality, rather than project it onto other people. Furthermore, Jung's dream theory centers around the idea of "compensation": the dream balances that which is dominant in waking life by pointing to its opposite. In Borofsky's case the awareness that he himself could be the gangster compensates for the racist element in everyday attitudes in American society.

Borofsky's *Dream* (1979), in the Ben Shahn Gallery, Wayne, New York, is a confrontation with another variant of himself in relation to Blacks: "I dreamed I was fighting (verbally) with a black man who was selling tickets" is an aggressive encounter. Here, rather than showing compassion for the Black ticket seller, "imprisoned" behind a grille,

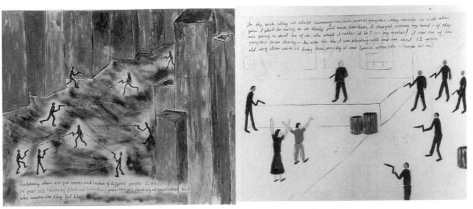

FIG. 95 and 96. Jonathan Borofsky, *Dream #1* (1972–73), oil on canvas, 48 x 60.
Collection of the artist, courtesy of Jonathan Borofsky.

Borofsky depicts himself as the aggressor. Again, as in the resolution of the gangster dream, it is through this awareness that the artist deconstructs racial stereotypes, admitting that aggression is part of himself and should not be simply projected onto the Black man. Jung's theory does not divide the world into good versus bad, but rather sees good and evil as two complementary aspects that should be admitted as constituting everybody's inner state. Thus, the notion of evil in Borofsky's dream does not serve only as a projection onto others, as in the case of minorities who serve as scapegoats, but as a moment of self-awareness. In another dream, which in the absence of a title I shall call "Subway Dream" (fig. 97, 1978), a young Black boy provides a shadow, a mirror-image of the dreamer:

> I dreamed I was walking down the stairs into the subway where a little black boy (light skin, 13 years old) was standing with an older woman and a younger woman. He asked me if I would be his older brother for this ride and that that way he would get on for a cheaper fare. I was about to tell him that he was black and I was white and that I didn't think we'd pass for brothers when I realized my color and hair were very much that of a black man—in fact we had similar features. The four of us talked for a while and I asked the little boy if he was a mulatto. He said he didn't know cause he was an orphan.

The subway, a modern symbol of travel, represents in dream language the descent into the subconscious.[5] It is here that the dreamer meets his shadow image, his "other," the complementary counterpart. Here once more there is a reversal of the "absolute" color division, as the hero realizes that he looks like the Black boy. Since no affect is expressed at the moment of realization, how does the protagonist judge his discovery? On the one hand, it expresses his symbiotic identification with the Black boy. The possibility of being "mulatto" suggests a meeting ground between the two. The need for a family ("brother," "brothers") expressed in the dream and the possibility that the boy is an orphan suggest that the boy needs a companion, a "new family," something the artist could provide. Furthermore, the young Black boy is thirteen years old, namely at the beginning of adolescence, a transitional period susceptible to the emergence of questions of identity.

Borofsky's dream, which centers on this age, the year of the Jewish bar mitzvah, is about that very moment of change of status from childhood to adulthood. The dream about a thirteen-year-old Black boy searching for a brother and Borofsky's awareness of the physical affinity between the two of them is thus part of his search for the Self, for his own identity.[6] According to his testimony, the artist in the dream feels like an orphan, fractured, not whole: "Bar mitzvah means you are a man on your own, no more tied to your parents, facing the unknown of the world on your own—an orphan."

On the other hand, there is the abrupt end of the dream: the Black boy does not know who he is and whether he is of mixed race (since he is an orphan and has no access to his personal roots). The prospect of a newly created family, based on the apparent

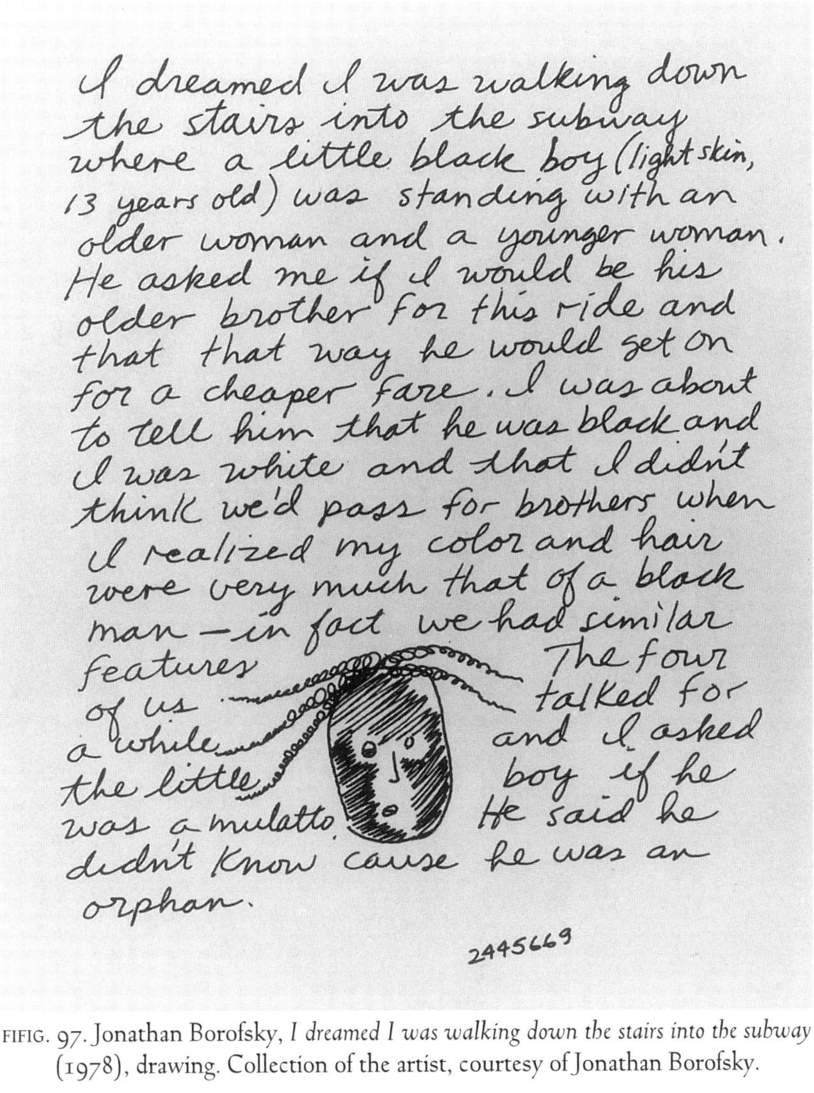

I dreamed I was walking down the stairs into the subway where a little black boy (light skin, 13 years old) was standing with an older woman and a younger woman. He asked me if I would be his older brother for this ride and that that way he would get on for a cheaper fare. I was about to tell him that he was black and I was white and that I didn't think we'd pass for brothers when I realized my color and hair were very much that of a black man — in fact we had similar features of us . . . a while the little was a mulatto. didn't know The four talked for and I asked boy if he He said he cause he was an orphan.

2445669

FIG. 97. Jonathan Borofsky, *I dreamed I was walking down the stairs into the subway* (1978), drawing. Collection of the artist, courtesy of Jonathan Borofsky.

likeness of the artist and his counterpart, proves short-lived. The color line reemerges as a potential barrier. The dream ends abruptly as a kind of "awakening" from the fantasy of inner and racial integration. On the whole, the dream portrays an inner dialogue that stages unity and disillusion concurrently.

In the context of American literature, the term "mulatto" stands for a light-colored character of mixed blood. The theme of the "tragic mulatto," very often "mulatta," is a recurrent subject in American literature. In Langston Hughes's poetry and plays it is a leitmotif for over a quarter of a century. "Cross," published in *The Weary Blues* (1925), stages the conflicts of the tragic mulatto, expressing the theme of anger and rejection. In *Fine Clothes to a Jew* (1927), Hughes named one of the poems "Mulatto" and later wrote a play (1935) and an opera (1949) with music by Jan Meyerowitz on the same theme—all portraying various aspects of his sense of being "a rejected son."[7] In his biography of the poet, Rampersad writes about Hughes's "tragic mulatto," pointing out that the theme serves as a metaphor for the "divided" poet representing "typically, a young man of mixed race ... caught disastrously between the black and white worlds," wishing to be accepted by his father. This unconscious identification with the mulatto, though neither of his own parents was White, represents Hughes's ambivalent family situation and sense of identity in a mixed society.[8]

By becoming part of his dream imagery, the mulatto theme in Borofsky expresses his own sense of split and his longing to be able to cross the color line (which also represents his inner self), although neither of his parents was Black. His own search for a (mulatto) brother (in the broad sense of brotherhood) can be compared to the theme of rejection implied in the most tragic lines of Hughes's "Mulatto":

> Naw, you ain't my brother.
> Niggers ain't my brother.
> Not ever.

"Mulattoes," writes Henry Louis Gates, are "most certainly . . . terms of mediation, partaking of two fundamentally opposed forces."[9] Borofsky's illustrated dream stages these irreconcilable forces. In contrast to the (White father's) complete rejection in Hughes's poem, Borofsky's open-ended final lines in the dream at least suggest that these forces may be reconciled. In spite of the ambivalence, the possibility of brotherhood and hence self-integration is hinted at.

In Borofsky's visual realm, symbiosis takes place through the portrait that illustrates the dream: a black face with long stiff curly locks, a hybrid of the artist and the Black boy. Whereas the verbal part of the dream plays out the various possibilities of merging and separation, in the visual image Borofsky and the Black boy fuse: the artist himself has become a mulatto.

We are reminded that this sense of union was also conveyed by Jean Toomer in his description of the fusion with the Jewish cantor, which is part of his characterization of

Fern's singing. We also saw that Henry Ossawa Tanner's search for a Semitic type conveyed his sense of identification with the Yemenite Jew.

When we compare the way Borofsky deals with his cravings for fusion with Raphael Soyer's vision of the unity of mankind, we can see the change in mode of thought between the two types of artists discussed in this book. It is the difference between the "engaged" artist who knows the answers (Soyer) and the "engaged/disengaged" artist whose works express conflict (Borofsky). Borofsky articulates his aspirations in the first person (in contrast to Soyer's image of the modern Madonna). It is noteworthy that themes of fusion between African-Americans and Jews played a role in African-American art of the end of the nineteenth century and the beginning of the twentieth, whereas Jewish-American artists carried the theme on throughout the twentieth century, even to the end of it.

A sharp line—the color line—divides the Black group from the crouching White girl in an illustration describing the following dream: (fig. 98, 1975): "I dreamed that blacks were marching for freedom and that one girl said she would tell the truth." This is a very curious dream with an unexpected conclusion in a form of a riddle. The girl in the role of the archetypal child who tells the truth, as in "The Emperor's New Clothes," triggers the viewer's questions: What does she know that the Black marchers and the viewers do not know? Does she know that they *are* marching for freedom, or the contrary truth that they are not marching for freedom? But the use of "she will tell the truth" sounds as if she were about to tell them off, to accuse them, although it is not clear of what.

The latter possibility may explain the deviation from the child in Hans Christian Andersen's tale, who could tell the truth because of his innocence and lack of awareness of social decorum. Here, it is a girl who is going to tell the truth, but in accordance with the dream's special logic, it remains untold. According to the artist, the marchers represent freedom, the girl represents truth; they are extrovert, she is introvert; she is closed within a private space, sitting with crossed legs, protected by the table: "She knows that Blacks as a race are struggling to deal with White man's oppression. A few generations since they were in chains, their spirituality has carried them through. Feeling free is also an internal state, feeling good about themselves."[10] The demand here is for both an external and an internal freedom.

However, a reading other than Borofsky's relates the dream to sexual-racial stereotypes. Frantz Fanon, the Black psychiatrist, reports typical dreams of Blacks as sexual aggressors.[11] Fanon also deals with another set of stereotypes that pertain to the division between Blacks and Whites. The White girl represents superiority over the Black marchers ("she knows, they don't"). In *Black Skin, White Masks*, Fanon attacks Jung's concept of the "collective unconscious" by saying that it is the sum of our prejudices and is therefore culturally constructed and acquired. He describes the Western archetypal image of the Black as the symbol of evil, of sin: "Satan is black, one talks of shadows, when one is dirty one is black. . . . Blackness, darkness, shadow, shades, night the labyrinths,

FIG. 98. Jonathan Borofsky,
*I dreamed that blacks were marching for
freedom* (1975), drawing. Collection of
the artist, courtesy of Jonathan Borofsky.

abysmal depth, and on the other side, the bright look of innocence, the white dove of peace, magical heavenly light." Fanon compares the joy, peace, and hope in the phrase "a magnificent blond child" with "a magnificent black child" in order to deny the possibility of such a comparison.[12] It seems that the White girl in Borofsky's dream would fit Fanon's description of stereotypes.

Borofsky's image is open to various readings. He himself takes it as a reconciliation of opposites, two aspects of one's own personality—the White girl complementing the Black marchers. Another reading, however, will see the stereotypical underlying racial aspect. His acceptance of Jungian patterns of thought may have made him see Black/White relations in a way that can be read as (unintentionally) stereotyping. Thus, the girl's enigmatic expressivity confronts even the most progressive viewer with prejudices.

The exhibition *Prisoners of Image: Ethnic and Gender Stereotypes*[13] displayed a collection of objects showing stereotypes of Blacks (e.g., "Mammy," "Sambo," Blacks eating watermelon). This exhibition, which was preceded by the show *Ethnic Notions: Black Images in the White Mind* (Berkeley Art Center, 1982), aimed at "providing an opportunity for people to reflect on the formation of ethnic attitudes and thereby to empower them to change."[14] Regarding these images of Blacks featured in various objects of Americana, Alice Walker coined a fitting phrase: "Prisoners without traditional bars, but prisoners of image."[15] The same mode of thought lies behind the work of the African-American artist Carrie Mae Weems. In images such as *Ain't Jokin* and *Black Woman with Chicken* (1987), she juxtaposes word and photograph, using racist imagery to fight stereotypes. Andrea Kirsch's analysis of the latter image as "words which, on their own, have a strongly derogatory connotation" and the attitude of the viewer to the former can be borrowed and applied to Borofsky's dream of the White girl who would tell the truth about the Black freedom marchers: "This work has a demonstrated capacity to upset both black and liberal white audiences. That discomfort is surely one measure of its importance."[16] For both Borofsky and Weems, uneasiness is an intentionally integral part of the work. This is also reminiscent of the challenging imagery of Philip Guston, who toward the end of his life used the image of the Klansman in his self-portraits, creating sensations of strong discomfort.

Borofsky's wavering between his attraction to Blacks and the fear of loss of his own identity lies behind the Whitney Museum installation of 1981. It includes the inscription of names and addresses of Black athletes, such as Floyd Patterson, the former heavyweight champion. Yet part of this installation was based on someone else's obsession. Borofsky describes the events leading to the installation as "the writing of someone we might possibly consider psychotic. I was writing what a stranger had written exactly."[17] According to the artist, the exhibition was based on anonymous letters that Borofsky used to get in his mailbox, letters containing the names and addresses of Black men. Borofsky collected the letters, and as the show got closer the number of letters he received increased. He found out that the person sending them was Black: "I saw a black man in an overcoat carrying a briefcase. He turned around for a moment, then walked on. . . . So what I have in my mind is the image of a black man who carries a briefcase, who walks the streets of New York, and who writes down whatever names he sees going on in his head."[18]

The Whitney's walls became commemorative panels, paying tribute to Black athletes in an intentionally "pseudo-graffiti" style. Borofsky's appropriation of the contents of the letters is an act of complete identification with the anonymous Black letter writer as well as with the Black personalities mentioned in the letters. They became his shadows. This identification is reflected in the installation, even down to the type of handwriting used. "If Floyd Patterson was written more heavily on the walls in charcoal, it was because that guy had doubly darkened it on his messages to me."[19] Furthermore, this almost symbiotic relationship with a projected (anonymous) Black person is reflected in Borofsky's sense of losing his own control and becoming a medium subjected to another person's power: "I was writing what he wrote exactly. I felt there was danger in doing this, and I was worried. . . . *Would I, could I, become one with him?* I felt it was very chancy becoming that person."[20]

The emphasized sentence in this quotation represents a leitmotif in Borofsky's dreams about Blacks. These dreams express a wish for union together with a parallel awareness of the danger of symbiotic identification that could amount to a loss of the

Self. In the installation, a figure of a dark "Hammering Man" looms large, representing "the shadow part of the soul, the shadow worker in all of us, the dark side of the man with whom I was in touch, the shadow of the marchers for freedom."[21]

Yet Borofsky also comments on actual political events. For instance, in his Whitney Museum installation of 1979, the name "Biko," the Black South African leader who was killed in his cell, is printed in red. Borofsky's feeling for the plight of Blacks in South Africa is clearly manifested in his *Riot Police in Capetown, South Africa. . .at 2,415.919* (fig. 99, 1987). The seemingly objective reportage plays on the irony of the situation. The White police are helping the Black couple at whom they have fired tear gas. The caption reads: "Riot police in Capetown, South Africa help an elderly mullato [sic] man and his wife who were overcome by tear gas fired to clear a street yesterday." The irony is enhanced by the fact that one of the policemen is wearing a white mask, probably alluding to the Ku Klux Klan. In one of the sketches for this scene, various shapes of the Star of David were inscribed, drawing an analogy with modern Jewish history.

On a more autobiographical note, Borofsky's own phrasing may best summarize his intense involvement with the Black condition: "I am an observer of the human condition. I feel about the down-trodden, the feeling of myself of being down-trodden, [and] part of myself feeling oppressed makes me identify with others! My dreams reflect these issues around. It is we who are living the dream."[22]

Wolfgang Max Faust has pointed out the inner contradiction at the end of the present millennium: on the one hand, global civilization seems to see "the very idea of 'national' art [as] mildly absurd," yet, on the other, "the present is marked by catastrophes arising from national, ethnic and religious conflicts."[23] Faust sees the American school of the "New Image" as having "a certain national touch." The artists included in this school, exhibited at the Royal Academy in London in 1993, were Jonathan Borofsky, Jean-Michel Basquiat, Philip Guston, David Salle, Julian Schnabel, and Keith Haring.[24] And indeed we can discover in Jonathan Borofsky and Jean-Michel Basquiat some common threads associated with this kind of ethnic awareness that merit a comparative examination.

Basquiat was born in 1966 in Brooklyn to a middle-class family. His father was from Haiti, while his mother was of Puerto Rican descent. In 1982, the year after Borofsky's commemoration of Black athletes in the Whitney Museum, Basquiat proclaimed his admiration of Black athletes in works such as *Famous Negro Athletes, Aaron,* and *St. Joe Louis Surrounded by Snakes* (fig. 100) He continued working on this theme in the following year with *Jack Johnson* (fig. 101), *Cassius Clay,* and *Sugar Ray Robinson.* Beyond this common focus on the theme of Black athletes, especially boxers, the artists share a language that combines words and images on an equal footing, the verbal and the visual complementing and reinforcing each other. Both show an interest in the fate of Black people, each one from his own perspective, Borofsky as a Jew and Basquiat as an African American. Each uses a direct mode of expression, an off-hand drawing next to a written

FIG. 99. Jonathan Borofsky, *Riot Police in Capetown* (1987), drawing, collection of the artist, courtesy of Jonathan Borofsky.

text indicating the name of the protagonists. For Basquiat the vulnerability of the athlete is also illustrated: the crown that represents his success is but a floating one, suggesting a kingdom but also the possibility of losing it.

Since George Bellows's *Both Members of This Club* (1909), the theme of the Black boxer occurs quite often in African-American art. The main difference between Bellows on the one hand and both the African-American tradition and Jonathan Borofsky on the other is that the artists of the 1980s do not show the fight itself but rather concentrate on the image of the Black fighter. Borofsky's boxers are included in a list of African-American athletes, but Basquiat's work deals with each one individually. However, both Basquiat's and Borofsky's treatments of the boxer are based on the long history of this subject in African-American art. Take for instance Richmond Barthé's *The Boxer* (fig. 102, 1942), displayed during the Second World War as part of the exhibition *Artists for Victory* at the Metropolitan Museum of Art.[25] Here we see an elongated elegant figure that conveys contemplative dignity and inner concentration.

Benny Andrews's *Champion* (fig. 103, 1968) is very different from either the physicality of Bellows's depiction of the Black boxer or the elegance of Barthé's. We are faced with the price of championship: the protagonist is seated in his corner, his face battered and his body drooping. In this collage, the towel over the head "is made of a piece of rumpled, pigment-stiffened cloth, giving an effect of physical mutilation and damage."[26] The image of the boxer is associated with martyrdom. The boxer becomes a modern Black martyr for Black self-assertion. Benny Andrews himself could identify with this sense of martyrdom since he paid a heavy price in his own struggles for artistic self-assertion. He was completely misunderstood by both students and faculty at the Art Institute of Chicago, where he studied. Only Jack Levine shared his artistic and political interests.[27]

FIG. 100. Jean-Michel Basquiat, *St. Joe Louis Surrounded by Snakes* (1982), acrylic, oil paintstick, and paper collage on canvas, 40 x 40. Private collection. Jean-Michel Basquiat © ADAGP, Paris 1997.

FIG. 101. Jean-Michel Basquiat, *Jack Johnson* (1982), acrylic and oil paintstick on
canvas, 47 2/3 x 38 1/4. Galerie Bruno Bischofberger, Zurich.
Jean-Michel Basquiat, *Jack Johnson* (1982) © ADAGP, Paris, 1997.

FIG. 102.
Richmond
Barthé, *The
Boxer* (1942),
bronze, H. 16.
Collection The
Metropolitan
Museum of
Art. The
Metropolitan
Museum of
Art, Rogers
Fund, 1942,
(42.180).

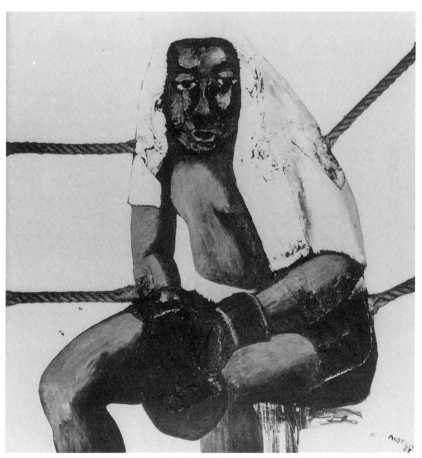

FIG. 103. Benny Andrews, *The Champion* (1968),
oil and collage on canvas, 50 x 50. Private Collection,
courtesy of Benny Andrews and Michael Rosenfeld Gallery, New York.

According to Benny Andrews his hero symbolizes "the strength of the black man, the ability to persevere in the face of overwhelming odds," but he adds:

> I cannot fail to remember my sense of indignation over the fate that has befallen the black man's Thors, and it is in this sense of indignation I tried to paint my heart out in "The Champion." The epitome of the sad fate that has engulfed Joe Louis came to surface a few weeks ago when it was reported that an official at the Colorado Psychiatric Hospital said that former world champion Joe Louis, 56, had been admitted on a "hold for treatment" order.[28]

The allusion to Thor signifies the fall of a tragic hero. The representation of the image of the boxer as both the champion and the fallen hero is shared by other African-American artists such as Raymond Saunders. In his *Jack Johnson* (1971), Saunders combines figurative and abstract language: the champion of the world fills the whole length of the canvas, which seems too small to accommodate him, while his head is partly cut off by the frame. At the same time, the boxer's hands, his main tools of expression, are eliminated under an expressive red coloring. The picture frame constraining the hero could also suggest his inability to conform to social demands in a segregated society. As a matter of fact, Jack Johnson never complied with the sexual customs of segregation. Eventually, he died in tragic circumstances.[29] In a concentrated conceptual image, *Champ* (1991), made after Basquiat's depiction of the boxer, David Hammons did an anthropomorphic leather jacket with red bloody boxing gloves and tubular forms hanging limply on the wall. It becomes "an emblem of deflated hopes and the certainty of going nowhere fast."[30]

In the light of these examples it can be said that both Borofsky's and Basquiat's commemorations of Black athletes continue an African-American involvement in the subject. In Basquiat's *St. Joe Louis Surrounded by Snakes* (1982), Joe Louis becomes beatified. This picture is an instance illustrating the artist's familiarity with traditional artistic conventions. Thus, the good supportive arm is on Louis's right, whereas the "snakes" are on his left. Rene Ricard associates the image of the boxer, drawn from an Irvine Penn photograph of Louis, with the "sacra conversazione"—Italian for "holy conversation," a theme in Italian Renaissance art showing the Madonna and Child surrounded by a group of saints—and contrasts the image of a boxer "dazed after a fight" with the "few predatory old white men, waiting for their eighty percent."[31]

The protagonists on either side of Joe Louis can be more specifically identified. Various critics have pointed out that as a child Basquiat used to go to museums in New York with his mother, and that books on art as well as history served him well while he was painting. The *St. Joe Louis Surrounded by Snakes* conveys a sense of awareness of visual traditions of the past and a knowledge of the boxer's life. Thus, the "good" right side may be read as representing Louis's Black trainer, Jack Blackburn, while the profiled image at his left with the "broken nose" could echo that of the typical "Jewish" profiles of flagellation scenes, "Ecce Homo," or even "the Kiss of Judas."[32] In Chris Mead's study of

Joe Louis's life, a profiteering type of relationship between Joe Louis and his promoter, Mike Jacobs, is described.

Mike Jacobs was the son of Isaac and Rachel Jacobs, East European Jews who emigrated to New York and earned a meager living in the sweatshops. Jacobs, who grew up in poverty and sold newspapers as a boy, ended up being "a hidden power at Madison Square Garden."[33] He is described in a biography of Joe Louis as having one sole motivation for existence: he "devoted his life to a single-minded, almost fanatic pursuit of money."[34] He was willing to bet on Joe Louis's boxing career from its beginnings in 1935 throughout his active years, which included Louis's victory against the German world champion, Max Schmeling, in a 1938 match that was taken to symbolize America's defeat of Nazism. Jacobs controlled and manipulated Louis's career, as well as the champ's income tax frauds. Moreover, Nat Fleischer, the editor of *Ring*, worked as a publicist for Jacobs, tailoring Louis's public image. Louis is quoted as saying, "Mike had no prejudice about a man's color so long as he could make a green buck for him."[35] Snake imagery is also used in Mead's book in connection with Jacobs: dealing with him is compared to "getting into bed with a rattlesnake,"[36] an evaluation that concurs with the title of the painting.

When we compare Borofsky's attitude to Blacks, both in his dreams and in his homage to Black athletes, with Basquiat's allusion to the snake-like, crooked-nosed Mike Jacobs, it can be seen that the attitude to the "other" is not reciprocal. Borofsky's depiction of Blacks is multilayered: the symbiotic identification, which arises from an inner involvement, is so charged that he fears the loss of his own identity. Borofsky is willing to deal with his own racial stereotyping, but is also engaged with the struggle of the Blacks in South Africa. As for the Black athletes, his installation expresses his admiration and need to commemorate them.

Basquiat, in *St. Louis Surrounded by Snakes*, is depicting a stereotype of the Jew, both in physical features and as "money hungry," a Judas—the betrayer of Christ for thirty pieces of silver. His point of departure regarding the Jew as the "other" is not that of identification but rather anger. Basquiat's stereotyping of the "other" can be compared to the work of another Jewish-American artist, Art Spiegelman, the illustrator of *Maus*. Dick Hebdige draws a perceptive analogy between Basquiat and Art Spiegelman regarding the discrepancy between content and mode of narration: in Basquiat harsh realities are expressed in often playful form, while in Art Spiegelman the portrayal of the Holocaust takes the form of comics characters in animal masks. For both artists the discrepancy only enhances the sense of horror.[37]

Moreover, another meeting point between the two that is relevant is the verbal stereotyping of Blacks. In *Maus: A Survivor's Tale*, racial stereotyping is brought into the open and critically questioned, so that a number of voices are heard simultaneously.[38] In a scene taking place in America within the frame story, which serves as background to the Holocaust story, the father (a survivor), his son (American born), and his son's wife

(French) return home in their car (fig. 104). Françoise, the daughter-in-law, stops for a hitchhiker—a Black man. The father's reaction is shocking: "A hitch-hiker? And—oy—it's a colored guy, a Shvartser!" When Françoise ignores these remarks and gives the Black man a ride, the father gets excited and mutters in Polish; and when the hitchhiker leaves the car, the father cannot stop using the derogatory term "shvartser" (in the singular as well as the plural form). An argument takes place between the older member of the family and the younger generation, who do not use the Yiddish word "shvartser" in challenging the father's racial prejudices. Each party is offended by the other's reaction. Françoise asks (fig. 105): "How can you, of all people, be such a racist! You talk about Blacks the way the Nazis talked about the Jews!" And the father answers: "It's not even to compare the Shvartsers and the Jews!" Spiegelman here uses the broken English of an immigrant, incorporating Yiddish exclamatory words like "Oy" to denote a sense of calamity. The American-born generation is ill at ease with the immigrant language and racial prejudices. It is the type of language that ought not to be used, the artist

FIG. 104. Art Spiegelman, *Maus II: And Here My Troubles Began* © 1986, 1990, 1991 by Art Spiegelman. Reprinted by permission of Pantheon Books, a division of Random House, Inc.

implies, and certainly should not be aired in front of outsiders. The irony is that this discriminatory language is used in a Holocaust story.

Alan Rosen has shown that on one level *Maus* "celebrates English. . . . English can master anything it confronts, can dominate whatever demands subjection." On another level it represents linguistic limitations: "Significantly, *Maus* enforces the limitations of English by representing as authoritative an English that is uniquely broken, incompetent, unmastered."[39] However, it can be argued that the universalism of English precludes it from being a private language. This is the case in the old world when the father says, "You know, you should be careful speaking English—A stranger could understand." This is also the case in the hitchhiker scene, when he reverts to Polish.

The sense of uneasiness conveyed by the hitchhiker scene is part of a predominant trend in the art of the 1980s, especially among artists using verbal texts as a major factor in making the viewer self-conscious and noncomplacent. As noted, in the case of the African-American artist Carrie Mae Weems, there is a sense that postmodern artists

FIG. 105. Art Spiegelman, *Maus II: And Here My Troubles Began* © 1986, 1990, 1991 by Art Spiegelman. Reprinted by Permission of Pantheon Books, a division of Random House, Inc.

wish to place the viewer in a disconcerted situation, to address both guilt and shame. Spiegelman confronts matters demanding tact in a nontactful way, so that even the most liberal reader cannot feel free of prejudice and therefore beyond shame when confronted with an awareness of her or his own stereotyping. Art Spiegelman is "uncompromisingly confrontational," to borrow Abigail Solomon-Godeau's analysis of Carrie Mae Weems *Black Woman with Chicken*.[40]

In other words, Spiegelman is intentionally politically incorrect in his unmasking of pejorative racial language as used by a Holocaust survivor. He deliberately avoids the attempt to create an image of a Jew who will look good to the outside world, putting aside the idea that Jews should not expose their weaknesses to other people because of "what will the others say about us." He opens up the disagreements and generation gaps within the family, the differences between the Holocaust survivor and the American- and French-born younger generation. Spiegelman is pessimistic about the older generation in his final conclusion regarding the father, when the son says, "Forget it, honey . . . he's hopeless," but is more optimistic about the younger generation, which is struggling against their parents' narrow-minded prejudices.

The use of the Yiddish word "schvartser" to single out Blacks is not unnoticed by African-American writers and artists. Author Michele Wallace, daughter of the artist Faith Ringgold, addresses this issue: "We all know in our hearts, as any mere child in our midst today must know, that 'nigger,' 'black,' and 'schwartze' are often used interchangeably in our language to mean an abject 'other,' and yet we persist in denying it."[41] Basquiat, too, was evidently fully aware of Yiddish pejorative language, and he too "unmasked" it in his work. Variations of columns ironically repeating the word "schwarz" occur in his monumental painting *Pegasus* (1987): "Schwarz, Schwarz, Schwarz, Black, Schwarz, Black." In another variation the word "Schwarz" is crossed out by a black line, and is then repeated seven times. Overall, the word "Schwarz" appears forty-seven times in *Pegasus*. The private taboo word is no longer private.

The name Pegasus is repeated, as is Andromeda, the Black princess his rider Perseus rescued, which is sometimes also crossed out. However, unlike the mythological figure, Basquiat's Pegasus is associated with "broken wings," which are also repeated many times in the canvas, often next to the reiterated "schwarz." Basquiat seemed to be saying that the Black Pegasus with broken wings, or with wings that have been broken (by racial prejudice), will not be able to help save Andromeda. In the two images discussed in which he relates to Jews, Basquiat both uses a stereotypical crooked-nosed image of a "money hungry" Jew (expressing anti-Semitic feelings) and exposes racist Jewish language in his work.

The crooked nose in profile also delineates Moses in Basquiat's *Moses and the Egyptians* (1983). The artist uses the traditional Jewish shape of the Tablets of the Law (often featured on the exterior of synagogues in New York, some of which were transformed into Black churches). Rather than writing out the Ten Commandments, Basquiat's graffiti-like inscription plays with Moses' name, enumerating his deeds: "Staff into serpent trick," "Leprosy Trick," "Water into Blood." He also plays with the spelling of "Israelites" and "Egyptians." The red coloring of Basquiat's *Tablets* suggests blood.

Basquiat's *Tablets* perform a dual role. The graffiti-like inscriptions with jokey spelling and casual drips of color devalue the biblical text and its symbolized Ten Commandment form, as if the artist were trying to "empty" and distance himself from its original meaning. (Basquiat also conflates the Ten Commandments with the ten plagues.) However, does he, through this ironic presentation, really neutralize the charged connotations of the image? Or rather, does he not convey (in spite of the fun) his own revived interest in the Exodus story by restating it, thus adding another layer to the ongoing involvement with the theme by both Jews and Blacks?

In discussing postmodernism, David Driskell has pointed out that African-American art is often autobiographical and "expresses the artist's open-ended attitude" about issues of race and ethnicity.[42] Adrian Piper, for example, employs the verbal medium in an autobiographical manner in her performances to address racial and ethnic stereotypes. In *My Calling Card #1* and *#2* (1986–90), the artist uses her professional business card to state that she is Black. The card is handed out at dinners and cocktail parties to those people in "good society" who make racist remarks. Her card intentionally begins in a friendly tone, leading to an element of surprise:

> Dear Friend,
> I am black.
> I am sure you did not realize this when you made/laughed at/agreed with
> that racist remark.

The card's function is to make the racist fill uneasy. It ends with an "apology," and plays on the gap between the two seemingly symmetrical statements of regret:

> I regret any discomfort my presence is causing you, just as I am sure you
> regret the discomfort your racism is causing me.[43]

Lowery Stokes Sims rightly sees the calling card as a warning alerting us not to misindentify "individuals [who] we think mirror ourselves."[44]

In light of *My Calling Card*, it is significant that for Adrian Piper anti-Semitism is a mirror image to racism, recalling Fanon's remark: "Whenever you hear anyone abuse the Jews, pay attention, because he is talking about you."[45] Piper's sensitivity to racial stereotyping is in line with her sensitivity to anti-Semitism. There are a number of references in her writings in which she draws an analogy between the two. For instance, describing the strategies used by some people in an attempt to make her feel accepted, Piper describes "the WASP colleague who attempted to establish rapport with me by making anti-Semitic jokes."[46] It is interesting that this is the first in a list of four examples reported by Piper of the underlying racism of these futile strategies.

Barbara Kruger is another artist of the last two decades who makes extensive use of verbal language in addressing stereotyping and whose work contains aspects reminiscent of Adrian Piper. Kruger was born in Newark, New Jersey, in 1945 to lower-middle-class American-born Jews. Her awareness of the marginalized segments stems from growing up in a Black neighborhood, and her identification with Black marginalization derives from her own marginalized background. Her understanding of racial questions is also associated with her childhood memories. According to the artist, she learned about race differences at an early point in life. Kruger's memories include the harassment of her father, who was the first Jew hired by Shell Oil in Union, New Jersey. The family would get midnight telephone calls, voices threatening the Jew for working with the company. Kruger draws an analogy between Jewish identity and Black identity: "Both ethnicities are defined as 'others' by society":

> I can't forget that culturally I am Jewish because nobody else is going to forget. The same goes for Blacks. Being Jewish constitutes my understand-ing of the marginalization of others. Jews have had many years of under-standing what that marginality is. The only way to exist is to objectify our experience. Marginality produces a kind of commentary on society, such as Jewish humor, Black speech. Both can alternate from marginality to the center.[47]

Barbara Kruger's installation at the Mary Boone Gallery, *All Violence Is the Illustra-tion of a Pathetic Stereotype* (fig. 106, 1991), demonstrates an escalation of the intensity and variety of verbal racial stereotypes in a work of art. The confrontation between the spectator and a wide array of the pejorative stereotyping vocabulary, covering race, mi-norities, and sex, comes to a dramatic peak in the show. The artist's knowledge of the variety and nuances of epithets is here manipulated to create an artistic "dictionary," a thesaurus of synonyms, containing the stereotypical derogatory slang language addressed to minority groups in American society. Thus, the various minority groups are con-densed into one panel. Jews are called "yid, hymie, Hebe, kike"—from the mildly de-rogatory "yid" (the only one used by Jews as well), through "hymie" (originating from the Jewish male name Haim), to "Hebe" (deriving from "Hebrews"), and to the most objectionable, "kike" (denouncing Jewish gestures and speech mannerisms). African Americans are named "sambo, nigger, boogie, spook"—"boogie" man as one of the names of the devil (but later associated with Boogie-Woogie and dance), "spook" associated with Black music and, as often the case, its insinuation is dependent on the user (Black or White).[48] Other derogatory words in Kruger's list include "wop," "spic," "dago"—"wop" connoting an ill-bred and aggressive person, used in derogatory refer-ence to Italians; "spic" a shortened version of "spaghetti," originally used for Italians and later adopted for people of Spanish ancestry; and "dago," stemming from Diego and there-fore originally referring to the Spanish but later applied to Italians. Orientals are called "slant"—the Japanese "jap" as well as "nip," and the Chinese "chink." As for sexual

FIG. 106. Barbara Kruger, *All Violence Is the Illustration of a Pathetic Stereotype* (1991), installation, Mary Boone Gallery. Courtesy of Barbara Kruger and the Mary Boone Gallery.

appellations, Kruger uses "homo," "fagot," and "fairy" for homosexuals, and "cunt," "gash," "snatch," and "pussy" for women as sexual objects.

This bombardment of a multicultural list of contemptuous language, in spite of its ethnic variety, points to a common denominator, a condensation of mostly monosyllabic sounds overwhelming the spectator's ethnic and sexual sensibilities and conceived in terms of violence: *All Violence Is the Illustration of a Pathetic Stereotype*. Aggression is set in a visual context, which is "sensational—an explosive wedding of hyperactive form and vehement polemic, a spectacular theater of dissent."[49] We are reminded of novelist Saul Bellow's hero Herzog, who while waiting for the uptown express stares at graffiti on mutilated posters that look like "blacked-out teeth and scribbled whiskers, comical genitals like rockets, ridiculous copulations, slogans and exhortations." The graffiti read: "Moslems the enemy is white. Hell with Goldwater, Jews! Spicks eat SHIT."[50]

The show was launched on the metal gate outside the Mary Boone Gallery. Here, the viewer immediately experienced role reversals. The American flag, the symbol of the American dream, was transformed into a board with questions addressed to the viewer: "Who is free to choose? Who is beyond the law? Who is healed? Who is housed?" Thus, the gallery gate and its interior create one continuum, in which the artist confronts the spectator with a barrage of phrases voicing the issue of stereotyping with a multivocal resonance. It is a turn-of-the-millennium image of a scream bursting from the three dimensions of the room: white-on-red slogans on the floor, ceiling, and aisles of the large hall. The scream is concretized through the double image of a photographed fragmented head. The spectator is assaulted by the excessive use of confrontational language, by the condensed visual images, and by the overall claustrophobic effect of the organization of the space.

Further, the experience includes a loss of balance due to the paradoxical instructions given from below, above, left, and right. Those on the ceiling are a case in point: "Don't look up. It begs for heroes. It brings you down." The double head stands for the dual experience of the viewer as a "you" in the singular and "you" in the plural form (an ambiguity typical of Kruger's language). One is asked to look at one's sense of identity as a private person as well as at the relationship between personal and group identities vis-à-vis racial stereotyping. The singular "you" implies that the spectator is directly addressed and cannot get away. However, the "you" in the plural is a "trap" in this enclosed space, which forces the viewer to ask herself/himself: "Do I belong to a group?" and if so, "To which group do I belong?" Or, to apply Craig Owens's insight regarding Kruger's art to the present installation: "Her work forces the viewer to shift uncomfortably between inclusion and exclusion."[51]

In confronting racial derogatory language, the viewer can find herself on both sides of the spectrum, both as the offended party or as the one that gives offense. In this experience one is forced to relive simultaneously the two sides of the racial experience. On the other hand, the cumulative effect of registering so many pejorative names takes the sting out of and nullifies the power of the racist language.

Ken Johnson saw the spectator's position in a different light, claiming that he did not feel attacked personally, and yet he suggests another stereotype: "Rather, the installation spoke to a fictive person, an imaginary someone who embodies the dark side of American society. That someone is, of course, a white male power figure, a personification of the negative aspect of mainstream American consciousness, which Kruger's program indicts as racist."[52] However, Johnson also conceives the installation in biblical terms: "And given the scale of this installation and the tone of portentous judgment, it seemed a voice of heroic stature, a booming voice of condemnation and retribution, the voice of the biblical prophet with a bullhorn."[53] For Grant Kester, the use of an excess of affective language "seems designed to overcome the indifference of the dominant culture to the issues of exploitation and oppression being explored by sheer rhetorical force." However, Kester believes that "the actual reception of these works has been largely rhetorical. The audience for . . . a Kruger installation knows that it isn't the 'real' target of the outraged pronouncements on sexism or racial oppression. Rather, they consume the work simultaneously in the first person and the third person; imagining themselves as the intended viewer while at the same moment reassuring themselves of their own ideological superiority to this point of view."[54]

The various possibilities of experiencing racial stereotyping in the Mary Boone installation convey Kruger's sophisticated use of word and image. The archetypal theme of the "Cry" in art, which was represented at the end of the nineteenth century by Munch (1894) as a private-cosmic expression of anxiety, is recharged and recontextualized by Kruger at the end of this century to signify an urban experience of social tension. And it should be added that the title *All Violence Is the Illustration of a Pathetic Stereotype* is self-referential: by being itself a re-created act of stereotyping, the exhibition plays out an act of violence on its viewers.

In a psychohistorical analysis, Sander Gilman links "pathology," "sexuality," and "race" as reflected in our need to create stereotypes. The stereotyped groups studied in his *Difference and Pathology* include Jews and Blacks.[55] Although Gilman deals with the close of the nineteenth century, his principal premises are applicable to the end of the twentieth. Consider, for instance, his notion of the universality of stereotyping as a means of coping with anxieties when "self-integration is threatened." He distinguishes between pathological stereotyping and that needed "to preserve our illusion of control over the self and the world." A further distinction between the two types lies in the in/ability to distinguish the "individual" from the stereotyped class. The pathological personality will not separate between the two.[56] Stereotyping is an anxiety projection. The "good" and "bad" within us are projected onto the "other." The "bad" Other becomes the negative stereotype; the "good" Other becomes the positive one. Gilman sets his subject in a cultural-historical context, since "every social group has a set of vocabulary of images for this externalized Other."[57] He also sees it in terms of power relationship since the "mental representation of difference is but the projection of the tension between control and its loss."[58]

Gilman's analysis is relevant to the experience the viewer undergoes in Kruger's installation. Furthermore, this author sees the fluidity of "texts" as the ideal source for studying stereotyping. "Texts" are seen in the broadest sense and include advertising and graffiti scratched on the wall. They are all "structured expressions of the inner world."[59] Kruger's textual installation is a case in point. It is a contemporary text, a slick postmodern graffiti, in which one is faced with derogatory words, concise and reductive in their very nature and thus in line with the evaluation that "when systems of representation are used to structure the projections of our anxiety, they are necessarily reductive."[60] We may conclude the experience of stereotyping in Kruger's installation with Gilman's final remarks: "Neither we nor any of our cultural artifacts are free of this taint."[61]

Following the Mary Boone installation, Kruger was engaged in a direct political agenda in the 1992 "Art and Politics: A Pre-Election Symposium":

Instead of bold new proposals we are witnessing tantrums of cynicism and blame, of us-versus-themisms and crassly unapologetic racism. We are being suffocated by the cloying smoke-screen of "the value thing," an avoidance of the issues of race, sex, money and power that are determining the look and feel of changing America. . . . Our government *must* begin to reflect the diversity of its racial, cultural and sexual constituency. . . . I would hope that those who have been unseen and unheard will represent themselves rather than be dumbly misrepresented by others, and that what they show and tell will create moments of compelling empowerment and righteous anger.[62]

However, though being marginalized has been a crucial part of her make-up, Kruger did not belong to leftist organizations in the 1960s because "they did not let women into the discourse," and her social commitment to minority questions, which should not be separated from her feminist struggle, came only later and became an integral part of her art. And, Kruger says, "America is a culture that struggles with its race differences. Racial issues are aiming to destroy the country. The power inclination of America is about destroying differences. A choreography of power."

In *Untitled (Speak for Yourself)* (fig. 107, 1986), a photomontage, Kruger addresses a feminist issue of marginalization through the image of a Black woman welder.[63] The image echoes that of Ben Shahn's poster *Welders, or, for full employment after the war, Register / Vote* (fig. 108, 1944), in which a Black male welder's head is seen next to the upper bust of a White one, who covers two-thirds of the canvas, while the Black image covers one-third. The White dominates the central scene and the Black is relegated to the side. Shahn is speaking here of equal opportunities as part of Roosevelt's presidential campaign, which called for equal opportunities on the basis of equal participation in the war. *Welders* was originally meant to serve the cause of antidiscrimination, but was considered "as not suitable for mass-communication." However, when it was used later by the CIO's Political Action Committee for the presidential campaign, it reached millions of people.[64] Rodman has shown that the poster was based on a photograph of two White welders, while Shahn's transformation of one of them was part of his anti-racial beliefs. Rodman compares the reflective, dignified Black head to a figure in Piero della Francesca's Arezzo frescos.[65]

The comparison between Shahn's and Kruger's images is an interesting example of the difference in tone between "an engaged artist" in the 1940s and a postmodern one. The two works share the use of word and image and the call for action. However, in contrast to the contemplative, respectful, Black welder in Shahn's poster, Kruger passes the torch to the female welder, whose image is active and in full command of the space. Unlike the unidimensionality of the earlier poster, which conveys a straightforward message, Kruger's title is ambivalent, since it plays with two possible interpretations of the meaning of "speak for yourself." The first is critical and restrictive, implying that you should not speak for me. The second is encouraging and is trying to raise the consciousness of the protagonist: "Speak for yourself rather than let others speak for you." According to the second meaning, if you do not speak for yourself, others will, which will force you to tell them to speak for themselves in the first sense!

The question here is also, Who is the speaker? Is it the welder, or is it Barbara Kruger herself? If it is Kruger telling the Black/woman/welder to speak for herself, there is an awareness of the irony of the situation, since it is a White woman matronizing a Black woman by telling her to speak for herself. If it is the welder who is speaking, it implies that Kruger should not speak for her. Moreover, double irony is implied here, since there is an echo of the American ethos: you have to speak for yourself in the sense that you have to care for yourself. In other words, "You have to stand up for yourself, and if you won't, no one will."

The possibilities raised in Kruger's statement are either overinvolvement (by telling others what to do) or no involvement at all. The ambivalence is part of the artist's postmodernist language. It serves as a means of problematizing the issue of support for others, and a means for circumventing a self-righteous preaching tone, in spite of, or rather because of, the artist's commitment to feminist as well as to minorities issues. It is particularly pertinent in an era perceived as expressing "a desire to think in terms sensitive to difference (of others without opposition, of heterogeneity without hierarchy)."[66]

Kruger's dilemma takes us back to the early days of the Black–Jewish relationship. Joel Spingarn, a leading member of the NAACP and cofounder of the Spingarn Medal, expressed his concern in *The Crisis* in 1917: "I said to myself then, and I say to you now: What the colored people need most of all is not money, or land or political power or patronizing friends, but unpurchasable leaders—leaders who would not sell their souls for the good will of their neighbors or for big buildings, any more than they would for a dollar or a job."[67] The Spingarn citation demonstrates the paradoxical position of friend and patron.

As a postmodern artist, Kruger does not separate her art from an engagement in cultural criticism. She is involved in organizing panel discussions, editing, and writing her own critical reviews. In October 1987 she organized panel discussions on contemporary culture as part of the Dia Art Foundation's activities in New York. These were published in *Remaking History*, which she coedited. The selection includes essays by people whose ideas she shares. She considers her artistic work to be in a constant dialogue with the texts published in this book, which contains articles addressing contemporary critical views on, among other things, Black culture.[68] Since these articles are relevant to postmodern art and to Barbara Kruger, I will note some of the main arguments of the writers dealing with Black culture.

An essay by Cornel West deals with the failure of postmodernism to address

FIG. 107. Barbara Kruger, *Untitled (Speak for Yourself)* (1986), photomontage.
Collection of the artist, courtesy of Barbara Kruger.

seriously the cultural and political practices of oppressed African Americans. West sees
Black music as the most unique cultural product of America "of any hue."[69] Michele
Wallace, in a biographical sketch, describes her part in resisting stereotypical racial tru-
isms, such as "If you're white, you're alright; if you're brown, stick around; and if you're
black, stay back," which was paramount for her art as well as for maintaining psychological equilibrium. This led her to initiate protest activities together with her mother, the
painter Faith Ringgold, against all-White-male exhibitions.[70]

Homi K. Bhabha's "Remembering Fanon: Self, Psyche, and the Colonial Condition,"[71] readdresses the psychoanalytical writer and philosopher of *Black Skin, White
Masks*,[72] Fanon's unforgettable text, which contains a daring and painful inner dialogue
dealing with desire. Bhabha is considered to be "at the forefront of the crucial recovery
and return of Frantz Fanon's writings to critical, scholarly gaze."[73] Bhabha's motto is

FIG. 108. Ben Shahn, *Welders, or, for full employment after the war, Register/Vote* (1944), tempera on card board, 22 x 39 3/4. The Museum of Modern Art, New York. © Estate of Ben Shahn/ Licensed by VAGA, New York.

Fanon's final dramatic and painful epilogue: "O my body, make of me always a man who questions!" Bhabha recounts how Fanon discovered the impossibility of his mission as a colonial psychiatrist in the psychiatric hospital at Blida-Joinville, in the divided world of French Algeria. And yet, in spite of Fanon's participation in the Algerian revolution and his influence on the politics of the 1960s and 1970s through his writings on race, "his work will not be possessed by one political moment or movement."[74] Fanon's questioning body is seen through his confrontation with "the white man's eyes. . . . I was battered down by tom-toms, cannibalism, intellectual deficiency, racial defects." As Bhabha extrapolates the text, vision contains "the displacement of the colonial relation. The black presence ruins the representative narrative of Western personhood: its past tethered to treacherous stereotypes of primitivism and degeneracy. . . . The white man's eyes break up the black man's body."[75]

As a critic of Fanon, Homi Bhabha comments on his failure to historicize the colonial experience. For Fanon the colonial subject, who is viewed from a psychoanalytic perspective, is "determined from without," through image and fantasy, rather than as "a question of political oppression." For "what is often called the black soul is a white man's artifact," as the colonial situation is that of a "constellation of delirium" and "the Negro enslaved by his inferiority, the white man enslaved by his superiority alike behave in accordance with a neurotic orientation."[76]

Bhabha reiterates the impact of Sartre's notion of the "anti-Semitic consciousness" on Fanon's writings: "This ambivalent identification of the racist world—moving on two planes without being in the least embarrassed by it, as Sartre says of the anti-Semitic consciousness—turns on the idea of Man *as* his alienated image, not Self and Other but the 'Otherness' of the Self.[77] In Fanon's text the analogy between the Black and the Jew is a leitmotif. He quotes Sartre's definition of the Jew as one whom other people consider a Jew. This definition holds true for Blacks, or putting it differently: "An anti-Semite is inevitably anti-Negro."[78] Overall, while addressing stereotypes, Fanon sees both the similarities and the differences between the Black and the Jew. He cites racial attributes assigned to both Jews and Blacks: "The Jew is feared because of his potential acquisitiveness. . . . They are everywhere. The banks, the stock exchanges . . . are 'infested' with them." As for the Blacks, they are feared because of their sexual powers: "They are really genital." Thus, "the Negro symbolizes the biological danger; the Jew, the intellectual danger."[79]

The Jew and the Black have to take their stand regarding the way each party sees itself while facing projections. Fanon once more quotes Sartre, admitting, "Certain pages of *Anti-Semite and Jew* are the finest that I have ever read. The finest, because the problem discussed in them grips us in our guts." In the paragraph cited by Fanon, Sartre is emphatically describing the Jew as a "haunted man, condemned to make his choice of himself on the basis of false problems and in a false situation." As for the question of who is to be blamed, Sartre's reply is equally applicable to the Black: "It is we who constrain him to choose to be a Jew *whether through flight from himself or through self-assertion*; it is we who force him into the dilemma of Jewish authenticity or inauthenticity."[80]

Barbara Kruger sees these texts as crucial for understanding her identity, as well as for understanding that of the Black minority. These concerns are an integral part of her art. Moreover, as a postmodern artist, she also engages in written criticism, much of which is concerned with Black issues, as well as with Jewish–Black relations. Thus for instance, she reviewed contemporary movies and videos for *Artforum* in the 1980s, and a selected number of her pieces were collected in *Remote Control.*[81] These include viewing Sankofa Film/Video Collective and Black Audio Film Collective. In her discussion of *Territories* (1985, directed by Isaac Julien), she speaks of the voices that meditate on "Who I am," while pointing out the contradiction between "us" and "them." Her review of *Passion*, in which a Black family is watching a television game show with a Black couple as contestants, underscores a phrase dealing with the private and public domain that could be relevant to other minorities: "Every time a black face appears we think it has to represent the entire race."[82]

But the review most relevant to this context is Kruger's analysis of Roger Deutsch's films *Dead People* and *Jews*, examined together. The former is a film about "Frank," an elderly Black man whom Deutsch actually befriended and who became the subject of a film. Kruger challenges the notion of friendship here, preferring to see the relationship in terms of "an object of fascination, a 'found object' upon which Deutsch could project his own stereotypes." This can be shown through the arbitrary end of the intensive fascination, just because the filmmaker leaves town: "Then I left town and never finished the film."[83] Kruger sees this candor in terms of self-critique, Deutsch's adoration of "otherness," and its relegation to the position of temporary fancy. It thus becomes a postmodern awareness and a way of deconstructing good intentions toward "otherness." On a broader level it also questions grand ideas of engagement with the "other."

Attempting an overview of the artists discussed in this chapter, we may reach some general conclusions. Jean-Michel Basquiat did not refrain from using stereotypical anti-Jewish images, and, through the use of language in his art, he also uncovered the racist language employed by Jews. Adrian Piper, while confronting racists with their views, also exposes anti-Semitic remarks. Jonathan Borofsky expresses a wide array of attitudes, conveying his identification with Blacks as well as his fear of losing his own identity. Art Spiegelman intentionally problematizes the usage of racial language, creating a generation gap between those Jews who do not draw the analogy between the Holocaust and the Black experience, and their liberal children. Barbara Kruger fights various stereotypical attitudes in her installations, political expressions, edited books, and reviews. Her reported sense of her own marginality may explain her particular sensitivity to the place of minorities in our modern culture. What is ultimately common to all five artists is their highly effective way of forcing the viewer to confront his or her own racial and ethnic prejudices. By adopting the critical, postmodern stance, the artists lead the viewer to adopt the same self-searching attitude that they manifest in their works of art.

· CHAPTER 7 ·

cONclusioN

The relationship between Jewish and African Americans and the artistic expression
that mirrors their relationship constitute an ongoing process which no book can
bring to a final cadence. Since this century-old interaction is currently assuming new
shapes and turns, one can only suggest tentative comments based on the past. A retrospective overview of the present study shows that there are more examples of Jewish-
American artists dealing with African-American themes in their art than vice versa.
Generally speaking it can be said that most African-American artists have concentrated
above all on the consolidation of their own identity, either by stressing their original
racial contribution, or by becoming part of the mainstream of American art. However, a
Jewish presence can be traced in the art of Henry Tanner, Winfred Russell, Romare
Bearden, Aaron Douglas, Jacob Lawrence, Cliff Joseph, David Hammons, Benny Andrews,
Jean-Michel Basquiat, Adrian Piper, and Pat Ward Williams.

It is not surprising that the historical starting point for Black artists' depictions of
Jews at the end of the nineteenth century centered around the Bible. This is in line with
the traditional role Jews have played in Western Christian art in general, but it also
manifests the specific African-American reading of the Bible. In African-American art
biblical images are a natural continuation of religious aspirations and of the spirituals
created during the period of slavery. Tanner traveled to the Holy Land, as did many
people of his time, often motivated by religious orientations. However, he differed from
other traveler-artists in his feeling for the subjugation of the Jewish people and in searching for a "Semitic type" to express his biblical themes and also in portraiture. The epitome
of this identification was conveyed, as we have seen, through the image of the Yemenite,
the dark-skinned Jew.

Following Tanner's interest in portraiture, but working in the realistic style of the
1920s and 1930s, W. Russell depicted a contemporary version of a "Jewish type," expressing a sense of sympathy with the portrayed. Romare Bearden continued this mode
of representation in the 1930s, illustrating the common life and hardships of Blacks and
Jews. Analogously, as the Harlem Renaissance was taking shape, biblical illustrations

centering around Exodus and rebirth flourished in the graphic art of Aaron Douglas and later in the art of Howard Johnson. In the *New Negro* parallels were drawn between the Black and the Jewish revivals, "Palestine full of a renascent Judaism."

The persecution of European Jews and the Holocaust brought John Biggers and Victor Löwenfeld together, and although Biggers did not depict Holocaust themes directly, some of his images of the plight of Black people allude to the Jewish experience. Cartoons in various African-American magazines also drew analogies between the fate of the two peoples by juxtaposing the Ku Klux Klan and Nazi Germany.

The 1960s, the next phase in which African-American artists depicted Jews, showed them acknowledging a sense of camaraderie between Jews and Blacks. Jacob Lawrence painted ministers praying together, with a rabbi wearing a talit (prayer shawl) situated in the center of the composition. Cliff Joseph's art is a turning point. On the one hand he depicts the common sacrifice of two young Jewish men and a young Black man murdered while fighting for the Black cause in Mississippi. Yet in a painting done a year later, he questions this alliance, accusing both Jewish and Christian leaders of betrayal. Here the religious biblical reference no longer reflects positive identification (as in Tanner, Douglas, and Johnson); the title "Heirs to the Kiss of Judas" shifts the traditional portrayal of the Jew in the New Testament to the present moment, as the archetype of betrayal. In the early 1960s David Hammons also depicted a rabbi in relation to African Americans. His portrayal of the rabbi is an ironic self-portrait: rather than a talit he is wearing the American flag, representing for the African-American artist America's oppressive power. Nagging doubts and ironic comments notwithstanding, David Hammons's rabbi is none other than himself. However, Benny Andrews's consistent depictions of rabbis and Jewish scholars demonstrate that to draw a sharp line of differentiation between the periods would be misleading.

A Jewish presence reappeared in African-American art in the 1980s. Jean-Michel Basquiat's stereotypically money-hungry Jew is a case in point. Here, the protagonist has moved from the previous religious context (Tanner, Joseph, Hammons) to a secular one. The Jew is depicted as profiteering from the martyrdom of Joe Louis. Moreover, through his use of verbal imagery, Basquiat also undertook to uncover racist language used by racist Jews. Adrian Piper, however, adds an approach opposite to Basquiat's, as she demonstrates her equal sensitivity to racism and anti-Semitism. For her the two are indivisible.

The use of the Holocaust reflects changing attitudes in the 1980s, as some artists invoked a sense of competition between the relative suffering of Jews and Blacks. By making an analogy between a photograph of a lynched man and adding questions relating to Hitler's treatment of the Jews, Pat Ward Williams raised the issue of who suffered more, Jews or Blacks, a kind of impossible comparison that nevertheless goes on haunting the numerous encounters and attempted dialogues between the two communities.

This brief survey of the development of the depiction of Jews in African-American art suggests a distinction between three modes of representation: positive identification

(Tanner, Douglas, Johnson, Bearden, Biggers, Lawrence, Joseph, Andrews), critical identification (Joseph, Hammons), and finally disillusionment (Basquiat). These changes in the depiction of Jews by African-American artists correspond to general social and political stages in the evolution of the relationship between the two groups. And yet artists such as Adrian Piper and Benny Andrews break up this neat categorization. In a way, they represent another voice in the African-American community.

In light of this retrospective analysis, can we interpret the meaning of contemporary works by African-American artists on Jewish subjects? Since we are situated in the middle of this evolving relationship and do not have enough historical perspective, I will present only one example to throw light on recent developments. Howardena Pindell's *Autobiography: Air/CS560* (fig. 109, 1988) communicates the changing tone in African-American art. In her case, no longer do we see a depiction of biblical figures, of Jewish-American orthodoxy or references to secular Jewish-American artists. Rather than these, she is personally engaged (as the title of her image suggests) in displaying her attitude to Israel and the Palestinians. In other words, we can see here a displacement of interest from the traditional direct depiction of American Jews to a critical depiction of Israel.

Pindell's painting was done in response to the Intifada, the Palestinian uprising. The work combines a number of media (acrylic, tempera, oilstick, paper, polymer photo transfer, and vinyl tape) on an irregularly shaped, cut-and-sewn canvas. The title is taken from the name of a tear gas manufactured in Salzburg, Pennsylvania. Into the opalescent pale ocher surface, alluding to a nautilus shell, Pindell sews her own life-size silhouette in four variations. She is floating in various directions: from above, from the sides, and in reverse with her body upside down. The four silhouettes, resembling police demarcation of corpses, float in the center of the composition. A photograph from the *New York Times* illustrating the uprising is placed next to messages such as "censorship," "assassination," "cheap labor," "slave market," and "plastic coated bullets." By hovering among the incriminating inscriptions, the artist identifies with the Palestinian point of view.[1]

Pindell points out that CS560 was the name of a gas made in America and used against the uprising: "The painting, though directly expressing my feelings about oppression of the Palestinians, also relates to all struggles in the world by people who do not wish for their land, resources, homes, labor, culture or lives to be stolen or destroyed."[2] Clearly this is a long way from the days of Tanner's depiction of "the Jews' wailing place" and his description of the subjugated Jews "under the scornful gaze of the . . . Turkish conqueror."

Jewish artists have been more involved with African-American social and racial causes than vice versa. The Black cause was pursued both as a vision for a better future (by Chaim Gross, Julius Bloch, Philip Evergood, Ben Shahn, and Raphael Soyer) and as an indictment of the harsh reality of lynching, segregation and inequality (e.g., Jacob Epstein, Peshka, William Gropper, Philip Evergood, Hugo Gellert, Julius Bloch, Reisman, Louis Lozowick, Harry Sternberg, Philip Guston, Adolf Wolff, Aaron Goodelman, and

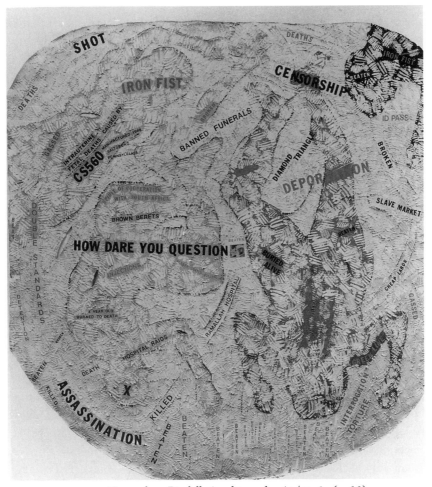

FIG. 109. Howardena Pindell, *Autobiography: Air/CS560* (1988),
Acrylic, tempera, oil stick, blood (the artist's), paper, polymer photo, transfer, vinyl
type on canvas, 87 x 84. Collection of the artist, courtesy of Howardena Pindell.

Seymour Lipton). This concern of the first half of the century was later rekindled in the
political and artistic involvement of Jewish artists in the civil rights movement (Gross,
Shahn, Soyer, Jack Levine, George Segal). In a sense, the distinction between the positive
vision and the moral condemnation of racial injustice is artificial and was drawn here for
methodological reasons, to emphasize the complementary concerns of the artists. Many
of these artists depicted both aspects, the bleak circumstances looming in the background
of the vision.

The vision itself frequently contained references to Jewish sources and conveyed
universalistic messages found in Psalms and the Prophets. It was a vision of an egalitarian society, free from discrimination and persecution, based on respect for every racial

and ethnic minority, that is to say opposed to the kind of particularism associated with White supremacy. By advocating these ideas, through the portrayal of the Black, the Jewish-American artists discussed in this book were also fighting their own battle. Their vision of the "other" also suggests a vision of the position of Jews in American society. It is a vision of America in which both Jews and Blacks could be integrated in a society that would accept them on their own merits.[3]

In the last three decades of the twentieth century, with artists turning to a more personal mode of expression, Philip Guston's identification with the Klansman, for biographical reasons, sets a questioning tone. However, Larry Rivers's continuous depiction of Black issues carries an autobiographical hue of a different nature. At times the artist seems to wish to experience the world as if he were himself Black. Like his predecessors, he engaged in depicting the cruelty of Black history. But Rivers went beyond that. His identification with Blacks led him to a reversal of traditional Eurocentric modes of perception that found a high point in the transformation of Manet's white Olympia into a black one. In his constructions, Rivers also provocatively addressed the issues underlying the libidinous relationship between the races.

Jonathan Borofsky's autobiographical art takes us to the realm of the subconscious. In Borofsky's depictions of dreams, done under the impact of a Jungian analysis, Blacks form a leitmotif, representing that part of himself which has to be integrated. His identification with Blacks reached such a degree that he expressed fears of loss of his own Self. But the dreams also express his own prejudices and racial stereotypes.

Borofsky, Art Spiegelman, and Barbara Kruger are all committed to simultaneous use of word and image. In their images they address issues of racial and ethnic stereotyping. Spiegelman points out the generation gap regarding racial attitudes within the Jewish community, and Kruger explores a variety of racist expressions assigned to minorities in America, Jews and Blacks included. Their art is meant to provoke, to raise questions, to confront viewers with their own prejudices.

Stepping beyond this review, it is well worth noting the sexually provocative images of two Jewish-American artists, Philip Pearlstein and Art Spiegelman, who in these works break away from social decorum in representing racial relationships. Pearlstein's *Model with Minstrel Marionettes* (fig. 110, 1986) revolves around uneasy ambiguous juxtapositions: two Black marionette entertainers, fully dressed, are seen next to a naked White woman. While they act their roles, they look at her jubilantly, whereas she is sulkily withdrawn, her eyes looking down. Various realms of existence are fused: the viewer is not quite sure where to draw the line distinguishing between the "real" world (her superrealist image) and the "stage" (the marionettes). Her enlarged arm, leaning on the Black musician's leg and heightening their physical proximity, blurs the distinction between the world and the stage. However, does her arm insinuate that the musician serves as an object, a prop she can use, or rather is it a sexual gesture that is the counterpart of the sexual metaphor suggested by playing the string instrument? Her expression is undetermined: on the one hand, in her unselfconscious nudity and self-absorption she seems not to be aware of the musicians' presence; on the other hand, she seems to be attuned to them, dependent on their archetypal musical ability to lift her from her dejected mood (as in the biblical story of young David playing music before the depressed King Saul). However, their grins and her nudity set the image apart from classical representations of the role of music in art and hence from art as therapy. Be that as it may, the incongruous juxtaposition of participants intentionally provokes the sexual dimension of the relations between the races (not unlike works by Larry Rivers and Jonathan Borofsky). Furthermore, in his choice of Black minstrel figures with exaggerated features, manipulated as marionettes (based on a piece of Americana he owns), Pearlstein uses a stereotypically degrading image implying the manipulation of Blacks. And yet, the title suggests that the scene can also be looked at as a representation of the artist's studio. From this angle, both Black marionettes and White nude are subjected to the same kind of treatment. They become materials in the hands of the artist-creator, and thus their common denominator is their status of "captivity": she in her frozen nude pose succumbing to the artist's demands, and they in their confinement to the role of marionettes. The complexity of the image and the multilayered possibilities of viewing it add to the deliberate sense of discomfort it creates.

Whereas Pearlstein portrays a relationship between the races, Art Spiegelman presents perhaps the most provocative visual image dealing with Jewish–Black relationships in recent years. His *Valentine's Day* (fig. 111), published as the cover of the *New Yorker* (February 15, 1993), stirred a heated controversy. It was done in the aftermath of riots in the Crown Heights section of Brooklyn, in which tensions soared between Blacks and Hasidic Jews. The image shows a Hasidic Jew and a Black woman in an erotic embrace, kissing each other on the lips. The first reaction to the image is astonishment: is this "unbelievable" picture a parody, and if so, what is its purpose? But this response quickly gives way to shock: how dare an artist portray an encounter that is seriously offensive to members of both communities? Spiegelman himself, in an editorial note, made an attempt to explain, even justify, his provocative image. Using the occasion of Valentine's Day to lead into the subject, as well as to separate it from everyday reality, Spiegelman wrote that he was expressing a wish for reconciliation. He admitted that this rather far-fetched symbolic kiss was hardly a practical solution to conflict, but rather an attempt, however naive, to show what it would be like if, for instance, Serbs and Croats, Arabs and Israelis, West Indians and Hasidic Jews, would make a simple gesture of forgiveness.[4]

Spiegelman was obviously conscious of the double taboo he was breaking: on the one hand an ultra-Orthodox Jew cannot be easily imagined in such a sexually explicit situation, not to speak of the fact that the woman does not come from his own milieu (where prearranged marriages within the community are the norm); on the other hand, it is hardly probable that a Black woman would want to lure a Hasidic Jew into an intimate relationship. And yet Spiegelman uses this image as an expression of a dream, a

FIG. 110. Philip Pearlstein, *Model with Minstrel Marionettes* (1986),
watercolor on paper, 42 x 30. Private collection, courtesy of Philip Pearlstein.

FIG. III. Art Spiegelman, *Valentine's Day* (1993), first published in the *New Yorker* (February 15, 1993). Reprinted by permission of the author and Deborah Karl, Inc.

sincere aspiration toward a world governed by love rather than by racial barriers of animosity and violence. The traditional "kitschy" wishes of Valentine's Day are superimposed on the harsh social conflict, creating a sharp dissonance.

However, does this image really work? Does the image achieve the intended effect of creating a temporary dreamlike haven from the realities of violent clashes? According to Patricia J. Williams, an African-American law professor, the illustration "offended everyone, it seemed; pleased no one."[5] Rather than initiating a serious public debate about the meaning of the Crown Heights riots, the cover illustration misfired. It suggested both a stereotype of the Jewish look and the old stereotype of Blacks as sexually promiscuous ("and imagine *how* transgressive the Jezebel was who could lure a devout Hasidic man from his pursuit of piety").[6] But most important, Williams believes that the fundamental failure of the Spiegelman illustration lies in its insensitivity to the particular cultural practices and sensibilities of the two groups. "Innocently assimilative, dehistoricized ideals only blur or aggravate rather than assuage."[7]

Nevertheless, because there is so much truth in Williams's critical analysis of *Valentine's Day,* the powerful (and indeed offensive) image does manage to arouse serious reflection about racial relations, their conditions and limits. The viewer's initial responses of amused astonishment and angry shock are likely followed by a third response, a cooler, self-reflective attempt to examine not so much the meaning of the picture but rather the meaning of one's response to it. The image goes a step beyond Alex Katz's *Vincent and Tony,* but rather than encouraging us to adopt a color blind perception of our social environment, it punches us in the face with a blatant image forcing on us a color-conscious experience.

Spiegelman's image and the uneasiness it creates are indicative of the role of the visual arts in the present complex relations between the two groups. Much art toward the end of the millennium in general tends to raise self-consciousness in the viewer and often does so by means of provocation and the creation of uneasiness, dissonance, and paradox. Conveying a direct vision in the style of Lucienne Bloch or Raphael Soyer would be regarded today as unacceptably sentimental and devoid of self-reflectivity. In its self-conscious, self-referential, critical nature, contemporary art has lost its capacity to make direct positive statements. As a coeditor of *CommonQuest* remarked, the romance of the Selma days is over.

Yet the ambiguous and "offensive" message of Spiegelman's cover forces spectators to sincerely test their perceptions, prejudices, and limits of tolerance, and thus proves the unique power of the visual to enhance genuine reflection about interracial relations. The Valentine's Day cover demonstrates that racial reflections are deeply rooted in mutual visual perceptions and hence the visual arts play an irreplaceable role in the articulation of these reflections. Due to the power of the visual, this lesson can be retrospectively applied to many artists who figure in the intricate story of the mutual reflection of Blacks and Jews in America.

We may thus conclude with a recent literal rendering of the power of the visual to characterize the complexity of Jewish–Black relationships. Unlike Pearlstein and Spiegelman, who reflect on reflected racial images, Gerda Meyer-Bernstein's *Phoenix* (fig. 112) focuses on the vehicle of reflection, the mirroring glass itself. It is a site-specific, twelve-by-thirteen-foot installation built for the 1994 exhibition *Bridges and Boundaries: Chicago Crossings* at the Spertus Museum, in which African-American and Jewish-American artists were invited to respond to the Jewish Museum's earlier show in New York.[8] The installation consisted of half black and half white walls with layers of shattered glass covering the floor and reflecting the black and white coloring of the walls. In the text accompanying the installation, the artist, who was born in Germany, says that her intention was "to mirror and reflect the shattering of our relations, the utter senselessness of Blacks and Whites destroying each other. In this process we are all equal."[9] There is a deep sense of despair in this work: not only have the social and political relations between the two communities been wrecked; the means of communication, the vehicles of mutual reflection, including the artistic ones, have been shattered. Language in general, and that of the visual arts in particular, have been put to an aggressive, divisive use. However, beyond the despair of the impossibility of reconstructing splintered glass, the work expresses in its title a hope of a healing process. The phoenix is, after all, the legendary bird that after being consumed by fire arises out of its ashes.

FIG. 112. Gerda Meyer-Bernstein, *Phoenix* (1994), installation with glass in the Spertus Museum *Chicago Crossings* exhibition. Courtesy of Gerda Meyer-Bernstein.

Notes

Notes to Introduction

1. Michael Lerner and Cornel West, *Jews and Blacks: Let the Healing Begin* (New York: Putnam, 1995), 4.

2. Jonathan Rieder, "Beyond Frenzy and Accusation," *CommonQuest* 1 (spring 1996), 2.

3. Milly Heyd and Ezra Mendelsohn, "Jewish Identity and the Artistic Representation of the Other," unpublished article.

4. Linda Nochlin, "Starting with the Self: Jewish Identity and Its Representation," in Linda Nochlin and Tamar Garb, eds., *The Jew in the Text: Modernity and the Construction of Identity* (London: Thames and Hudson, 1995), 8.

5. Ibid., 18.

6. Sander L. Gilman, "The Jew's Body: Thoughts on Jewish Physical Difference," in Norman L. Kleeblatt, ed., *Too Jewish? Challenging Traditional Identities* (New York: The Jewish Museum, and New Brunswick: Rutgers University Press, 1996), 61–63. See also the illustration, p. 70.

7. W.E.B. Du Bois, *The Souls of Black Folk*, edited with an introduction by David W. Blight and Robert Gooding-Williams (Boston and New York: Bedford Books, 1997), 38.

8. William Zorach, *Art Is My Life: An Autobiography* (Cleveland and New York: World Publishing Company, 1967), 130.

9. Heyd and Mendelsohn, "Jewish Identity."

10. See Milly Heyd and Ezra Mendelsohn, " 'Jewish' Art? The Case of the Soyer Brothers," *Jewish Art* 19–20 (1993–94), 200.

11. Ezra Mendelsohn, *On Modern Jewish Politics* (New York: Oxford University Press, 1993), 134–137.

12. Jonathan Kaufman, *Broken Alliance: The Turbulent Times Between Blacks and Jews in America* (New York: Charles Scribner's Sons, 1988). The book cover mentioned belongs to this edition. Jack Salzman, with Adina Back and Gretchen Sullivan Sorin, eds., *Bridges and Boundaries: African Americans and American Jews* (New York: George Braziller in association with The Jewish Museum, 1992).

13. Jack Salzman, "Introduction," in *Bridges and Boundaries*, 15–16.

14. Clayborne Carson Jr., "Blacks and Jews in the Civil Rights Movement," in *Bridges and Boundaries*, 36, 38. This article was originally published in Joseph R. Washington, ed., *Jews in Black Perspective: A Dialogue* (Rutherford, N.J.: Fairleigh Dickinson University Press, 1984).

15. Taylor Branch, "Blacks and Jews: The Uncivil War," in *Bridges and Boundaries*, 50–70.

16. Du Bois, *Souls of Black Folk*, 209. For the full elaboration of the various editions and Du Bois's confusion and indecision in his use of "Jews," see 209–210. I am grateful to Robert Gooding-Williams

for drawing my attention to the nuances in the various editions of the text. The quotation about the Jew as the heir is on p. 112.

17. Kenneth B. Clark, "Candor about Negro–Jewish Relations," in *Bridges and Boundaries*, 95.

18. James Baldwin, "The Harlem Ghetto," in *Notes of a Native Son* (Boston: Beacon Press, 1955), 69.

19. Clark, "Candor about Negro–Jewish Relations," 93.

20. Baldwin, "Harlem Ghetto,"66–72.

21. Avram Kampf, *Jewish Experience in the Art of the Twentieth Century* (South Hadley, Mass.: Bergin and Garvey, 1984), 66. On the impact of the prophets, such as Amos, on Jewish-American artist, see Heyd and Mendelsohn, "'Jewish' Art," 201–203; and Mendelsohn, *On Modern Jewish Politics*, 30–31.

22. Du Bois, Of Our Spiritual Strivings, *Souls of Black Folk*, 40. On the biblical dimension of the spirituals, see 185–194.

23. Albert J. Raboteau, *Slave Religion* (Oxford: Oxford University Press, 1978), 311–312.

24. Michael Walzer, *Exodus and Revolution* (New York: Basic Books, 1985). Walzer's point of departure is a sermon he heard while writing about the Black student sit-ins, in a Baptist church in Montgomery, Alabama, in 1960: "I listened to the most extraordinary sermon that I ever heard on the Book of Exodus and the political struggle of southern blacks. There on his pulpit, the preacher, . . . acted out the 'going out' from Egypt and expounded its contemporary analogues: he cringed under the lash, challenged the pharaoh, hesitated fearfully at the sea, accepted the covenant and the law at the foot of the mountain" (3).

25. See Arnold Rampersad, *The Life of Langston Hughes* (Oxford: Oxford University Press, 1986), vol. 1, 136. He also points out that Knopf accepted the book, but not without balking at the title(138). In his autobiography, the poet mentions Jewish ancestry. See *The Big Sea* (1940; reprint, New York: Thunder's Mouth Press, 1986), 11.

26. These patrons did not set up parallel funds to support Jewish American artists in the same period of the earlier decades of the twentieth century.

27. On the Amy Spingarn Fellowship awarded to Laura Wheeler Waring, see further Samella Lewis, *African American Art and Artists* (Berkeley: University of California Press, 1990), 55.

28. A. A. Schomburg, "Forward," *Exhibition of the Work of Negro Artists* (New York: Harmond Foundation, 1931), 6.

29. Romare Bearden and Harry Henderson, *A History of African-American Artists: From 1792 to the Present* (New York: Pantheon Books, 1993), 204, 253, 255.

30. Ibid., 253.

31. A quotation from the *New York Herald Tribune: Books* (November 12, 1939) reads: "He agreed with Booker Washington that it is education in the industrial field that the Negro needed but he disagreed with his Jewish friends that Jews needed a homeland" (Schomburg Center for Research in Black Culture). Rosenwald supported Jewish causes such as the Jewish Charities of Chicago, Hebrew Union College in Cincinnati, and Jewish settlers in Russia.

32. Julius Rosenwald, "The Business of Giving Money," *Atlantic Monthly* (May 1924). Rosenwald is estimated to have given $70 million to various Black enterprises. When he died, the Black press compared him to Moses. Thus, for instance, the obituary in the Chicago Defender (January 16, 1932): "The Negro race has lost a Moses who has given fully of his vision, his love and his means." In some cases he was hailed for being a Jew and in others for overcoming this. The same obituary continues: "He was a Jew and, therefore, it was easy for him to take in greatness like Moses. . . . He surveyed a promised land, and unlike Moses, improved it." On the other hand, the *Nashville Tennessean* on the same date declared, "Despite the fact that he was a Jew, Mr. Rosenwald practiced the principles of Christianity to the degree seldom reached by Christians" (Schomburg Center for Research in Black

Culture). For an account of his enterprises which includes a chapter on "Race Relations," see Edwin R. Embree, *Investment in People: The Story of the Julius Rosenwald Fund* (New York: Harper and Brothers), 1949.

33. Lewis, *African American Art and Artists*, 84. See also Bearden and Henderson, *History of African-American Artists*, 172, 178–179.

34. Bearden and Henderson, *History of African-American Artists*, 139.

35. Ibid., 133. See also Amy Helene Kirschke, *Aaron Douglas: Art, Race and the Harlem Renaissance* (Jackson: University Press of Mississippi, 1995), 116.

36. Bearden and Henderson, *History of African-American Artists*, 275. See also Lewis, *African American Art and Artists*, 127; Elton C. Fax, *Seventeen Black Artists* (New York: Dodd, Mead, 1971), 88.

37. Bearden and Henderson, *History of African American Artists*, 300.

38. Fax, *Seventeen Black Artists*, 68–69.

39. Bearden and Henderson, *History of African-American Artists*, 422.

40. Lewis, *African American Art and Artists*, 72–73.

41. Bearden and Henderson, *History of African-American Artists*, 141.

42. Ibid., 339.

43. Alvia J. Wardlaw, *The Art of John Biggers: View from the Upper Room*, with essays by Edmund Barry Gaither, Alison de Lima Greene, and Robert Farris Thompson (New York and Houston: Harry Abrams in association with the Museum of Fine Arts, Houston, 1995).

44. Gabrielle Simon Edgcomb, *From Swastika to Jim Crow: Refugee Scholars at Black Colleges* (Malbar, Florida: Krieger Publishing, 1993), xiii.

45. Ibid., xiv. The quotation is from a letter by Ernst Manasse to Carla Boden, June 14, 1984. Manasse taught German, Latin, and philosophy at North Carolina Central College (now University) in Durham, North Carolina.

46. Ibid., 97.

47. Ibid.

48. Viktor Löwenfeld, *Creative and Mental Growth: A Textbook on Art Education* (New York: Macmillan, 1947). The section titled "Mural Painting and Its Techniques," discussing mural painting as part of architecture, is illustrated by works by Biggers (201). Another example is a group work done at the Hampton Institute in the center of which is a shackled group of Black people surrounding a crucifix (203).

49. John Biggers and Carrol Simms, *Black Art in Houston: The Texas Southern University Experience* (College Station: Texas A&M University Press, 1978), 7–8.

50. Wardlaw, *Art of John Biggers*, 28.

51. Interview with Biggers in Edgcomb, *From Swastika to Jim Crow*, 98–99.

52. Bearden and Henderson, *History of African-American Art*, 431.

53. Edgcomb, *From Swastika to Jim Crow*, 79.

54. On depictions of wanderers with sacks on their backs and images of the Wandering Jew in the context of the Holocaust, see Ziva Amishai-Maisels, *Depiction and Interpretation: The Influence of the Holocaust on the Visual Arts* (Oxford: Pergamon, 1993), 19–27, 158–159.

55. See, for instance, Viktor Löwenfeld's article, "New Negro Art in America," *Design* (September 1944): 20–21, 29. The article is illustrated by John Biggers's mural, *Dying Soldier*.

56. Interview with Biggers in Edgcomb, *From Swastika to Jim Crow*, 99.

57. Samella Lewis, *The Art of Elizabeth Catlett* (Los Angeles: Hancraft Studios and The Museum of African American Art, 1984), 17.

58. On Hagar in African-American art, see Bearden and Henderson, *History of African-American Artists*, 68.

59. Edmonia Lewis's *Hagar* (1875), marble 52 5/8 in. x 15 1/4 in. x 17 in., is in the National Museum of American Art, Washington, D.C.

60. David Driskell, *Lila Oliver Asher: The Years at Howard* (Washington, D.C.: Howard University Gallery of Art, 1991), 5.

61. The sculptures were published by Vallière Richard Auzenne, *The Museum of African American Art: The Catalogue of the Barnett-Aden Collection* (Tampa: 1995).

62. Press release from The Jewish Museum, New York, March 18, 1991.

63. Amei Wallach, "Blacks and Jews United and Divided," *Newsday* (March 22, 1992): 13.

64. Ron Harrigan, "Bridges and Boundaries: African Americans and American Jews," *Black Ivory: The Pan-African Magazine* (April 4, 1992), 39.

65. Hasia Diner, *In the Almost Promised Land: American Jews and Blacks, 1915–1935* (Westport, Conn.: Greenwood Press, 1977), whose important analysis is based on newspapers, magazines, and press data, ignores the visual material found in her sources. The renewed interest in these relationships can be seen in Jack Salzman and Cornel West, eds., *Struggle in the Promised Land* (New York: Oxford University Press, 1997), which contains one article dealing with a visual image: Patricia J. Williams, "On Imagining Foes, Imagining Friendship." The article analyzes Art Spiegelman's *Valentine Day* (1993). The illustration itself is not given.

66. John Wilmerding, "When Does Modern American Art Begin?" unpublished lecture, Princeton May 3, 1997,

67. An important exhibition at the Jewish Museum was devoted to the artists of New York's Lower East Side; on this see Norman L. Kleeblatt and Susan Chevlowe, eds., *Painting a Place in America: Jewish Artists in New York, 1900–1945* (Bloomington: Indiana University Press, and New York: The Jewish Museum, 1991). See also Milton Brown, "An Explosion of Creativity: Jews and American Art in the Twentieth Century" and Matthew Baigell, From Hester Street to Fifty-Seventh Street: Jewish American Art in New York," both in Kleeblatt and Chevlowe, eds., *Painting a Place in America*, 22–28, 28–29.

68. Aaron Douglas, "The Negro in American Culture," in Matthew Baigell and Julia Williams, eds., *Artists Against War and Racism: Papers of the First American Artists' Congress* (New Brunswick: Rutgers University Press, 1986), 83. Also compare Abraham Walkowitz's *East Side Figures* (1903) with Palmer Hayden's *Midsummer Night in Harlem* (1938).

Notes to Chapter One

1. Alain Locke, "The Legacy of the Ancestral Arts," *The New Negro* (1925; reprint, New York: Atheneum, 1922), 264.

2. Ibid., 261.

3. Dewey F. Mosby, *Henry Ossawa Tanner* (Philadelphia: Museum of Art, 1991), 11–13.

4. Cedric Dover, *American Negro* (New York: American Graphic Society, 1960), 29.

5. Joseph Pennell, *The Adventures of an Illustrator* (Boston: Little Brown, 1925), 54 (emphasis added). Since we know that there was only one Black student, Henry Tanner, in Pennell's class, we can infer the identity of the person referred to in the quotation.

6. Autobiographical recollections by Tanner were published in "The Story of an Artist's Life," *The World's Work* 18 (May–Oct. 1909): 11774 (part 2).

7. Ibid., 11773.

8. John Wilmerding, *American Views: Essays on American Art* (Princeton, N.J.: Princeton University Press, 1991), 3.

9. Tanner, "The Story of an Artist's Life," 11774.

10. Benjamin Tucker Tanner, *The Negro's Origins and Is the Negro Cursed* (Philadelphia: African M.E. Book Depository, 1869), 22.

11. Albert Boime, "Henry Ossawa Tanner's Subversion of Genre," *Art Bulletin* 75 (1993): 436. Boime's article is part of the larger important study in *The Art of Exclusion: Representing Blacks in the Nineteenth Century* (Washington, D.C.: Smithsonian Institution Press, 1990).

12. Ibid., 437.

13. Mosby, *Henry Ossawa Tanner*, 94.

14. John W. Work, *American Negro Songs and Spirituals* (New York: Bonanza Books, 1940), 22.

15. Tanner, "The Story of an Artist's Life," 11774.

16. Boime, "Tanner's Subversion of Genre," 436.

17. Quoted by Walter Augustus Simon, "Henry O. Tanner—A Study of the Development of an American Negro Artist: 1859–1937" (Ph.D. dissertation, New York University, 1961), 87. Simon was the first to explore the impact of Tanner's mixed blood on his development, basing his assumption on two texts: Franklin Frazier, *Negro Youth at the Crossroads* (Washington: American Council for Education, 1940); and Maurice R. Davies, *Negroes in American Society* (New York: MacGraw Hill, 1949).

18. There was no Ethiopian Jewish community in Palestine at the turn of the century.

19. Reuben Aharoni, *Yemenite Jewry: Origins, Culture, and Literature* (Bloomington: Indiana University Press, 1986), 161. The Yemenite community in Jerusalem consisted of 650 people, some of whom lived in the Kidron Valley, which is the background of Tanner's painting. See Yehuda Nini, *The Jews of Yemen: 1800–1914* (Chur: Harwood Academic Press), 1991.

20. Henry Louis Gates Jr., *Figures in Black: Words, Signs, and the "Racial" Self* (New York: Oxford University Press, 1987), 92.

21. Mosby, *Henry Ossawa Tanner*, 168–169.

22. Romare Bearden and Harry Henderson, *A History of African American Artists: From 1792 to the Present* (New York: Pantheon Books, 1993), 95.

23. Moseby, *Henry Ossawa Tanner*, 170.

24. Bearden and Henderson, *History of African American Artists*, 104, n.106, 492.

25. Anon., "Howard Wants His Art," *Baltimore Afro-American* (January 30, 1937): 12.

26. Linda Nochlin, "Starting with the Self: Jewish Identity and Its Representation," introduction in *The Jew in the Text* (London: Thames and Hudson, 1995), 11.

27. Bearden and Henderson, *History of African-American Artists*, 92.

28. Mosby, *Henry Ossawa Tanner*, 136.

29. Francis C. Holbrook, "A Group of Negro Artists," *Opportunity* 1 (July 1923): 211.

30. Arnold Rampersad, "Introduction," in *The New Negro*, ix.

31. Ibid., xii.

32. Alain Locke, "Foreword," ibid., xxv.

33. Alain Locke, "The New Negro," ibid., 14.

34. Arnold Rampersad, ed., *The Collected Poems of Langston Hughes* (New York: Alfred A. Knopf, 1994), 52–53. "America" was first published in *Opportunity* (June 1925, 175) where it won third prize in a literary contest.

35. Arnold Rampersad, personal communication.

36. W. A. Domingo, "Gift of the Black Tropics," in *The New Negro*, 345.

37. Kelly Miller, "Howard: The National Negro University," in *The New Negro*, 318.

38. Charles S. Johnson, "The New Frontage of American Life," in *The New Negro*, 293.

39. James Weldon Johnson, "Harlem: The Culture Capital," in *The New Negro*, 309.

40. Alain Locke, "The Negro Spirituals," in *The New Negro*, 200.

41. Jean Toomer, "Fern," from *Cane*, in *The New Negro*, 103.

42. *The New Negro*, "Introduction," xxi.

43. Gates, *Figures in Black*, 208.

44. Alain Locke, "The Legacy of the Ancestral Arts," in *The New Negro*, 254–267.

45. Mary Schmidt Campbell, introduction to *Harlem Renaissance Art of Black America*, essays by David Driskell, David Levering Lewis, and Deborah Willis Ryan (New York: The Studio Museum in Harlem, Abradale Press, Harry Abrams Publishers, 1994), 13.

46. Boris Schatz, *Yerushalayim Ha'benuya* (Jerusalem rebuilt) (Jerusalem: Bezalel, 1924).

47. Houston Baker, Jr., *Modernism and the Harlem Renaissance* (Chicago: University of Chicago Press, 1987), 76.

48. In a recently published book, *Black Art and Culture in the 20th Century* (New York: Thames and Hudson, 1997), the author, Richard J. Powell, asks whether it was ironic to choose Winold Reiss, "a Caucasian artist of German nationality—to portray this modern, black persona." He sees this artist's cultural distance from American racism as legitimizing his participation in *The New Negro*; *Black Art*, 43.

49. James A. Porter, *Modern Negro Art* (New York: Arno Press and the New York Times, 1969), 105.

50. Amy Helene Kirschke, *Aaron Douglas: Art, Race, and the Harlem Renaissance* (Jackson: University Press of Mississippi, 1995), 42–43.

51. Gregory Holmes Singleton, "Birth, Rebirth, and the 'New Negro' of the 1920s," *Phylon* 43 (March 1982): 29–45.

52. The stretching of the neck toward heaven is a leitmotif in Douglas' art. See for instance the advertisement for Carl van Vechten's *Nigger Heaven* (1926) in *The Creation* (1927).

53. "The Legacy of the Ancestral Arts," in *The New Negro*, 266.

54. Campbell, *Harlem Renaissance Art of Black America*, 27.

55. David Driskell, "The Flowering of the Harlem Renaissance: The Art of Aaron Douglas, Meta Warrick Fuller, Palmer Hayden, and William H. Johnson," in *Harlem Renaissance Art of Black America*, 108–109.

56. Albert J. Raboteau, *A Fire in the Bones* (Boston: Beacon Press, 1995), 41–42. Raboteau's discussion of the significance of Psalm 68:31 in African-American Christian thought revolves around three major themes: "the African race," "the redemption of Africa," and "the mission of the darker races." For a full discussion of the three themes see 37–56.

57. Smadar Tirosh, "The Canaanite Hero," *Mishkafayim* 22 (October 1994): 17–19 (Hebrew).

58. Yigal Zalmona, "The Art Collections," in *The Israel Museum*, with a preface by Martin Weyl (London: Lawrence King Publishing, 1995), 203. See also Avram Kampf, *Jewish Experience in the Art of the Twentieth Century* (South Hadley, Mass.: Bergin and Garvey, 1984), 150–156. For a comprehensive book on Danziger, see Mordechai Omer, *Itzhak Danziger* (Tel Aviv: Tel Aviv Museum of Art, 1996), especially p. 101.

59. Meta Warrick Fuller also depicted images of suffering. A similar duality existed among artists concerned with the image of the New Jew. A most interesting comparison can be made between her sculpture of the *Refugee* (c. 1940), bearded and carrying a stick as he roams the world (for a reproduction see *Harlem Renaissance Art of Black America*, plate 28), and the recurrent theme of the Wandering Jew.

60. See also the discussion in Richard J. Powell, "Biblical and Spiritual Motifs," in Judith E. Stein, ed., *I Tell My Heart: The Art of Horace Pippin* (Philadelphia: Pennsylvania Academy of the Fine Arts, 1993), 124.

61. For a reproduction see David Driskell, with catalogue notes by Leonard Simon, *Two Centuries of Black American Art* (New York: Alfred A. Knopf and Los Angeles County Museum of Art, 1976), 153.

62. David Driskell, "The Flowering of the Harlem Renaissance," in *Harlem Renaissance Art of Black America*, 152–153. For an illustration see plate 51.

63. Meyer Schapiro, "Race, Nationality and Art," *Art Front* (March 1936): 10–12.

64. Alain Locke, "Freedom through Art: A Review of Negro Art, 1870–1938," *The Crisis* 45 (July 1938): 227–229.

65. For a study of Romare Bearden and his illustrations in various magazines, see Myron Schwartzman, *Romare Bearden: His Life and Art*, in particular "The Eagle Flies on Friday—Harlem in the 1930s," (New York: Harry N. Abrams, 1990), 62–95.

Notes to Chapter Two

1. Matthew Baigell et al., *American Art: 1930–1970*, (Milan: Fabbri, 1992), 47.

2. See also Milly Heyd and Ezra Mendelsohn, "'Jewish' Art? The Case of the Soyer Brothers," *Jewish Art* 19–20 (1993–94): 200.

3. Henry A. Milton and Linda Nochlin, eds., *Art and Architecture in the Service of Politics* (Cambridge, Mass.: MIT Press, 1978), ix.

4. Jacob Epstein to Arnold L. Haskell, *The Sculptor Speaks* (New York: Doubleday, Doran and Co., 1932), 84.

5. Ibid., 104.

6. Ibid., 87.

7. Hugh Honour, *The Image of the Black in Western Art*, vol. 4, Part 2 (Cambridge, Mass.: Harvard University Press, 1989), 242.

8. Ibid., 243.

9. Quoted in D. Graftly, "Gill and Epstein," *The American Magazine of Art* (June 1934): 328. For a discussion on Epstein's reception in England see Elizabeth Barker, "The Primitive Within: The Question of Race in Epstein's Career, 1917–1929," in *Jacob Epstein: Sculpture and Drawings* (Leeds: City Art Gallery, 1987), 45–48.

10. Frank Getlein, *Chaim Gross* (New York: Harry Abrams, 1974), 61.

11. Josef Vincent Lombardo, *Chaim Gross Sculptor* (New York: Dalton House, 1949,) 217. The Dogon sculpture is in the University Museum of the University of Pennsylvania.

12. Ziva Amishai-Maisels, *Depiction and Interpretation: The Influence of the Holocaust on the Visual Arts* (Oxford: Pergamon Press, 1993), 141.

13. Chaim Gross, *The Technique of Wood Sculpture* (New York: Vista House, 1957), 51.

14. Writing retroactively, Lipchitz explained that he realized that the image had emerged from his subconscious. It evoked a memory of a crippled beggar woman without legs in Russia. He does not refer to the African format of the facial features. Jacques Lipchitz and H. H. Aranson, *My Life in Sculpture* (New York: Viking Press, 1972), 148, 151. For an elaboration of Lipchitz's *Mother and Child* in the context of the Holocaust, see Maisels, *Depiction and Interpretation*, 28, 48, 142–143.

15. J. A. Rogers, "Jazz at Home," in *The New Negro* (1925; reprint, New York: Atheneum, 1992), 216.

16. Lombardo, *Chaim Gross Sculptor*, 150.

17. Ibid., 122.

18. Interview with Mrs. Renee Gross (February 2, 1997).

19. Chaim Gross's papers, Archives of American Art, Roll 924. Gross writes: "Raphael Soyer painted a portrait of me with this figure, painting in my collection." The text is illustrated by a drawing of the *Walking Negress* who is also called "Black Woman."

20. Arnold Rampersad, "Langston Hughes and His Critics on the Left," *The Langston Hughes Review* 5 (spring 1980): 34–35.

21. "My people," in Arnold Rampersad, ed., *The Collected Poems of Langston Hughes* (New York: Alfred Knopf, 1944), 36.

22. The *Opportunity* poem was reproduced in Langston Hughes and Arna Bontemps, *The Poetry of the Negro 1746–1949* (New York: Doubleday, 1949), 145. According to Arnold Rampersad, it was never titled "How Beautiful She Is" in any original English version. I am grateful to Arnold Rampersad for enlightening me on Waring Cuney's poetry.

23. Alain Locke, "The Legacy of The Ancestral Arts," in *The New Negro*, 264.

24. Jewish immigration to Birobidzhan began in 1928. It was established as a district in 1930, and was granted the status of "Jewish Autonomous Region" in 1934.

25. Alma Jones Waterhouse, "The Yeses of Chaim Gross: Art Collecting as Autobiography," *Connoisseur* 215 (May 1985): 128.

26. A photograph of the wall in the original site is preserved in the Archives of American Art, Roll N DA 3.

27. For a reproduction of the lost fresco as well as the artist's comments, see Lucienne Bloch, "Murals for Use," in F. V. O'Connor, ed., *Art for the Millions* (Greenwich, Conn.: New York Graphic Society, 1973), 77. The essay was written in 1936. The artist wrote further: "Some of the more articulate girls even used this [the sharing of an apple] and other themes from the murals as subjects of letters to their friends and relatives in the outside world. Such response clearly reveals to what degree a mural can, aside from its artistic value, act as a healthy tonic on the lives of all of us."

28. Paul von Blum, *Other Visions, Other Voices: Women Political Artists in Greater Los Angeles* (Lanham, Md.: University Press of America, 1994), 5.

29. Anonymous, "Art for Psychic's Sake in Our New Prisons," *New York Post* (May 8, 1935). Archives of American Art, Ben Shahn, D147.

30. Michele Vishney, "Lucienne Bloch: The New York City Murals," *Women's Art Journal* 13 (spring–summer 1992): 24–25.

31. A statement in the artist's handwriting, Archives of American Art, Evergood Roll 1346.

32. A statement by Philip Evergood, undated, Archives of American Art, Evergood Roll 1349.

33. Philip Evergood, "Art Is Not a Popsicle," *American Dialog* 1 (July–August, 1964): 15.

34. Archives of American Art, Evergood Roll 1346.

35. A letter from Jacob Lawrence to Philip Evergood reads: "Your painting of course was sold. We were able to give the students about $4,000 (four thousand dollars) from the sales thanks to such artists as you," signed "Regards Jake and Gwen Lawrence." November 17, 1963, Archives of American Art, Evergood Roll 1348.

36. Philip Evergood, "Building a New Art School," *Art Front* (April 1937): 21.

37. V. R., "Individualists," a review of the artist's show at the ACA gallery, *Arts Magazine* 36 (September 1962): 54.

38. Elizabeth Cattlet, "Comments on an Exhibition in Mexico City," (May 29, 1953): 2. Archives of American Art, Evergood Roll 1346.
The source gives no details of the film referred to.

39. Archives of American Art, Evergood Roll 1352.

40. Kendall Taylor, *Philip Evergood: Never Separate from the Heart* (London and Toronto: Associated Universities Presses, 1987), 159.

41. Ibid., 160.

42. Evergood's illustration can be seen in Goodelman's papers, Archives of American Art Roll 4935.

43. Archives of American Art Evergood Roll 1350. The text in the artist's handwriting is undated.

44. The discussion of the Soyer brothers, not including their relationship with Jacob Lawrence and Benny Andrews and an analysis of their mutual portraits, was published in Heyd and Mendelsohn, "'Jewish' Art? The Case of the Soyer Brothers," 200–205.

45. Marvin S. Sadik, *The Portrayal of the Negro in American Painting* (Brunswick, Me.: Bowdoin College, 1964), figure 78.

46. Raphael Soyer, *Diary of an Artist* (Washington: New Republic Books, 1977), 135.

47. Frank Gettings, *Raphael Soyer: Sixty-Five Years of Printmaking* (Washington, D.C.: Smithsonian Institution Press, 1982), 64.

48. Archives of American Art, Raphael Soyer Roll 0597.

49. *New Masses* (November 7, 1944), 27.

50. Epstein to Haskell, *The Sculptor Speaks*, 150.

51. *New Masses* (June 26, 1945), 30.

52. Stephen Gardiner, *Epstein: Artist Against Establishment* (London: Michael Joseph, 1992), 283–284.

53. Jerome Klein, "Twenty-One Gun Salute," *Art Front* (May 15, 1935): 4.

54. On the three Soyer brothers' struggle for the Black cause, see Heyd and Mendelsohn, "'Jewish' Art? The Case of the Soyer Brothers," 203–205.

55. Charles Childs, "Larry Ocean Swims the Nile, Mississippi and Other Rivers," in *Some American History*, exhibition commissioned by the Menil Foundation (Houston: Rice University Institute for the Arts, 1971), 18.

56. Jan Nederveen Pieterse, *White on Black: Images of Africa and Blacks in Western Popular Culture* (New Haven: Yale University Press, 1992), 155.

57. Ann Holmes, "'Some American History,' Consideration of Black?" *Houston Chronicle* (February 5, 1971): 4. I am grateful to Guyle De Gregori from the Menil Foundation for her generous assistance.

Notes to Chapter Three

1. Langston Hughes, "The Town of Scottsboro," in Arnold Rampersad, ed., *The Collected Poems of Langston Hughes* (New York: Vintage Books, 1995), 168.

2. I am grateful to Albert J. Raboteau for drawing my attention to this book.

3. Ralph Ginzburg, *100 Years of Lynchings* (Baltimore: Black Classic Press, 1962), 5.

4. Margaret Rose Vendryes, "Hanging on their Walls: An Art Commentary on Lynching. The Forgotten 1935 Art Exhibition," *Race Consciousness* (New York: New York University Press, 1997), 168.

5. Ibid., 172.

6. On the Holocaust and modern art see Ziva Amishai-Maisels, *Depiction and Interpretation: The Influence of the Holocaust on the Visual Arts* (Oxford: Pergamon, 1993).

7. Amei Wallach, "A Museum Show Digs for the Roots of a Relationship," *Newsday* (March 22, 1992): 12. I have problematized this issue in the introduction.

8. Jack Salzman with Adina Back and Gretchen Sullivan Sorin, eds., *Bridges and Boundaries: African Americans and American Jews* (New York: George Braziller in association with The Jewish Museum, 1992), 192.

9. Milly Heyd and Ezra Mendelsohn, "Jewish Identity and the Artistic Representation of the Other," unpublished article.

10. August L. Freundlich, *William Gropper: Retrospective* (Los Angeles: Ward Ritchie Press, 1968), 16.

11. Ibid., 28.

12. Albert P. Blaustein and Robert L. Zangrado, eds., *Civil Rights and the American Negro: A Documentary History* (New York: Trident Press, 1968), 346–347. See also James Goodman, *Stories of Scottsboro* (New York: Pantheon Books, 1994).

13. The original Yiddish poem and its translation into English were published in Benjamin and Barbara Harshav, *American Yiddish Poetry; A Bilingual Anthology* (Berkeley: University of California Press, 1986), 646–647.

14. Marlene Park, "Lynching and Antilynching: Art and Politics in the 1930s," *Prospects* 18 (1993): 311–365.

15. Patricia Likos, "Julius Bloch: Portrait of the Artist," *Bulletin of Philadelphia Museum of Art* 79 (summer 1983): 11. The quotation is from the artist's journals, no. 3 (March 10, 1933), n.p.

16. The painting is in the collection of the Philadelphia Museum of Art.

17. Letter from Langston Hughes to Julius Bloch (January 31, 1934). Reproduced in Patricia Likos, "Julius Bloch," 13.

18. Milton M. James, "The Negro Paintings of Julius Bloch," *Negro History Bulletin* 18 (December 1956): 51.

19. Alain Locke, *The Negro in Art* (1925; reprint, New York: Hacker Art Books, 1971), 140.

20. Malcolm Warner, *The Prints of Harry Sternberg* (San Diego: San Diego Museum of Art, 1994), 62. Sternberg's statement is ambiguous: did he unconsciously feel guilty about the blatant image? In woodcuts published in 1991 he used an opposite style for the lynch scene, as if he felt the need to compensate for his aggressiveness. Here the image centers around the discrepancy between content and form. A childlike, seemingly naive woodcut shows four little Klan children in the foreground with four black silhouettes hanging from a tree, under the title *Strange Fruit* (reproduced in Warner, 104). It seems that the artist could not make up his mind about the "right" tone for depicting lynch scenes.

21. Letter to Dr. Francis V. O'Connor, June 9, 1972, cited in Janet Flint, *The Prints of Louis Lozowick: A Catalogue Raisonné* (New York: Hudson Hills Press, 1982), 119. The quotation is based on the letter in the Lozowick papers, Archives of American Art, Lozowick Roll 1334. Park's citation in "Lynching and Antilynching," 344, is rather selective; it omits the reference to Nazism, thus missing a crucial connection.

22. Francis M. Naumann and Paul Avrich, "Adolf Wolff: 'Poet, Sculptor and Revolutionist, but Mostly Revolutionist,'" *Art Bulletin* 67 (1985): 486–500. The authors suggest that perhaps another sculpture was bought by the museum in Birobidjan, since it is mentioned in the artist's résumé. If this was indeed the case, it was probably part of the collection which included Chaim Gross's *Shulamit* (see chapter 2).

23. Adolf Wolff, *Songs of Rebellion, Songs of Life, Songs of Love* (New York: Albert and Charles Boni, 1914), n.p.

24. The statuette is reproduced in Matthew Baigell, "From Hester Street to Fifty-Seventh Street: Jewish-American Artists in New York," in Norman L. Kleeblatt and Susan Chevlowe, eds., *Painting a Place in America: Jewish Artists in New York 1900–1945* (New York: Jewish Museum, 1991), 59.

25. For the drawing, see the Archives of American Art, Goodelman Roll 4934.

26. The press reviews are part of Aaron Goodelman's file at the Jewish Museum, New York. I am grateful to Susan Chevlowe for her help.

27. J. L., "Sculpture in Wood: A First Showing by S. A. Lipton," *Art News* 37 (November 5, 1938): 17.

28. Roberta K. Tarbell, "Seymour Lipton's carvings: A New Anthropology for Sculpture," *Arts Magazine* 54 (October 1979): 80.

29. Marlene Park, "Lynching and Antilynching," 324.

30. Roberta Tarbell, "Seymour Lipton's Carvings," 79.

31. "Philip Guston: 'A Day's Work,' 1970," *Art Now* 2 (1970): n.p.

32. The picture was lost and only a photograph remained.

33. Dore Ashton, *Yes, but . . . : A Critical Study of Philip Guston* (New York: Viking Press, 1976), 27. The drawing for *Conspirators* can be seen on p. 8, the oil painting on p. 10, and the fresco panel on p. 28. Dore Ashton and later Robert Storr describe the raiding incident. The quotation is from Robert Storr, *Philip Guston* (New York: Abbeville Press, 1986), 13.

34. Ashton, *Yes, but . . .* , 8.

35. Musa Meyer, *Night Studio: A Memoir of Philip Guston by His Daughter* (New York: Alfred A. Knopf, 1988), 12.

36. Ibid., 22. The artworks of Philip Guston are not reproduced here, since copyright permission was not granted by "The Estate of Philip Guston." The artist's change of name and his need to hide it can be compared to Man Ray, another American Jew who left for Paris to live under a camouflaged identity. On this, see Milly Heyd, "Man Ray/Emmanuel Radnitsky: Who is Behind *The Enigma of Isidore Ducasse?*" *Israel Museum Journal* 11 (spring 1993): 31–46. For the broader context see Sander L. Gilman, *Jewish Self-Hatred: Anti-Semitism and the Hidden Language of the Jews* (Baltimore: Johns Hopkins University Press, 1986), especially the introduction, "What is Self-Hatred?," which includes a discussion of the name change of Eric Erikson (Homburger), 1–22. Philip Guston's identification with his father's occupation as a junk collector is sublimated in his late works, where piles of junk objects are depicted.

37. Philip Guston, in a letter of request for support written to Philip Evergood, signed Philip Guston (chairman) and Lloyd Goodrich (co-chairman), March 14, 1966. Archives of American Art, Evergood Roll 1345.

38. Quoted in Renée McKee, ed., "Philip Guston Talking," in *Philip Guston Paintings 1969–1980*; exhibition catalogue (London: Whitechapel Art Gallery, 1982), 52.

39. Irving Sandler, *Art of the Postmodern Era: From the Late 1960s to the Early 1990s* (New York: Icon Editions, 1996), 196.

40. Musa Meyer tells about family recollections of the pogroms in Odessa: "There were scary stories of crouching in the cellars, in fear for their lives, hiding from the violent attacks against Jews that raged through the city" (*Night Studio*, 10).

41. Maurice Berger, *How Art Becomes History* (New York: Icon Editions, 1992), 86.

42. I am grateful to Marta Aizenman for discussing this issue with me.

Notes to Chapter Four

1. Milton Brown, *Jack Levine* (New York: Rizzoli, 1989), 100.

2. Lerone Bennett Jr., *What Manner of Man: A Biography of Martin Luther King, Jr.* (Chicago: Johnson Publishing Company, 1968), 125.

3. Ibid., 162. About 250,000 people, some 60,000 of them White, came to the Lincoln Memorial.

4. I am indebted to Ezra Mendelsohn for drawing my attention to the theme of the taboo on interracial handshake.

5. Richard Wright, *Native Son* (1940; reprint, New York: Harper and Row, 1966), 66–67.

6. Ibid., 297.

7. *The Crisis* 73 (April 1966): 228.

8. John Oliver Killens, *Youngblood* (1954; reprint, Athens: University of Georgia Press, 1982), 119. The book was first published by Dial Press and was reissued by Trident Press in 1966.

9. Ibid., 151.

10. A discussion of this work can be found in Milly Heyd and Ezra Mendelsohn, "'Jewish' Art? The Case of the Soyer Brothers," *Jewish Art*, 19–20 (1993–94): 201. However, the article does not discuss the context of the image, namely the portfolio devoted to the murder of the three students in Mississippi and the archival material concerning Shahn's activities in the civil rights movement.

11. Jonathan Kaufman, *Broken Alliance* (New York: Charles Scribner's, 1988), 17.

12. Rabbi Arthur Gilbert, "Moral Dimensions in the Struggle for Racial Justice," *The Crisis* 71 (January 1964): 5–11. Gilbert also writes: "Blackness does have something to say to me. It has something to say about man's capacity to endure suffering, about the gaiety that can transform limitation in life into life affirmation. It has something to say to us about man's ability to repress anger and to convert it into righteous conviction" (9–10).

13. Archives of American Art, Ben Shahn Roll D 147.

14. Avram Kampf, *Jewish Experience in the Art of the Twentieth Century* (South Hadley, Mass.: Bergin and Garvey, 1984), 72. For an important analysis of the Hebrew tradition and other works by Ben Shahn, see 71–74.

15. For Ben Shahn's reflections on the mosaic and its imagery, see Archives of American Art, Ben Shahn Roll D 147.

16. Eric F. Goldman, moderator, "A Profile of Ben Shahn," transcript of an interview with Ben Shahn for *The Open Mind*, WNBC television (January 17, 1965), Archives of American Art, Ben Shahn Roll 3471, 33–34.

17. Gretchen Sullivan Sorin, in Jack Salzman with Adina Back and Gretchen Sullivan Sorin, eds., *Bridges and Boundaries: African Americans and American Jews* (New York: George Braziller, in association with the Jewish Museum, 1992), 224. See also Heyd and Mendelsohn, "'Jewish' Art?: The Case of the Soyer Brothers," 201.

18. Milly Heyd and Ezra Mendelsohn, "Jewish Identity and the Artistic Representation of the Other," unpublished article.

19. Kneeland McNulty, *The Collected Prints of Ben Shahn* (Philadelphia: Philadelphia Museum of Art, 1967), 104.

20. Stephen Spender, *Poems* (London: Faber and Faber, 1933), 45.

21. Letter from Clark Foreman, *Southern Conference for Human Welfare* (March 15, 1945), Archives of American Art, Ben Shahn Roll D 147.

22. The letter is signed "Jim" (October 4, 1945). Archives of American Art, Ben Shahn Roll D 147.

23. Letter from J. Joseph to Ben Shahn (January 3, 1952). Archives of American Art, Ben Shahn Roll D 143.

24. Ben Shahn's statement, Archives of American Art, Ben Shahn Roll D 143.

25. John Bartlow Martin, letter to Ben Shahn (December 15, 1949), Archives of American Art, Ben Shahn Roll D 146.

26. Shahn talked about the social aspect of these drawings in his interview with Eric Goldman.

27. Letter from Milton Meltzer to Ben Shahn (July 15, 1954), Archives of American Art, Ben Shahn Roll D 146. The book, *A Pictorial History of the Negro in America*, by Langston Hughes and Milton Meltzer, has become a classic. It was first published in 1956 and was reissued in a revised edition in 1963.

28. A letter from Carey McWilliams of *The Nation* (September 8, 1954) requests the artist's permission to reproduce the design. Archives of American Art, Ben Shahn Roll D 146.

29. Press release "A.I.G.A. A Medal to Ben Shahn" (March 1, 1957), Archives of American Art, Ben Shahn Roll D 143.

30. The letter to Ben Shahn was written by Henry Lee Moon, Director of NAACP Public Relations (March 28, 1955). On it Shahn noted, "Drawing already done." Archives of American Art, Ben Shahn Roll D 146. The NAACP badge is inscribed on the letter: "NAACP Fight For Freedom." The image shows the scales of justice and an open book.

31. SCEF press release (July 21, 1958), Archives of American Art, Ben Shahn Roll D 147.

32. Letter from Eleanor Roosevelt to Mr. and Mrs. Ben Shahn, (February 6, 1958). The Shahns were invited to a reception in honor of the SCEF activities. Archives of American Art, Ben Shahn Roll D 147.

33. Letter to Ben Shahn from Ralph G. Martin, the editor of *Bandwagon* (October 29, 1957), Archives of American Art, Ben Shahn Roll D 143.

34. Letter to Ben Shahn from Jack Barnett of the Treason Trial Defense Fund, Cape Town (February 16, 1959), Archives of American Art Ben Shahn Roll D 147.

35. Letter to Ben Shahn from Ann Morrissett, acting secretary of the South Africa Defense Fund (March 5, 1959), Archives of American Art, Ben Shahn Roll D 147.

36. Letter to Ben Shahn from Ann Morrissett, acting secretary of the South Africa Defense Fund (April 7, 1959), Archives of American Art, Ben Shahn Roll D 147.

37. Letter from Graphic Artists for SANE, addressed to "Dear Friend" and signed by Fran Elfenbein (December 5, 1962), Archives of American Art, Ben Shahn Roll D 145.

38. Letter to Ben Shahn from the chairman of the Department of Fine Arts, Hofstra College, Hempstead, New York (February 10, 1961), Archives of American Art, Ben Shahn Roll D 145.

39. Letter to Ben Shahn from Warren M. Robbins, Department of State, Foreign Service Institute, Washington, D.C. (December 14, 1962), Archives of American Art, Ben Shahn Roll D 147.

40. Letter to Ben Shahn, "Dear Friend of the SCEF," from SCEF president Edgar A. Love (January 8, 1963). Archives of American Art, Ben Shahn Roll D 147.

41. Martin H. Bush, *Ben Shahn: The Passion of Sacco and Vanzetti*, with an essay by Shahn (Syracuse: University of Syracuse Press, 1968), 69–70.

42. Author's interview with Cliff Joseph (January 12, 1997). All quotations are from this interview.

43. Cliff Joseph was a personal friend of the Goodman family and gave them the original drawing.

44. Cliff Joseph, "Art, Politics, and the Life Force," *Forward: Journal of Socialist Thought* 9 (spring–summer 1989), 47.

45. This image was brought to my knowledge by Ezra Mendelsohn and led me to further research into Lila Asher's work (as discussed in the introduction).

46. Author's interview with Renee Gross (February 2, 1997).

47. Letter from Hale Woodruff to Chaim Gross (February 7, 1942), Archives of American Art, Chaim Gross Roll 925.

48. A fuller, though not conclusive list of Jacob Lawrence's paintings includes *John Brown* series (1941), *Harlem* series (1942–43), and *War* series (1946–47).

49. Milton Brown, *Jacob Lawrence*, exhibition catalogue (New York: Whitney Museum of American Art, 1974), 11.

50. Ellen Harkins Wheat, *Jacob Lawrence: American Painter*, exhibition catalogue (Seattle Art Museum: University of Washington Press, 1986), 63.

51. Ibid., 74.

52. R. B., "Jacob Lawrence," *Art News* 63 (February 1965): 17.

53. Wheat, *Jacob Lawrence*, 108–109.

54. "The Black Artist in America," *The Metropolitan Museum of Art Bulletin* 27 (1969): 259.

55. Wheat, *Jacob Lawrence*, 109.

56. Matthew Baigell, *A Concise History of American Painting and Sculpture* (New York: Harper and Row, 1984), 359.

57. Phyllis Tuchman, *George Segal* (New York: Abbeville Press, 1983), 28.

58. For a more comprehensive description of the movement, see Lenwood G. Davis, *I Have a Dream: The Life and Times of Martin Luther King, Jr.* (Westport, Conn.: Negro Universities Press, 1969).

59. James Porter, *Ten Afro-American Artists of the Nineteenth Century* (Washington, D.C.: Howard University Gallery of Art, 1967), 11. See also David Driskell, *Two Centuries of Black American Art* (Los Angeles County Museum of Art, 1976), 123.

60. Author's interview with George Segal (April 6, 1997).

61. Henry A. Millon and Linda Nochlin, eds., *Art and Architecture in the Service of Politics* (Cambridge, Mass.: MIT Press, 1979), ix.

62. For "Lord I want to be a Christian," see John Wesley, *American Negro Songs and Spirituals* (New York: Bonanza Books, 1940), 76.

63. Russell Adams, "As the Twig Is Bent," *CommonQuest* 1 (spring 1996): 11.

64. Cf. Samella Lewis, *African American Art and Artists* (Berkeley: University of California Press, 1990), 165–166.

65. Kellie Jones, "The Structure of Myth and the Potency of Magic," in *David Hammons: Rousing the Rabble*, exhibition at the Institute for Contemporary Art, New York, curated by Tom Finkelpearl, December 1990–February 1991 (Cambridge, Mass.: MIT Press, 1991), 16–17.

66. On the American flag in African-American art, see Mary Schmidt Campbell, *Tradition and Conflict: Image of a Turbulent Decade, 1963–1973* (New York: The Studio Museum in Harlem, 1985), 54–55.

67. Jones, "The Structure of Myth," 16.

68. Author's interview with David Hammons (February 22, 1997). All quotations are from this interview.

69. Joanne Silver, "Benny Andrews' 'America' Has Human Touch," *Boston Herald* (November 4, 1994).

chapter Five

1. Larry Rivers with Arnold Weinstein, *What Did I Do? The Unauthorized Autobiography* (New York: HarperCollins, 1992), 306.

2. Charles Childs, "Larry Ocean Swims the Nile, Mississippi and Other Rivers," *Some American History* (Houston: Institute for the Arts, Rice University, 1971), 12.

3. John Wilmerding, *American Art* (Harmondsworth: Penguin Books, 1976), 218.

4. Robert Hughes, "Bronx is Beautiful," *Time* (February 8, 1971): 68.

5. David Shapiro, "Strawberry Cake with the Psyche of a Good Camera," *Art News* 69 (December 1970): 68.

6. Frank Bowling, "If You Can't Draw, Trace," *Arts Magazine* 45 (February 1971): 21.

7. Haya Friedberg, "Identity Problems in the Art of Larry Rivers: 1945–1964" (Hebrew), Ph.D. diss., Hebrew University, Jerusalem, 1997.

8. Larry Rivers with Arnold Weinstein, *What Did I Do?*, 434–443. Haya Friedberg studied Rivers's involvement in Africa as reflected in his various maps of the continent, in terms of the political events in the area. For an illuminating analysis see "Identity Problems," 214–222.

9. William J. Harris, *The Jazz Aesthetic: The Poetry and Poetics of Amiri Baraka* (Columbia: University of Missouri Press, 1985), 128.

10. *The Autobiography of LeRoi Jones Amiri Baraka* (New York: Freundlich Books, 1984), 155.

11. Ibid., 162.

12. Rivers, *What Did I Do?*, 431–432. My reading of the relationship between Jones and Rivers follows that of Haya Friedberg, "Identity Problems," 269–273. My emphasis, however, is on their autobiographies and Jones's plays.

13. *The Autobiography of LeRoi Jones*, 189. In 1962 Jones published a collection of aphorisms concerning the art scene. In one of them he parodies the mutual admiration of Larry Rivers and the poet Kenneth Koch. "'Larry Rivers is the finest painter in America.'—Kenneth Koch. 'Kenneth Koch is one of the finest poets in America.'—Larry Rivers." From "Voices from the Art World (Or, Bright Sayings)," *The Floating Bear* 26 (1962): 8–9.

14. Rivers, *What Did I Do?*, 432.

15. Amiri Baraka, *Selected Plays and Prose of Amiri Baraka/LeRoi Jones*, "The Slave" (New York: William Morrow, 1979), 118.

16. Werner Sollors, *Amiri Baraka/LeRoi Jones: The Quest for a "Populist Modernism"* (New York: Columbia University Press, 1978), 137. According to the playwright himself, the play aims at showing "the missionaries and wiggly liberals dying under blasts of concrete."

17. Amiri Baraka, *The Baptism and the Toilet* (New York: Grove Press, 1967), 62. For an interesting analysis of the play see Werner Sollors, "The Toilet," in *Amiri Baraka/LeRoi Jones: The Quest for a "Populist Modernism"*, 107–117.

18. Rivers, *What Did I Do?*, 432.

19. Ibid., 430, 432.

20. On this see Friedberg, "Identity Problems," 20.

21. Rivers, *What Did I do?*, 222.

22. Sam Hunter, *Larry Rivers: Supplement to the First Edition* (New York: Harry Abrams, 1971), 265.

23. Bowling, "If You Can't Draw, Trace," 20.

24. Frantz Fanon, *Black Skin, White Masks*, trans. from the French by Charles Lam Markmann (New York: Grove Press, 1967), 170 (originally published as *Peau noire, masques blancs*, Paris, Editions du Seuil, 1952).

25. Ibid., 159.

26. Press release, *Rice University News* (January 1971): 1.

27. Ralph Ellison, *Invisible Man* (1947; reprint, New York: Random House, 1980), 3.

28. Dale McConathy, "Paint it Black," *Vogue* (April 15, 1971): 127.

29. Anon., "A White Look at the Black Experience," *Coronet* (May 1971): 119.

30. Ibid., 122.

31. Walter Jones, "Critique to Black Artists," *Arts Magazine* 44 (April 1970): 20.

32. Bowling, "Some Notes Toward an Exhibition of African-American Abstract Art," in *The Search for Freedom* (New York: Kenkeleba Gallery, May 19–July 14, 1991), 127.

33. Walter Jones, "Critique to Black Artists," 18.

34. Bowling, "Some Notes Toward an Exhibition of African-American Abstract Art," 127.

35. Childs, *Some American History*, 9.

36. Ibid., 10.

37. "The Negro Speaks Of Rivers," in Arnold Rampersad, ed., *The Collected Poems of Langston Hughes* (New York: Vintage Books, 1995), 23.

38. Childs, *Some American History*, 10.

39. Ibid., 13.

40. Ibid., 14. Another review that connected Rivers's participation in *Some American History* to his Jewishness was that of Louis Chapin, "By Channels of Coolness," *Christian Science Monitor* (March 26, 1971): 8. "It was therefore with some courage and uninhibited insight that Larry Rivers, an artist of Jewish background, has undertaken such a project."

41. Eleanor Freed, "Larry Rivers and the Black Experience," *Houston Post* (February 14, 1971): 14.

42. For an interesting analysis of Amiri Baraka's *The Slave Ship*, see Kimberly W. Benston, "Vision and Form in *Slave Ship*," *Imamu Amiri Baraka (LeRoi Jones)* (Englewood Cliffs, N. J.: Prentice Hall, 1978), 174–185.

43. For diagrams of slave ships, see Langston Hughes and Milton Meltzer, *A Pictorial History of the Negro in America* (New York: Crown Publishing, 1963), 11. For a more detailed description of conditions on the slave ships see W.E.B. Du Bois, *The Souls of Black Folk*, ed. David W. Blight and Robert Gooding-Williams (1903; reprint, Boston: Bedford Books, 1997), 247–48.

44. Chapin, "By Channels of Coolness," 8.

45. Benjamin Quarles, *The Negro in the Making of America* (New York: Macmillan, 1969), 22.

46. Childs, *Some American History*, 19.

47. Shirley Woodson, "The Middle Passage: Matrix and Memory; The Art of Richard Hunt," in *Walter O. Evans Collection of African American Art* (Savannah: Beach Institute King-Tisdell Museum, 1991), 32–33. For an illustration, see p. 77.

48. Richard Wright, *Native Son* (1940; reprint, New York: Harper and Row, 1966), xxi. The quotation is from the author's introduction, "How 'Bigger' Was Born."

49. Ibid.

50. Ralph Ginzburg, *100 Years of Lynchings* (Baltimore: Black Classic Press, 1962).

51. Childs, *Some American History*, 21.

52. Ibid., 17.

53. Richard J. Powell, *Black Art and Culture in the 20th Century* (Thames and Hudson: New York, 1997), 146.

54. Hughes, "Bronx Is Beautiful," 68.

55. James Thrall Soby, *Ben Shahn: His Graphic Work* (New York: George Braziller, 1957), 16.

56. Barbara J. Bloemink, *The Life and Art of Florine Stettheimer* (New Haven: Yale University Press, 1995), 192. According to Bloemink (7), Florine Stettheimer's reaction to *Nigger Heaven* was that it was "honest and courageous but I fear it will do them no good."

57. Ibid., 193.

58. Hammons's installation was featured in the exhibition *The Blues Aesthetic: Black Culture and Modernism* (Washington, D.C.: December 1, 1989); *The New York Times* reported the act of vandalism on January 12, 1989, 14.

59. Darrell Moore, "The X Factor," *New Art Examiner* 20 (April 1993): 19.

60. Kellie Jones, "Malcolm X: Man, Ideal, Icon," in *Malcolm X: Man, Ideal, Icon* (Walker Art Center: December 1992–April 1993), n.p.

61. Moore, "The X Factor," 20. Emphasis added.

62. Sam Hunter, *Alex Katz* (New York: Rizzoli, 1992), 14. On Alex Katz and portraiture in the second half of the twentieth century see Robert Rosenblum, "Alex Katz's American Accent," in Richard Marshall, *Alex Katz* (New York: Whitney Museum of American Art, Rizzoli, 1986), 25–33.

63. Author's interview with the artist, January 8, 1997. For examples of Philip Pearlstein's multiracial nude portrayals see Russell Bowman, *Philip Pearlstein: The Complete Paintings* (New York, London: Alpine Fine Arts Collection, 1983), 134, figure 56, *Standing Male, Sitting Female Nude* (1969), *Two Female Models with Drawing Table* (1973).

64. Author's interview with the artist.

Notes to chapter six

1. Ziva Amishai-Maisels writes about Borofsky's dream imagery relating to the Holocaust. She also elaborates on Borofsky's constant use of numbering, both as a means of escaping from compulsive thoughts and as alluding to the tattooed numbers on the arms of concentration camp inmates. See her *Depiction and Interpretation: The Influence of the Holocaust on the Visual Arts* (Oxford: Pergamon Press, 1993), 330–335.

2. Author's interview with Jonathan Borofsky (December 12, 1996). All quotations are from this interview, unless otherwise indicated. See also the exhibition catalogue: Mark Rosenthal and Richard Marshall, *Jonathan Borofsky* (Philadelphia: Philadelphia Museum of Art with the Whitney Museum, 1984).

3. Carl G. Jung, M. L. von Franz, Joseph L. Henderson, Jolande Jacobi, Aniela Jaffé, *Man and his Symbols* (London: Aldus Books, 1964). According to Jonathan Borofsky, his analysis in 1970 was threefold: in a group, individually, and with a partner. It lasted a year and a half: "You were encouraged to get in touch with your anger. . . . I took the direct experience to the studio."

4. C. G. Jung, *Dictionary of Analytic Psychology* (London and New York: Ark Paperbacks, 1987), 96–97. (The text is excerpted from *Psychological Types*, vol. 6 of the Collected Works of C.G. Jung.)

5. On this, see M. L. von Franz, "The Process of Individuation," in *Man and His Symbols*. Franz writes: "The maze of strange passages, chambers, and unlocked exits recalls the old Egyptian representation of the underworld, which is a well-known symbol of the unconscious with its unknown possibilities." For instance, she interprets Giorgio de Chirico's railway image in *The Anxious Journey* as the encounter with the unconscious, 170–171.

6. For comparison, see for instance Spike Lee's movie *Getting on the Bus*, where an African American recounts his acts at the age of thirteen and asks: "Do you know what Jewish children are doing at that age?"

7. For an elaboration of the theme of the "tragic mulatto," see Arthur P. Davis, "The Tragic Mulatto Themes in Six Works of Langston Hughes," *Phylon* 16 (1955): 195–204.

8. Arnold Rampersad, *The Life of Langston Hughes*, vol. 1 (New York: Oxford University Press, 1986), 4–5, 75, 104, 191–192, 282, 314–315.

9. Henry Louis Gates Jr., *Figures in Black: Words, Signs, and the "Racial" Self* (New York: Oxford University Press, 1987), 148.

10. Author's interview with the artist.

11. Frantz Fanon, *Black Skin, White Masks*, trans. from the French by Charles Lam Markmann (New York: Grove Press, 1967), 101–107. Originally published as *Peau noire, masques blancs* (Paris: Editions du Seuil, 1952). Fanon's writings include *The Wretched of the Earth* and *Toward the African Revolution*. Fanon is also discussed in Chapter 5 in the context of Larry Rivers.

12. Fanon, *Black Skin, White Masks*, 188–189.

13. Robbin Legere Henderson and Geno Rodriguez, *Prisoners of Image: Ethnic and Gender Stereotypes* (New York: Alternative Museum, 1989).

14. Ibid., 6.

15. Ibid., 7.

16. Andrea Kirsh, *Carrie Mae Weems* (Washington, D.C.: National Museum of Women in the Arts, 1993), 13.

17. Joan Simon, "An Interview with Jonathan Borofsky," *Art in America* 69 (November 1981): 164.

18. Ibid.

19. Ibid.

20. Ibid. Emphasis added.

21. Author' interview with the artist.

22. Ibid. Borofsky is also engaged in artistic activities in places other than museums and galleries. One such case is his mural in a men's shelter (New York 1977). He was interested in the prison not only as an image in a dream, but also as actual prison in real life. In 1985–86 he traveled together with Garry Glassman to various American prisons. Their film, *The Prisoners* (1987), consists of interviews with inmates of San Quentin State Prison, many of whom were Blacks. The film opens with Borofsky's thoughts about his project: "Why am I doing this? Why am I talking to prisoners? Well, we are all learning to be free but these are people who make our lives less free. They make us lock our doors and put bars on our windows. . . . But, I know that these people are human beings not very different from myself and I feel for them. . . . They couldn't have been born like this. Something has happened in their lives, in their minds."

23. Wolfgang Max Faust, "Shattered Orthodoxy: The Energy of Transformation," in Christos M. Joachimides and Norman Rosenthal, eds., *American Art in the 20th Century* (London: Royal Academy of Art, 1993), 139.

24. Ibid., 141.

25. Francis Henry Taylor, *Artists for Victory* (New York: Metropolitan Museum of Art, 1942), n.p. There were six parallel prizes, for both sculpture and painting. Barthé's sculpture received sixth prize for sculpture, and Jacob Lawrence's *Pool Parlor*, a watercolor, received sixth prize for painting.

26. Holland Cotter, "Benny Andrews at the Studio Museum in Harlem," *Art in America* 77 (September 1989): 211–212.

27. Elsa Honig Fine, *The Afro-American Artist* (New York: Holt, Rinehart and Winston, 1973), 253. This sense of being misunderstood as a Black artist carries on into the 1970s. In commenting on the exhibition *Afro-American Artists: Boston and New York*, curated by Barry Gaither and Barney Rubinstein (1970), Benny Andrews questioned Hilton Kramer's lack of understanding of African American art, the latter having claimed (from a modernist formal position) that it cannot be understood in aesthetic terms but only in political ones. Andrews asks: "One can immediately ask why in the hell is it so damn confusing to see the Black artist expressing his feeling about his people, his environment and life as something unfathomable, if artists like Goya, Picasso. . . . Dürer, Grosz, Ben Shahn, etc. can be dealt with critically." Benny Andrews, "On Understanding Black Art," *New York Times* (June 21, 1970): D21.

28. Ibid., 22.

29. See also Samella Lewis, *African American Art and Artists* (Berkeley: University of California Press, 1990), 149, which contains a reproduction of the painting.

30. Ralph Rugoff, "David Hammons: Public Nuisance, Rabble Rouser, Hometown Artist," in *David Hammons in the Hood* (Chicago: Illinois State Museum, 1993), 19.

31. Rene Ricard, "World Crown: Bodhisattva with Clenched Mudra," in Richard Marshall, ed., *Jean-Michel Basquiat* (New York: Whitney Museum of American Art, 1992–93), 48–49.

32. See for instance Spinello Aretino's *Flagellation of Christ* in the Metropolitan Museum (no. 13.175), a fifteenth-century work of the Florentine school.

33. Chris Mead, *Champion: Joe Louis Black Hero in White America*, (New York: Charles Scribner's Sons, 1985), 40–41.

34. Ibid., 40.

35. Ibid., 42.

36. Ibid., 40.

37. Dick Hebdige, "Welcome to the Terrordome: Jean-Michel Basquiat and the 'Dark' Side of Hybridity," in Marshall, *Jean-Michel Basquiat*, 65.

38. Art Spiegelman, *Maus: A Survivor's Tale*, part 2 (New York: Pantheon Books, 1991), 258–259. I am grateful to Zvi Jagendorf for drawing my attention to the hitchhiker scene.

39. Alan Rosen, "English as a Metaphor in Spiegelman's *Maus*," *Prooftexts* (September 15, 1995): 259–260.

40. Abigail Solomon-Godeau, *Mistaken Identities* (University of California, Santa Barbara: University of Art Museum, 1992), 28–29.

41. Michele Wallace, "Modernism, Postmodernism and the Problem of the Visual in Afro-American Culture," in Russell Ferguson et al., eds., *Out There: Marginalization and Contemporary Cultures* (New York: New Museum of Contemporary Art; Cambridge, Mass.: MIT Press, 1990), 40.

42. David C. Driskell, ed. "The Progenitors of a Postmodernist Review of African American Art," in *African American Visual Aesthetics: A Postmodernist View* (Washington D.C.: Smithsonian Institution Press, 1995), 2.

43. Adrian Piper, *Out of Order, Out of Sight*, Volume 1: *Selected Writings in Meta-Art 1968–1992* (Cambridge, Mass.: MIT Press, 1995), 220.

44. Lowery Stokes Sims, "The Mirror the Other: The Politics of Esthetics," *Art Forum* 28 (March 1990): 113.

45. Quoted in Caryl Phillips, *The European Tribe* (New York: Farrar, Straus and Giroux, 1987), 54.

46. Adrian Piper, *Out of Order*, vol. I, 281.

47. Author's interview with Barbara Kruger (November 16, 1996). All quotations are from this interview unless otherwise indicated.

48. For an elaboration of the origins of black "namism," see H. L. Mencken, "Designations for Colored Folk," in *Mother Wit From the Laughing Barrel*, ed. Alan Dundes (New York: Garland, 1981), 142–156.

49. Ken Johnson, "Theater of Dissent," *Art in America* 79 (March 1991): 129.

50. Saul Bellow, *Herzog* (New York: Viking Press, 1964), 176.

51. Craig Owens, "The Medusa Effect or, The Spectacular Ruse," in *We Won't Play Nature to Your Culture: Works by Barbara Kruger* (London: Institute of Contemporary Arts, 1983), 6.

52. Johnson, "Theater of Dissent," 131.

53. Ibid. Yet another perspective was added when Kruger's variation of the American flag was incorporated incidentally as part of the decor in a CBS television show, *The Trials of Rosie O'Neal*. As the Jewish, liberal, skullcap-wearing boss looks at the questions on the wall ("Who is beyond the law? Who is bought and sold? . . ."), he says: "One could spend an entire lifetime doing nothing but investigating those questions." David Deitcher, "Barbara Kruger: Resisting Arrest," *Artforum* 29 (February 1991): 86.

54. Grant Kester, "Rhetorical Questions: The Alternative Arts Sector and the Imaginary Public," *Afterimage* 20 (January 1993): 14.

55. Sander L. Gilman, *Difference and Pathology: Stereotypes of Sexuality, Race and Madness* (Ithaca, N.Y.: Cornell University Press), 1985.

56. Ibid., 18.

57. Ibid., 20.

58. Ibid., 21.

59. Ibid., 26.

60. Ibid., 27.

61. Ibid., 239.

62. Barbara Kruger, "Issues and Commentary," *Art in America* 80 (October 1992): 40.

63. Maurice Berger, *How Art Becomes History* (New York: IconEditions, 1992), 83.

64. Kenneth W. Prescott, *The Complete Graphic Works of Ben Shahn* (New York: Quadrangle, 1973), 125.

65. Selden Rodman, *Ben Shahn: Portrait of the Artist as an American* (New York: Harper and Brothers, 1951), 64.

66. *The Anti-Aesthetic: Essays on Postmodern Culture*, edited with an introduction by Hal Foster (Seattle, Wash.: Bay Press, 1983), xv.

67. J. E. Spingarn, "The Editor, January 5th," *The Crisis* 13 (February 1917): 1.

68. Barbara Kruger and Phil Mariani, eds., *Remaking History* (Seattle: Bay Press, 1989).

69. Cornel West, "Black Culture and Postmodernism," ibid., 87–97.

70. Michele Wallace, "Reading 1968 and the Great American Whitewash," ibid., 97–109.

71. Homi K. Bhabha, "Remembering Fanon: Self, Psyche, and the Colonial Condition," ibid., 131–151.

72. See n. 11.

73. Gilane Tawadros, *Mirage Enigmas of Race, Difference and Desire* (London: Institute of Contemporary Arts, 1995), 11.

74. Bhabha, "Remembering Fanon," in Kruger and Mariani, *Remaking History*, 132.

75. Ibid., 135.

76. Ibid., 137.

77. Ibid.

78. Fanon, *Black Skin, White Masks*, 93, 122.

79. Ibid., 165–166.

80. Ibid., 181–182. Original emphasis.

81. Barbara Kruger, *Remote Control: Power, Cultures and the World of Appearances* (Cambridge, Mass.: MIT Press, 1993).

82. Ibid., 117–120.

83. Ibid., 136.

Notes to Chapter Seven

1. On this complex issue see Gary E. Rubin, "African Americans and Israel," in Jack Salzman and Cornel West, eds., *Struggles in The Promised Land* (New York: Oxford University Press, 1997), 357–371.

2. Howardena Pindell, *Paintings and Drawings: A Retrospective Exhibition 1972–1992* (New York: University of New York, 1992), 69.

3. Milly Heyd and Ezra Mendelsohn, "'Jewish' Art? The Case of the Soyer Brothers," *Jewish Art* 19–20 (1993–94): 200.

4. The editorial is in the *New Yorker* (February 15, 1993): 6. I am indebted to Ezra Mendelsohn for drawing my attention to this magazine cover.

5. Patricia J. Williams, "On Imagining Foes, Imagining Friendship," in Salzman and West, *Struggles in the Promised Land*, 373. Williams also questions whether the "horrible debacle" of the two communities in Crown Heights—Hasidic Jews and immigrants from the West Indies and the Caribbean—is "really about 'Black–Jewish relations,'" pointing out that both groups are far from representing the mainstream of the Jewish-American and African-American communities, respectively (372).

6. Ibid., 374.

7. Ibid., 375.

8. Morris A. Fred, *Bridges and Boundaries: Chicago Crossing* (Chicago: Spertus Museum, 1994),

with curatorial essays by the African American and Jewish American artists Othello Anderson and Claire Wolf Krantz. The atrocities of World War II inspired Anderson's wall installation; it focused on a time when "American Jews and American blacks . . . have worked so diligently together to eradicate the obstacles of race in our society" (11). Krantz's installation *The Book of Life* (1994) raises questions that are inscribed on the wall: "Who Makes Whom 'The Other'?" and "Is the Question Black and White?" (19). Kerry James Marshall, in *Reinterpretation*, superimposed African-American history with Jewish symbolism by the fusion of the Star of David with the symbol of a Black street gang in Chicago. In the Chicago *Bridges and Boundaries* he writes: "The work for this exhibition grows out of the search for some signs that mark the place where African American and Jewish American worlds intersect" (21).

9. Ibid., 13.

index

A.C.A. Gallery, 8, 69, 70, 106, 107, 138
Africa, 13, 62, 64, 69, 152–154, 155, 163–164,
    165–166
African art, 10, 18, 31, 32, 33, 44, 50, 52, 53,
    54, 55, 64, 152
African Methodist Episcopal Church, 18, 22, 23
aggression, 88, 113, 156, 179–180, 183, 199, 217
Alabama, 91, 101, 117, 119
alliance, 4, 9, 64, 88, 122, 132, 209
Alston, Charles
    Walking, 140, 142
ambivalence, 4, 5, 25, 150, 156, 157, 171, 177,
    182, 202–203, 206
America, 29–30, 119
American flag, 144–147
An Art Commentary on Lynching, 99, 100
Andrews, Benny, 79, 83, 147–150, 207, 209, 210
    Portrait of Raphael Soyer, 79, 82
    The Seder, 147–148
    The Student, 147, 149
    Champion, 187, 191–192
anti-Semitism, 3, 4, 5, 19, 28, 44, 53, 87, 89,
    112, 196, 197, 206, 207, 209
art
    and distancing positions (detachment),
    150, 152, 161, 171, 174, chap. 6 *passim*
    and questions, 16, 114–115, 116, 139,
    142–143, 144, 150, 159, 164, 170, 177, 180,
    183, 199, 209, 212
    and discomfort (uneasiness), 185,
    195–196, 213, 216
Asher, Lila Oliver, 13–15, 134–135
    Expulsion of Hagar, 13–14
    Homage to Ben Shahn, 135
autobiography, 154–155, 156, 157, 165–167,
    177–186, 197, 212

Baldwin, James, 5, 6, 133
Baltimore Afro-American, 28, 88, 89, 92, 115

bar-mitzvah, 164, 180
Baron, Herman, 8, 69, 70, 138
Barthé, Richmond, 8, 9, 73, 87, 187
    The Boxer, 187, 190
Basquiat, Jean-Michel, 177, 186–187, 192–193,
    196–197, 207, 208, 209, 210
    St. Joe Louis Surrounded by Snakes, 186,
    188, 192–193, 209
    Jack Johnson, 186, 189
Bearden, Romare, 13, 23, 41, 44, 89, 91, 92,
    138, 139, 208, 210
    Sermons: The Walls of Jericho, 44, 47
    Eighth Avenue Market, 46–47
    The Ghost Walks, 91, 93
    The Real Judge at Scottsboro, 92, 99
Bezalel Art School, 23, 32, 44, 64
Bible (see also Hebrew Scriptures), 5, 6, 24, 32,
    41, 51–53, 55, 61, 64–65, 73, 75, 120,
    122–124, 141–142, 144, 150, 169, 197, 200,
    211, 213
biblical narrative, 18, 22
biblical themes, 28, 208
Biggers, John, 9–13, 209, 210
    Crossing the Bridge, 10–11
    Middle Passage, 10, 12
Birobidzhan, 64
birth and rebirth, 23, 33, 38, 41, 209
Black athletes, 185, 186–193
Black beauty, 55, 62, 64, 69–70, 84, 100, 163,
    165, 169
Black Power, 5, 150, 173
Black press, 16, 88, 89, 90, 91, 93, 97, 209
Bloch, Julius, 99, 100, 210
    The Lynching, 100, 102
    Horace Pippin, 100, 103
Bloch, Lucienne, 66–67, 71, 175, 216
    The Playground, 66–67
Borofsky, Jonathan, 177–186, 193, 207, 212,
    213

Dream # I, 178–179
  *I dreamed I was walking down the stairs into
    the subway*, 180–183
  *I dreamed that blacks were marching for
    freedom*, 184
  Riot Police in Capetown, 186
Bowling, Frank, 161, 163, 165–167
  Middle Passage, 165–167
Bridges and Boundaries (Jewish Museum, New
  York), 4, 15, 93, 100, 124, 140, 217

Canaanite Movement, 32, 41
Catlett, Elizabeth, 8, 13, 69, 173
Chaney, James, 121, 123, 125, 128, 133–134,
  209
childhood, 13–14, 50, 53–54, 66, 70, 71, 72, 73,
  74, 75, 79, 80–81, 84–85, 156, 184
Christian imagery, 5, 6, 11, 19, 22, 28, 31, 41,
  48, 52, 54, 70–71, 87, 88–89, 99, 100, 101,
  106, 111, 139, 142–144, 147, 192–193, 208,
  209
civil rights movement, 4, 16, 44, 112, chap. 4
  passim, 155, 211
color reversal, 169–173
color-consciousness, 174, 178–186, 216
CommonQuest, 1, 2, 17
Cook, Timothy, 1
  Untitled, 1–2
CORE (Congress for Racial Equality), 112,
  132–133
Cuney, Waring, 55, 62

Danziger, Dan
  Nimrod, 41, 43
Depression era, 47, 73, 101
Der Hammer, 55, 62–63
Der Tog, 89, 91, 92
discrimination, 70, 86, 93, 118, 119, 211
disillusionment, 14, 47, 50, 154, 182, 210
Douglas, Aaron, 8, 17, 32, 41, 55, 131, 208,
  209, 210
  Untitled, 32, 35
  Invincible Music: The Spirit of Africa, 33, 36
  Into Bondage, 38, 39
Douglass, Frederick, 125, 127, 173
dreams, 15, 30, 38, 66, 67, 70, 71, 84, 86, 107,
  119, 145, 177–185, 193, 212, 213
Du Bois, W.E.B., 3, 4, 6, 7, 31, 161, 165

Eakins, Thomas, 18
Educational Alliance, 53, 55, 73

Egypt, 5, 24, 29, 38, 41
Ellison, Ralph, 161
empathy, 4, 5, 20, 22, 79, 117, 155
"engaged" and "engaged/disengaged" artists, 16,
  135, 176, 183, 202
Epstein, Jacob, 18, 50–54, 64, 73–74, 125, 210
  Cursed Be the Day Wherein I Was Born,
    50–53
  Head of Paul Robeson, 73–74, 78
equality, 48, 50, 64, 67, 73, 122, 123, 133, 134,
  143, 147, 202, 210
Ethiopia, 32, 38, 41, 73, 154
Evergood, Philip, 53, 67–71, 99, 138, 152, 210
  Dream Catch, 67–68, 70
Exodus, 5, 6, 41, 44, 147, 197

Fanon, Frantz, 86, 159–161, 183, 197, 204–206
fragmentation, 44, 101, 115, 159, 200
freedom, 1, 5, 38, 48, 55, 64, 70, 87, 106, 117,
  125, 133, 134, 135, 136, 143, 147, 183, 185,
  186
Freedom Fighters (button), 119
Fuller, Meta Warrick,
  Ethiopia Awakening, 38, 41, 42

Garvey, Marcus, 3, 161
Gellert, Hugo, 91–92, 99, 210
  Spike lynch terror! Save the Scottsboro Boys,
    91–92, 96
ghetto, 29, 30
Goodelman, Aaron, 99, 106–107, 210
  Necklace, 106, 109
Goodman, Andrew, 121, 123, 125, 133, 209
Gottlieb, Harry, 64
  I am Black But Comely, 64–65
Goya, Francisco, 88, 91
Graffiti, 185, 186, 196–197, 199, 201
Gropper, William, 69, 91, 110, 132, 138, 210
  Political Cartoon, 91, 94
  Southern Landscape, 91, 95
  Lynch, 91, 95
Gross, Chaim, 53–66, 73, 135–136, 152, 210, 211
  Mother Carrying Child, 54, 56–57
  Jazz, 54–55, 58
  Walking Negress, 55, 59
  Pregnant Negress, 55, 64, 60
  Shulamit, 55, 61
  Martin Luther King, 136–137
  Namibia, 136, 138
Guston, Philip, 15, 99, 110–113, 116, 154, 185,
  186, 212

Halpert, Edith, 8, 69, 138
Hammons, David, 144–147, 172–173, 192, 208, 209, 210
  Rabbi, 145–146
Hampton Institute (College) 9, 13
hands, symbolism of, 118–125, 133–135
Harlem, 3, 29, 30, 32, 69, 133, 135, 136, 163
Harlem Renaissance, 15, 18, 29, 31, 32, 33, 38, 47, 54, 55, 172, 208
Harlem, Studio Museum of, 135
Harmon Foundation, 7
Harris
  Christmas in Georgia, A.D., 88–89
Hebrew Renaissance, 31, 32
Hebrew Scriptures, 5, 6, 18, 22, 23, 24, 25, 28, 32, 41, 50, 52, 53, 55, 64, 73, 122–123, 124, 141–142, 144, 150, 169, 197, 200, 208, 210, 211, 213
Herzl, Theodor, 29, 32
Hirshhorn, Joseph, 69
Holocaust, 4, 10, 53, 54, 87, 114, 115, 116, 136, 155, 193, 195, 196, 207, 209
Holy Land, 19, 20, 208
homosexuality, 152, 155, 156, 157
Howard University, 1, 13, 15, 30, 100, 133, 134
Hughes, Langston, 6, 29, 55, 69, 86, 100, 119, 131, 133, 164, 182

identification, 5, 17, 22, 31, 41, 47, 70, 81, 91, 112, 116, 150, 152, 154, 164, 165, 166, 173, 182, 183, 185, 186, 187, 193, 198, 206, 207, 208, 209, 210, 212
identity, 1, 6, 16, 19, 22, 25, 28, 29, 32, 47, 48, 50, 53, 112, 113, 116, 133, 156, 163, 164, 180, 198, 200, 207, 208
irony, 88, 92, 106, 107, 115, 118, 144, 145, 147, 150, 152, 154, 156, 157, 159, 161, 168, 169, 173, 176, 182, 185, 186, 192, 193, 195, 196, 197, 203, 209
Israel (State of), 5, 29, 41,

Jacobs, Mike, 193
Jazz, 54–55, 151, 152, 154, 157, 163
Jerusalem, 22, 23, 32
Jewish art, 17, 44, 64
Jewish Negro, 23
Jewish nose, 2, 28, 31, 32, 192, 193, 196
Jewish symbols
  Star of David, 143, 144, 186
  Tablets of the Law, 4, 22, 196
John Reed Club, 3, 64, 99, 101, 106, 111

Johnson, Cornelius
  Prejudice, 88, 90
Johnson, Howard William, 41, 44, 138, 209, 210
Johnson, La Rue Daniel, 80, 161
  Over Here, Over There, 80–81, 84–85
Jones, LeRoi (Amiri Baraka), 71, 154–159, 165
  The Slave, 156, 157
  The Toilet, 156, 157
  The Slave Ship, 165
Joseph, Cliff, 133–134, 142, 144, 147, 176, 208, 209, 210
  Hands of Freedom, 133–134
  Heirs to the Kiss of Judas, 142–144, 147, 209
  My Country Right or Wrong, 144–145
Judas, 28, 101, 142–144, 147, 192, 193, 209

Katz, Alex, 174–175, 216
  Vincent and Tony, 174–175, 216
King, Martin Luther, 119, 125, 131, 133, 136, 142, 173
Kruger, Barbara, 198–201, 212
  All Violence Is the Illustration of a Pathetic Stereotype, 177, 198–207, 212
  Untitled (Speak for Yourself), 202–204
  Remaking History, 203–206
  Remote Control, 206–207
Ku Klux Klan, 88, 89, 91, 93, 106, 107, 111, 112, 113, 116, 147, 185, 186, 209, 212

Lawrence, Jacob, 7, 8, 69, 79, 133, 136–139, 147, 208, 210
  Praying Ministers, 139–140, 147
left wing ideologies, 4, 5, 16, 17, 44, 47, 49–50, 55, 56, 64, 69, 73, 91–92, 99, 106, 107, 111, 144, 172, 175, 176
Levine, Jack, 69, 73, 117–118, 136, 138, 139, 147, 187, 211
  Birmingham '63, 117–118
liberation, 2, 6, 38, 47, 48, 50
Lilien, E. M., 32, 33, 34
  Joshua, 32, 34
  The Jewish May, 33, 38
Lipton, Seymour, 99, 106, 107, 211
  Lynched, 106, 110
Locke, Alain, 7, 18, 22, 29, 31, 33, 38, 47, 50, 62, 100
Louis, Joe, 192–193, 209
Löwenfeld, Viktor, 9, 10, 11, 13, 209
Lower East Side (New York), 52, 53, 101, 147
Lozowick, Louis, 99, 101, 122, 210
  Lynching (Lynch Law), 101, 104

lynching, chap.3, *passim*, 117, 131, 161, 165, 168, 209, 210

Malcolm X, 161, 173
martyrdom, 88, 125, 187, 209
Meyer-Bernstein, Gerda
    Phoenix, 217
Middle Passage (slave ship), 10, 165–167
minister (church), 13, 125, 139, 144, 147, 209
minorities (marginalization), 4, 5, 13, 16, 17, 31, 44, 47, 53, 178–180, 198, 202, 203, 206, 207, 211, 212
minstrel show, 170–171, 212–213
mirroring, 6, 15, 47, 48, 49, 50, 79, 171, 180, 197, 208, 217
Mississippi Freedom Summer, 118, 121, 123, 124, 125, 133, 155, 209
modernism, 16, 33, 52, 110
mother and child, 33, 53, 54, 55, 71, 73, 79, 80–81, 84, 119
mulatto, 23, 180–182

NAACP (National Association for the Advancement of Colored People), 4, 7, 15, 88, 99, 118, 122, 124, 131, 203
Nazism, 9, 10, 87, 93, 101, 164, 193, 194, 209
New Jew, 15, 31, 32, 33, 64
New Negro, 15, 31, 32, 33
New Testament, 6, 23, 25, 28, 100, 111, 116, 142–149, 209

Opportunity, 29, 32, 38, 62, 88
oppression, 4, 9, 22, 41, 49, 50, 66, 87, 88, 107, 125, 156, 164, 183, 186, 200, 204, 209, 210
"other" (the), 1, 2, 3, 15, 16, 18, 28, 101, 115, 116, 152, 157, 170, 174, 180, 193, 196, 198, 201, 206, 207, 212

Palestine, 23, 24, 29, 30, 31, 32, 41, 64, 209
Palestinians, 210
Pann, Abel, 23
    The Sacrifice of Isaac, 24, 25
    The Creation, 33, 37
Parks, Rosa, 140
particularism, 6, 16, 30, 33, 73, 211, 216
patronage (in art), 6, 7, 203
patronizing, 5, 53, 124, 163, 203
Pearlstein, Philip, 174, 212–213, 217
    Model with Minstrel Marionettes, 212–214
pejorative language, 194–196, 198–200, 201
Pennell, Joseph, 19

Pennsylvania Academy of Fine Arts, 7, 18, 19
persecution, 5, 9, 10, 22, 29, 41, 50, 86, 91, 93, 209, 211
Peshka, 89, 91, 92, 210
    Black on White (May 1936), 89, 92
    Black on White (July 1937), 92–93, 98
Pindell, Howardena, 166, 167, 172, 210
    Autobiography: Air/CS560, 210–211
Piper, Adrian, 177, 197, 198, 207, 208, 209, 210
prejudice, 64, 70, 88, 172, 179, 183, 184, 193, 194, 196, 207, 212, 216
projection, 86, 115, 179–180, 201, 205, 206, 207

Queen of Sheba, 38, 41

race and racial, 2, 4, 16, 17, 18, 22, 29, 30, 31, 44, 66, 67, 70, 71, 73, 80, 84, 86, 87, 91, 93, 100, 115, 121, 123, 131, 140, 155, 156, 157, 159, 169, 170, 172, 174, 175, 212
racism, 3, 5, 19, 70, 89, 170, 171, 173, 196, 200, 206, 207, 211
religion, 2, 5, 6, 19, 22, 23, 47, 48, 52, 70, 87, 88, 99, 100, 139, 143, 144, 147, 150, 208, 209
Rivers, Larry, 15, 80, 99, 151–174, 212, 213
    African Continent and African, 152–153
    Imamu Baraka Reading, 157–158
    America's Number One Problem, 159–160
    Caucasian Woman Sprawled on a Bed and Eight Figures of Hanged Men on Four Rectangular Boxes, 161–162, 168–169
    The Slave Ship, 165–166
    I Like Olympia in Black Face, 169–172
Rosenwald, Julius, 7, 8
Russell, Winfred
    A Study, 27–29, 208

Saunders, Raymond, 192
Savage, Augusta, 8
Schatz, Boris, 32
Schomburg, Arthur, 7
Schwerner, Michael, 122, 123, 125, 133, 209
Scottsboro, 86, 91–93, 99, 100, 107, 111, 168
scream (cry), 52, 53, 125, 200, 201
Segal, George, 139–142, 211
    The Bus Riders, 139–141
segregation, 9, 67, 118, 192, 210
self (the), 180, 206, 212
Shahn, Ben, 48, 66, 121–142, 176, 202, 210, 211
    The Credo, 48–49
    Thou Shalt Not Stand Idly By, 120–134

Martin Luther King, 125–126
Frederick Douglass, 125, 127
James Chaney, 125, 128
Andrew Goodman, 125, 129
Michael Schwerner, 125, 130
May 5, 170–171
Welders, 202–204
slavery, 5, 6, 13, 20, 23, 38, 41, 48, 81, 88, 107,
125, 155, 165, 169, 208
SNCC (Student Nonviolent Coordination
Committee), 69, 168
Some American History, 80, 157, 161–170, 173
South (the), 9, 29, 67, 87, 91, 101, 112, 124,
125, 131, 132, 139, 140, 141, 147
Soyer, Isaac
Employment Agency, 73, 77
Soyer, Moses, 53, 69, 71, 73–74, 79
Portrait of Eartha Kitt, 79–80
Gwen and Jacob Lawrence, 79, 81
Soyer, Raphael, 53, 55, 69, 71–73, 79, 117, 119,
122, 176, 183, 210, 216
City Children, 71–72
Village East Street Scene, 71, 74
Amos on Racial Equality, 73, 75
Waiting Room, 73, 76
Portrait of Benny Andrews, 79, 83
Spiegelman, Art, 15, 177, 193–196, 207, 212,
213, 217
Maus II: And Here My Troubles Began,
193–196
Maus II: And Here My Troubles Began,
194–196
Valentine's Day, 213, 215–216
Spingarn, Amy, 7
Spingarn, Arthur, 7
Spingarn, Joel, 4, 7, 203
spirituals, 20, 22, 31, 44, 143, 208
stereotype, 2–3, 28, 32, 69, 80–81, 86–87, 169,
chap. 6 *passim*, 209, 212, 213, 216
Sternberg, Harry, 99, 101, 210
Southern Holiday, 101, 105
Stettheimer, Florine, 171–172
Stieglitz, Alfred, 52
suffering, 5, 6, 41, 53, 54, 87, 101, 122, 131,
135, 137, 155, 209
symbiosis, 1, 13, 54, 180, 182, 185–186, 193

Tanner, Benjamin Tucker, 18, 22, 53
Tanner, Henry Ossawa, 15, 18–29, 31, 48, 116,
138, 147, 183, 209, 210
A View in Palestine, 19–20

The Wailing Wall, 20–22
Nicodemus Visiting Jesus, 22–25
Head of a Jew in Palestine, 24, 26, 28
The Crisis, 3, 7, 33, 62, 64, 87, 88, 93, 101, 118,
121, 122, 124, 203
The New Negro, 15, 29, 30, 32, 33, 47, 55, 64, 209
Toomer, Jean, 31, 182–183, 207
types, 18, 23, 25, 28, 29, 73, 116, 147, 164, 183,
208

universalism, 3, 6, 17, 19, 33, 50, 71, 73, 117,
133, 195, 211

Vaynshteyn, Berysh, 99
vision, 15, 30, 32, chap.2 *passim*, 119, 175, 210,
211, 212

W.P.A. (Works Progress Administration), 8, 66
Weems, Carrie Mae, 185, 195, 196
White, Charles, 8, 13, 70
Williams, Pat Ward, 113–115, 208, 209
Accused/Blowtorch/Padlock, 113–115, 116,
209
Wolff, Adolf
The Lynch Law, 106
Woodruff, Hale, 7, 136
word and image, 15, 16, 115, 122, chap.6 *passim*
Wright, Richard, 121, 167–168

Yemenite Jews, 22–25, 183, 208
Yiddish, 16, 30, 55, 62, 64, 88, 89, 91, 93, 99,
194, 196

Zionism, 3, 5, 32, 33, 44, 64,
Zorach, William, 3

About the Author

Milly Heyd teaches in the department of the history of art at the Hebrew University of Jerusalem. She specializes in modern art, modern Jewish and Israeli art, and art and psychoanalysis. Her publications include *Aubrey Beardsley: Symbol, Mask and Self-Irony*, as well as articles on Odilon Redon, Man Ray, Giorgio de Chirico, Alberto Savinio, Salvador Dali, George Segal, Lilien, and Reuven Rubin.